# Theatre for Youth Third Space

# Theatre for Youth Third Space
## Performance, Democracy, and Community Cultural Development

Stephani Etheridge Woodson

**intellect** Bristol, UK / Chicago, USA

First published in the UK in 2015 by
Intellect, The Mill, Parnall Road, Fishponds, Bristol, BS16 3JG, UK

First published in the USA in 2015 by
Intellect, The University of Chicago Press, 1427 E. 60th Street,
Chicago, IL 60637, USA

Copyright © 2015 Intellect Ltd

All rights reserved. No part of this publication may be reproduced, stored in a retrieval system, or transmitted, in any form or by any means, electronic, mechanical, photocopying, recording, or otherwise, without written permission.

A catalogue record for this book is available from the British Library.

Series: Theatre in Education
Series ISSN: 2049-3878

Cover designer: Stephanie Sarlos
Copy-editor: MPS Technologies
Production manager: Jessica Mitchell
Typesetting: Contentra Technologies

Print ISBN: 978-1-78320-531-8
ePDF ISBN: 978-1-78320-532-5
ePUB ISBN: 978-1-78320-533-2

Printed and bound by Short Run Press, UK

I dedicate this book to the Hudson Manor Culture and Mayhem Society, who over the years have taught me to understand engaged children and youth: Chelsea, Alix, Lenox, Max, Getamesay, Laxmi, Prakash, Mia, Johnny, Ava, Lily Z. Luca, Aurora, Iris, Adele, Maeve, Esmée, Tehya, Forest, Lily R., Emma, Claire, Louis, and especially Maddie T. who once, when I really needed it, was impressed.

# Contents

| | |
|---|---|
| Acknowledgments | xi |
| Foreword—Michael Rohd | xiii |
| Introduction | 1 |
| **Section 1: Field Building—or—the Twenty Principles of TFY Third Space** | **9** |
| 1.1   TFY Third Space | 12 |
| 1.2   Public Art and Communities of Belonging and Location | 17 |
|     1.2.1   Words over Water | 18 |
|     1.2.2   River Then, River Now, River Future | 20 |
| 1.3   Children and Youth | 23 |
| 1.4   Further Defining "Public" | 26 |
| 1.5   Placemaking as a Function of Public-Making | 28 |
|     1.5.1   Physical Space and Social Place | 28 |
|     1.5.2   Placemaking | 29 |
| 1.6   Community Cultural Development | 32 |
| 1.7   Deliberative Democracy and the Politics of Representation | 34 |
| 1.8   Defining Community | 37 |
| 1.9   A Pause to Build Field Theory in CCD with Children and Youth | 42 |
| 1.10  A Brief Introduction to Capital and Cultural Economies | 46 |
| 1.11  Expanding Capital Systems | 49 |
| 1.12  Defining Development | 58 |
|     1.12.1  Positive Youth Development | 58 |
|     1.12.2  Defining Development within the Capabilities Approach | 66 |

| 1.13 | Good Work | 73 |
| 1.14 | Field Theory in CCD with Children and Youth, Part 2: Linking Capital and Development | 78 |

## Section 2: Ethics, Leadership, and Facilitation — 83

Introduction — 85

| 2.1 | Starting From Where You Are: Ethics and Pluralism | 88 |
| 2.2 | Culture, Values, and Beliefs | 90 |
| 2.3 | Diversity and Difference | 95 |
| 2.4 | Power and Status | 103 |
| 2.5 | Hegemony | 107 |
| 2.6 | Putting Ethics and Pluralism Together | 111 |
| 2.7 | Authentic Leadership | 114 |
| | 2.7.1 Openness and Emotional Honesty | 116 |
| | 2.7.2 Lateral Management Structures | 116 |
| | 2.7.3 Reciprocity | 117 |
| 2.8 | Healthy Ensembles | 119 |
| | 2.8.1 Dialogue and Positive Communication | 124 |
| 2.9 | Fostering Creativity | 129 |
| | 2.9.1 Domains, Fields and Circulating Symbolic Meanings | 131 |
| | 2.9.2 Individual Creativity | 133 |
| | 2.9.3 Raw Materials and Group Creativity | 135 |
| | 2.9.4 Creative Processes | 138 |
| 2.10 | Theatre and Performance Skills | 142 |
| 2.11 | Facilitating Creative Processes and Products | 146 |
| | 2.11.1 Studio as a Space of Games and Play | 146 |
| | 2.11.2 Spiral Devising | 154 |
| | 2.11.3 Compositional Practices and Aesthetic Considerations | 157 |

## Section 3: Partnering, Project Management, Planning, and Evaluating — 161

Thinking through *Community* — 163

| 3.1 | Partnering to Foster Change and Social Transformation | 166 |
| 3.2 | Barriers to Working Together | 173 |

| | | |
|---|---|---|
| 3.3 | Qualities Helpful to Overcoming Barriers | 177 |
| 3.4 | Conceptualizing Projects | 180 |
| 3.5 | Project Frames | 184 |
| 3.6 | Articulating a Theory of Social Change | 186 |
| | 3.6.1 Reeler's "Emergent Change" | 188 |
| | 3.6.2 Reeler's "Transformative Change" | 190 |
| | 3.6.3 Reeler's "Projectable Change" | 193 |
| 3.7 | Project Planning, Proposals, and Management | 197 |
| | 3.7.1 Project Planning | 197 |
| | 3.7.2 Proposal Components | 207 |
| | 3.7.3 Project Proposal Example | 211 |
| | 3.7.4 Project Management | 217 |
| 3.8 | Documentation, Evaluation, and Assessment | 220 |
| | 3.8.1 Documentation | 221 |
| | 3.8.2 Specialized Research Terminology | 222 |
| | 3.8.3 Rigor | 225 |
| 3.9 | Final Project/Partnership/Program Reports | 233 |
| Works Cited | | 237 |

## Acknowledgments

I would not have been able to complete this work without the learning environment and deep history of Arizona State University's (ASU) School of Film, Dance and Theatre's Theatre for Youth program. The students and faculty there demand the best of themselves and others. They ask the hard questions and creatively challenge themselves—and me. Thank you. In particular, I want to recognize past and present CCD artists: Ashley Hare, Elizabeth Sullivan, Haley Honeman, Megan Flod Johnson, Megan Hartman, Miranda Giles, Rivka Rocchio, Leslie Stellwagen, Sarah Sullivan, and Xanthia Walker. I especially acknowledge Megan Alrutz who told me, "Yeah, interesting, but I miss all the personal stories. Where are all your stories?" Megan, I put them all back in for you (plus one fart reference for Andy Waldron). I also want to thank my beta readers who gave generously so that this text might be better: Elizabeth Johnson, Linda Essig, Pam Korza, Sylvia Gale, and Tamara Underiner, and the students in the 2014 and 2015 community-based theatre classes, y'all rock. Special thanks to the Dark Circle who fed me butter, sugar, and booze, kept me honest, and once put out a fire in my kitchen. I could not ask for a better community. And of course, my family but particularly Kyle Woodson, who shows me every day how to be a better person with his grace, mad skills in garbage disappearance, delight in the ridiculous, and snarky sense of humor.

# Foreword

Recently, I was working with employees of a Chicago City Department on a project described as an arts-based collaborative visioning process. After lots of small group work, it brought together supervisors and staff from this department's sites around the city for the first time to engage together in identifying shared challenges and build problem-solving strategies. As the work progressed, something became clear: these city employees experienced their role in a large bureaucracy as so disempowering that when it came time to imagine possible visions and tactics, they could not release the voices of the system in which they were embedded. They could not enable themselves to see possibilities outside their daily lived experience.

In this instance, it was my job to help craft a space where possibility was present. Crafting that space is:

- To participate in a collective act that moves from invitation to engagement to reflection, again and again.
- To consider self, and group, and theory, and practice.
- To do, to learn, to grow, and to change.

When we make art, when we teach, when we guide—when we lead—we take on the responsibility of intentionality. Intentionality requires an awareness of self, action, and consequence. It requires the ability to assess and respond. This is hard, complex work. With this book, Stephani Etheridge Woodson has generously contributed to the field (or fields, as I will suggest below) a map. Not a recipe, nor a formula, but a set of considerations and proposals. Which is exactly what we need when we make space.

I met Stephani years ago; I actually don't remember when and where. We may have taken a Theater of the Oppressed workshop together (Augusto Boal) in the mid-1990s. We may have crossed paths at an annual Association of Theater and Higher Education conference. We may have first connected at ASU when her colleague Johnny Saldaña brought me in to give master classes on the work of my theatre company, Sojourn Theatre. Regardless of when and how we met, I've known her a little for a long time. And Stephani has always been someone whose work I've heard about and thought, "Wow, that seems really interesting. I wish I knew more about that." In particular, I was fascinated with what I observed as a passionate interest in the leadership of arts-based work with young people.

I had no idea that she was, over those years, developing her own unified take on leadership that brings together theatre, education, community, and social/political theory. At the heart of that unified take is a profoundly specific belief in the rights and capacities of young people. At its heart also rests a body of practice that articulates, in detail, the role of planning and facilitation in service to that belief.

I have spent much of my adult life studying and teaching facilitation in the context of artistic and community-engaged practice. It's a skill set that I see as crucial in all sorts of settings. Certainly a teacher, in my mind, is a facilitator. As is any artist whose work depends on other collaborators to achieve their own particular vision and desired outcome. I work in community and civic contexts with regularity, but I also co-lead the MFA directing program at Northwestern University, where I'm responsible for teaching core courses and mentoring student productions. It's the combination of activities I engage in on a daily basis—teaching in a university, running a not-for-profit ensemble-based theatre company, leading a Center (Center for Performance and Civic Practice) that supports artist/community partnerships around the nation—that makes my appreciation for Stephani's achievement deep, and my excitement about its cross-field implications high. I think the framework Stephani sets up in these pages offers an incredibly complex but highly accessible, ethical framework for deeply humane project practice at the intersection of youth-focused cultural development work, community-engaged artistic practice, and participatory pedagogies in fields as varied as urban planning, environmental justice, and neighborhood coalition building. I plan to teach it, and I plan to share it as a translation tool to use with community partners in non-arts sectors when we imagine and plan projects together.

I haven't addressed the most intriguing term in Stephani's title in this foreword: third space. I haven't, and I won't, because this book is fundamentally an investigation and explication of the term's meaning, and of the opportunity she states that it affords us as practitioners and as global citizens. I'm thrilled to take what I have learned from this book into the work I am doing with the city of Chicago on the project I described at the beginning of this foreword. I am thrilled with the promise of sharing vocabulary, experiences, and challenges with colleagues and students in multiple fields who are able to find in this book a landscape of common values and goals. I am thrilled for you to engage in the conversation

## Foreword

Stephani's work in these pages invites. And I'm thrilled I was asked to wish you well as you begin.

Michael Rohd
Founding Artistic Director, Sojourn Theatre
Founder/Director Center for Performance and Civic Practice
Assistant Professor, Northwestern University

# Introduction

*Never doubt that a small group of thoughtful, committed, citizens can change the world. Indeed, it is the only thing that ever has.*
— Margaret Mead

In the early-to-middle 1990s, when I first began working with children and youth to co-construct performances, I really struggled to put a name to my particular practice. Trained as a K-12 theatre educator and a Theatre for Youth (TFY) specialist, I labeled what I did as "performance art," and I leaned heavily on the "radical." For my Master's thesis at the University of Texas, I gleefully created a residency program in a local high school steeped in performance art. We studied Butoh, Dada, and Bread and Puppet Theater. We created Futurist performance manifestos and built a giant vagina on stage. Later, I realized, while I found the transgressive a useful wedge, I relied heavily on combative aesthetics, carelessly short-circuiting the possibility of social transformation and the emotional engagements I really wanted. We had a lot of fun devising performance art, but I did not create the possibility for lasting social change.

Additionally, I began to question my ethical stance and how I practiced power through being "radical" and "progressive." Those terms turned out to be more about me, and how I wanted to understand my art, than the communities of children and youth with whom I worked. So I shelved my "performance art" and focused on grounding myself in the theory, history, and pedagogy of children's theatre, childhood studies, and what is now often called applied theatre. When I finished my dissertation in 1999, I became anxious to creatively process my theoretical work with real children and youth. I enjoy scholarship immensely, but I learn and theorize best when I combine traditional scholarship with studio practices. My scholarship is focused on the realm of childhood and youth studies, particularly the social constructions and circulation of childhood. I study how cultures create and enforce the meaning of "child" and "youth." But I needed to work with real people of diverse ages, who negotiate these prescribed identity structures on a daily basis. Like most TFY specialists, I had never abandoned my creative practice, but my concentrated philosophical work helped me to understand that the stakes were much higher than I had originally thought. That effort also enabled me to name and map my unease with my previous actions, aesthetic choices, and facilitation strategies. This book is one answer to that negotiation. Here, I take readers through concentrated philosophical discussions alongside real-life examples and planning/assessment protocols drawn from both the project management field and international development practices. The ideas we all carry inside influence how we interpret and represent the world around us. For those of us who want to use our art to change the world (and what TFY artist does not at heart want to change the world?), we need to pay eagle-eyed attention to how change occurs and what theatre/performance can actually accomplish in the world.

TFY is an inherently conservative field, drawing heavily from educational practices as well as performance traditions. Much of the TFY literature and research pulls from one of two dominant streams:

1. Work that explores theories, concerns, and questions of presentation to young people—*children as audience.*
2. Work that revolves around theatre education and social theories, concerns, and questions—*children as learners.* Even work that emphasizes children and youth as performers tends to privilege the benefits accrued to the child because of and/or through engagement in performance.

In no other theatre practice is the primary audience as distant from the production processes as in TFY. Few professional TFY companies have child/youth advisory boards, let alone child playwrights, directors, designers, and performers. Economically, children and youth rarely purchase their own tickets to theatre shows. Contextually, the United States is only one of two United Nations members not signed onto the U.N. Declaration of the Rights of the Child. We literally do *not* guarantee young people's civil and human rights in the United States, let alone their right to culture. At a policy level, we have a schizophrenic relationship to children and youth legally based in property rights and future economic status, which takes precedence over individual and collective freedoms. In addition, as a culture, we are uncomfortable with children's entertainment for the sake of entertainment—art for fun, or what Thompson (2009: 9) would call the "affective range." Children's art (e.g., television, film, theatre, and music) is expected to inform and educate and only secondarily to entertain. Expanding the "children/youth as audience" and "children/youth as learners" literature, this text offers,

- Children/youth as artists
- Children/youth as citizens/publics
- Children/youth as community/civic assets

# Introduction

In this text, I will demonstrate an expanded model of "childhood" and "youth," focus on democratic facilitating and relationship-building strategies, and build a theoretical foundation for how youth arts can function in public space. My shorthand label for the practices I explore here is "TFY third space". TFY third space uses theatre and performance in partnership with young people to consciously affect society in legitimate and measurable ways.

What does TFY third space look like? An example: I worked two summers in a row with the San Solano Youth Exchange at Topawa, a small village located on the Tohono O'odham Indian Reservation in southern Arizona. This program partnered youth from St. Pius Catholic parish in Tucson with Topawa youth from the San Solano Mission's community. Living together for a week in the San Solano mission dorms, these young people from starkly different socioeconomic and cultural backgrounds focused on leadership training, service, and cultural exchange. The first year I was asked to participate, adult leaders wished to address a Topawa community problem. The parish school at Topawa—which had for almost eighty years been the only school in the village—had recently burned, an arson that was linked to young people in the village. Many adults and community elders received their K-12 education at the Topawa School and were distraught by the physical destruction. The burned building contributed to ongoing tension between families, elders, and youth. Many elders in the community felt the arson to be a slap in the face as well as representative of young people's casual attitudes toward education. The youth-exchange adult leaders wanted to focus on the Topawa School to acknowledge the school's history in the village as well as to explore participating youth's attitudes toward education. The adults approached me with a well developed plan of action; this *problem-solving residency* resulted in a digital story with documentary elements telling the history and meaning of the Topawa School while also exploring education itself. The young people had little involvement in either the original concept or subsequent preplanning. Nevertheless, we created engagement and facilitation structures that encouraged the youth to develop and explore through their own understandings. We did not shy away from controversial discussions, and the young people freely aired discordant and pessimistic views on the value of the education provided at the local school—and for their future. Youth engaged in substantive conversations with their community elders and spiritual leaders.

A year later, the exchange leaders contacted me to participate again. They did not have a specific agenda but were interested in how we could partner with the Tohono O'odham Cultural Center. Including youth in our planning this time, my partners (both adults and youth) decided to focus on *himdag*, which roughly translates to mean the practice of Tohono O'odham living/way. Feeling the lack of casual opportunities for complex and positive interactions between generations, my partners expressed a desire to bridge that gap experientially, while also positioning youth as leaders, rather than receivers. In this case, the group decided to create a children's *himdag* picture book, built from stories gathered throughout the community. The group collected stories, decided on four they wished to explore further, then wrote and illustrated them—primarily through the use of digital media. The stories showcased a diversity of *himdag*, including two traditional tales, one story about desert plants and one biographical story about a beloved local kindergarten teacher. We had the book printed and the youth exchange donated them to reservation elementary schools and Head Start programs, while the Cultural Center offered them for purchase in the museum. Youth leaders took a much more substantive role in planning and devising an art action *building effective connections and shared values*. Project partners returned repeatedly to their desire to leverage cultural resources while focusing on youth agency and leadership capabilities to refine the planning.

I enjoyed both these residencies, but believe I did a better job of crafting *participatory publics* (a term I explore further in Section 1) in the *himdag* residency. This success was partially due to the trust relationships built through the previous encounter. By working through difficult conversations during the first residency, we were able to achieve the second. However, both residencies exemplify TFY third space—crafting space for youth to speak to their communities honestly and with deliberation. Youth claimed public. In both cases, theatre and performance happened throughout the entire process although the outputs were both crafted digitally. We devised and improvised narrative. We used gesture and image to explore symbolism: we wrote and performed spoken word, monologues, and choral events. A community celebration/presentation/dialogue was also a part of each of these events. In each case, youth invited community elders, parents, civic leaders, spiritual leaders, et cetera to a meal. The youth prepared and served the meal and then hosted conversation around their art action.

TFY third space is a particular form of Community Cultural Development (CCD) that places youth in the center of their communities as active players, movers, and shakers. In TFY third space we acknowledge the gifts of children and youth, and leverage them to make the world a better place.

This book answers the question: How do we use our art to make the world a better place together? W.E.B. Du Bois famously wrote, "Now is the accepted time, not tomorrow, not some more convenient season. It is today that our best work can be done and not some future day or future year." I believe this. I also believe art is the crucible where cultures come together and perceive in different and new ways. I believe that children and youth have unique assets and abilities to make the world a better place *in the now*, and that cultural expressions can provide a medium for adults and communities to listen deeply to their wisdom. If you walk into a room full of adults and ask for a show of hands from those who define themselves as creative artists, the number raising their hands will be far below that of a room of young people. I believe children and youth have more creative capacity than adults. They are an untapped creative force for CCD. This text builds theory on *why* and *how* to co-construct both ethical and artistic work with children and youth that functions to advance the collective good. This is an academic text and a philosophical one, as well as offering practical advice built from theoretical sources. I offer new frames to think through old processes.

This text reflects how I have shaped and refined my artistic engagement practices and philosophy to build spaces of community exchange and reciprocity. Thus, this is a deeply personal text. In community-based theatre and performance, decisions have to be made contextually. Having a solid philosophical and theoretical understanding of *why* helps me know that as I make decisions in the moment, I do the best possible job. I ask *why* in order to create the conditions for positive, lasting change and social action. This text starts with asking why. Why think about TFY in new ways? Why think about *publics* and *ethics* and *placemaking*? And, how can thinking about those things help us create art actions with more possibility for social and cultural impact?

After asking *why*, I move to addressing *how*. How do we structure residencies? What do healthy partnering relationships look like? How do we know if we have succeeded or failed? What can theatre and performance actually accomplish in the world?

This book does not use a chapter structure, but follows an organizing scheme constructed around foundational principles, the ethics and practice of leadership in creative collaboration, and finally, principles of project design and evaluation. Writing builds things left to right; beginning to end; front to back. I struggled over ways to organize this book trying to capture the organic nature of the form itself. I ultimately settled on concepts as overall structuring devices. The internal logistics of the three sections, however, move back and forth between field building (laying the theoretical groundwork for why), ethics and leadership in multicultural environments, and what both have to do with organizational structures. Many of the ideas discussed pull from multiple fields of study and complex concepts (in philosophy, law, economics, development practices, human rights, performance studies, et cetera); thus, I keep the subsections shorter in order to be more easily digestible as well as to focus deeply on individual concepts. When workshopping the text with my graduate students, they asked for key idea pull-outs after all relevant subsections. They pointed out that while reading they would flip back and forth between sections to refresh their understandings of particular terms or to approach ideas differently, and they wanted a quick reference. These key terms sections recognize the circular nature of the text as a whole, as well as some readers' experiences navigating through the book.

So, what can you expect as you read this text? First, I build field theory for TFY third space, using multiple fields and philosophical traditions: performance theory, postcolonialism, sociology, psychology, democracy studies, economics, international development, history, applied ethics, et cetera. Rather than promoting a singular kind of practice, I work to build a solid theoretical foundation for a diversity of creative possibilities. Second, I make assumptions about my readership and audience. In particular, I assume readers are accomplished artists or teaching artists with a solid understanding of their own creative practices and preferred methodologies. This is not a handbook on how to be a TFY artist, but rather asks readers to contemplate using their art in a different way. I envision this text as a conversation between readers and myself and I use direct address. Finally, I pull extensively from my own life and practice. One of my graduate students questioned whether or not I really wanted to include my kids' names or so much personal information, and I struggled with his question. I deeply believe, however, that the personal *is* the political, and my children, in so much as they can, have given permission for me to include their stories here. Again, the organizational structure and narrative elements reflect my thinking patterns and life experiences. In particular, I do not fundamentally distinguish between my artistic practices and my philosophical ones—both are deeply important. Finally, there will be stories or experiences that do not (cannot) reflect all readers' beliefs or life paths. I hope you will approach such moments with a spirit of critical generosity. But I also hope that you do not let me off easy when you think I am wrong.

When I first began working in what I now call TFY third space, I had no idea what I was doing, and I made bad mistakes. This book is the text I wish I could have found to help me articulate both processes and the *whys* of the processes. I hope this book will be the first of many texts on this subject. And so, I invite you to continue the conversation with me, to turn my monologue into dialogue, either through your own research or your artistic practice or your writing. I invite you to contact me via e-mail at ASU. If you are reading this book, I claim you as a part of my community, and I look forward to hearing from you.

## Section 1

Field Building—or—the Twenty Principles of TFY Third Space

*Our deepest fear is not that we are inadequate. Our deepest fear is that we are powerful beyond measure.*
— Marianne Williamson

Section 1 defines my terms, while grounding Theatre for Youth (TFY) third space in contemporary development practices, deliberative democracy, and community-based art. Here, I will outline and explain the principles of TFY third space while offering an expanded discussion of capital systems, diverse development practices, and good work. I posit TFY third space as a viable, exciting, and challenging method of making a difference. I explain how theatre and performance can be a robust intervention into social life. In particular, I build the theoretical foundations for twenty principles of TFY third space, which I list below. In sections 1.1 through 1.8, I explore the first ten of these principles. In sections 1.10 through 1.13, I explore the second ten. Below I list the twenty principles, although the specialized language I use is explained throughout this section rather than parsed below in the list.

1. Culture is action.
2. Children and youth are competent cultural producers.
3. Children and youth are acknowledged experts on both being themselves and the meanings of their lives.
4. Childhood is understood as socially constructed, not biologically innate; and thus, processes do not place artificial limits on the scope of the work or on the assumed abilities of the participants.
5. Primary unit of concern is the community and public-making not individual achievement.
6. The work consciously builds the social, political, economic, and/or cultural power of the communities involved.
7. Facilitation and participatory techniques are understood through principles of deliberative democracy rather than pedagogy, consensus, or traditional directorial relationships.

8. Participants have express relationships to the content of the work developed.
9. Children and youth are civic publics.
10. The public sphere is a collective and discursive space built on and around human environments.
11. Children and youth are participatory publics.
12. TFY third space understands children and youth as social beings with human capabilities.
13. Overall community well-being depends on interdependent and complex flows of capital, collective placemaking, and human agency.
14. TFY third space claims publics with children and youth.
15. TFY third space nurtures children and youth as capable agents, able to collectively engage in the public sphere and civic environments.
16. Good work in TFY Community Cultural Development (CCD) pays equal attention to practice, product, and public-making.
17. TFY CCD builds community wealth and well-being through asset development and human capabilities development.
18. Deliberative democratic and communitarian principles guide all aspects of TFY third space.
19. TFY third space works toward change.
20. Children and youth are agents and assets within their communities.

## 1.1 TFY THIRD SPACE

TFY third space focuses on children and youth as artists and creators, acknowledging their proficiencies rather than their artistic, educational, or social deficiencies. Art functions differently than other spaces in our lives. We can combine the uncombinable, mix the unmixable, and think the unthinkable. Herman Melville's 1922 poem allows:

> In placid hours well-pleased we dream
> Of many a brave unbodied scheme.
> But form to lend, pulsed life create,
> What unlike things must meet and mate:
> A flame to melt—a wind to freeze;
> Sad patience—joyous energies;
> Humility—yet pride and scorn;
> Instinct and study; love and hate;
> Audacity—reverence. These must mate,
> And fuse with Jacob's mystic heart,
> To wrestle with the angel—Art.

Art connects minds and bodies while presenting multiple realities and layered meanings. "To create a play" and "to play" relate deeply with both occupying in between space—neither real life, nor not-real-life. This is TFY third space: a powerful spot to occupy, an in-between that allows us to experiment with choices, consequences, and ways of being and interact where "unlike things must meet and mate." Theatre expresses the "unbodied scheme." The in-between has risk, but that risk is contained between and to speak from the in-between suggests diverse engagement practices. After all, there is no ONE way to interpret a painting, a play, or a poem. Through the generative and playful possibilities of TFY third space, groups can rapidly see the consequences of their actions and how individual choices transform the whole. This space of "play" also works as an educational environment, allowing us to step outside of our lives for brief moments and into the worlds of others. In addition, we can more fully encompass our own stories by looking at them from other vantage points, allowing us to see through-lines, metaphors, and significant structures rather than experiencing life at breakneck speed. Theatre practices are particularly well suited to this realm, partly because performative storytelling employs multiple communication structures: narrative, embodiment, spectacle, sound and music, time or duration, space, and the reenactment of the intangible original—performance folds all the other arts into itself. In the 2010 young adult novel, *Cassie Draws the Universe*, P.S. Baber lyrically captures this power of theatrical engagement:

> The stage is a magic circle where only the most real things happen, a neutral territory outside the jurisdiction of Fate where stars may be crossed with impunity. A truer and more real place does not exist in all the universe.
> (204)

Real and not-real, contained but limitless, theatre is magic made manifest.

TFY third space pulls from the fields of positive youth development, builds on deliberative democratic principles, and expands understandings of "public" and "civic" work. TFY third space appreciates culture as action—*the act of coming together to create community, public space, and humanness*. TFY third space is also a political space that defines action in terms of social power. The president of Civic Change, Inc. at the Pew Charitable Trust, Suzanne Morse notes,

> A study, "Citizens and Politics: A view from main street America," in the early 1990s by the Harwood Group (1991) for the Kettering Foundation found [...] that Americans could not find their place in public life, not because they are apathetic as the common wisdom holds, but because they

were politically impotent. That is, they felt unable to make any difference at all in public decisions.

(Morse 2004: 144)

TFY third space labors to make a difference. By this I mean that TFY third space is *interactive* and *purposeful*.

*Interactive*—because power resides in networks rather than in individual humans, TFY third space understands children and youth as collective social actors who can work toward social good and civic change. The performances created in TFY third space then function within a system of cultural exchange and cultural development. I follow the CRAFT (Contact, Research, Action, Feedback, Teaching) model created by Keith Knight and Mat Schwarzman and a team of graphic journalists (2005) in their *Beginner's Guide to Community-Based Arts*. The CRAFT model places art at the center of a CCD process, not as the end result. Art is action and action points to social power. Within the CRAFT model, an art action interactively and consciously builds the social, cultural, civic, and/or economic power of the community. The art action adds social and cultural capabilities in—and to—social, cultural, and civic systems. By its very nature, TFY third space cannot be separated from communities because TFY third space focuses on collectives rather than individuals.

*Purposeful*—intended to affect social, cultural, and political structures in a certain way, TFY third space purposely intervenes in systems, working to increase the public good and social justice. Tom Borrup of Creative Community Builders writes, "The term *creative community building* describes efforts to weave multiple endeavors and professions into the never-ending work of building and rebuilding the social, civic, physical, economic, and spiritual fabrics of communities" (Borrup 2006: xv, original emphasis). William Cleveland (2012) defines Arts-Based Community Development (ABCD) as "community-based arts activities that equitably and sustainably advance human dignity, health, and productivity" (298). Each of these understandings applies here. The TFY third space empowers and engages children and youth as civic equals in the shaping of society. TFY third space functions as a form of social power based on collective action and social action. In this, I take to heart the warnings of Harry Boyte and Nancy Kari (1996). They write,

> Today, most adults in the youth development field—including teachers, youth workers, counselors, clergy and others—see young people as clients to be served or as consumers of the knowledge they "need to know." Although their intentions are far different than simply marketing to young

people, their practices can unwittingly reinforce the patterns which see youth as passive recipients, not active creators.

(173)

TFY third space acknowledges children and youth as active creators who contribute significantly to their communities and the larger society.

My use of the term TFY third space depends heavily on the scholarship of Homi Bhabha (1990, 2004), as well as an understanding of cultural processes and performances as what political theorist Harry Boyte calls "free-space" and of performance artist Guillermo Gómez-Peña's call for a "Fourth World." A postcolonial theorist, Bhabha's work uncovers the underlying meanings contained in seemingly simple moments. His concept of the third space acknowledges that while western cultures often polarize identities and structures (e.g., boys/girls, men/women, work/play, child/adult, and public/private), an engagement with these binaries and boundaries can create gaps between. This "between" landscape calls into question fixed categorizations and fosters new possibilities for cultural meanings. Bhabha's work is not concerned with revolution or with ideological evolution—both of which are still contained on the line between thesis and antithesis—rather, his work looks at expanding creative possibilities and cultural mash-ups. Bhabha's third space adds a third dimension to the limited possibilities of polarized understandings. He moves us off the page and into space.

Boyte, in his 2004 book, *Everyday Politics: Reconnecting Citizens and Public Life*, writes, "free space, rooted in everyday life settings, are places in which powerless people have a measure of autonomy for self-organization and engagement with alternative ideas" (61). There are few classes of people in the United States with less power than children and youth. As a society, we regulate children and youth's lives, but we do not allow them a political voice in that control. From the federal to local levels, they have no say in funding allocations or the way space is designed or regulated. Children account for 73.5 million US Americans (24%), but only 8% of federal expenditures. Boyte points out,

> Free spaces are places where people learn political and civic skills. They are also culture-creating spaces where people generate new ways of looking at the world. In free spaces, people simultaneously draw upon and rework symbols, ideas, themes, and values in their traditions and the culture to challenge conventional beliefs.
>
> (2004: 61–62)

A CCD practice understood as a "free space" can create opportunities for children and youth to find "discussions of meaningful differences and non-market-based democratic identities" while consciously acknowledging young people as powerful cultural workers (Giroux 2000: 11). Children and youth are highly regulated in educational and civic settings, which position them most often as spectators rather than agents (i.e., audience not actors). Boyte's notion of "free space" opens up the function of public art-making to simultaneously understand and *act* on the world. A creative process understood as a "free space" supports an unromantic respect for the abilities and expressive forms of young people highlighting capacities not deficiencies. "Free space" also supports young people's diversity of experience as a type of knowledge with just as much validity as traditional written or adult conceptions.

Finally, my use of the term third space depends on Gómez-Peña's call for a "Fourth World" unconfined by conceptions of "Old World", "New World", "First World", or "Third World". He writes that in the "Fourth World"

> there is very little place for static identities, fixed nationalities, "pure" languages, or sacred cultural traditions. The members of the Fourth World live between and across various cultures, communities and countries. And our identities are constantly being reshaped by this kaleidoscopic experience.
>
> (Gómez-Peña 1996: 7)

Gómez-Peña points out the playful and fluid processes of self and cultural formation. His work emphasizes the complicated and messy web of identities, relationships and stories while highlighting possibilities for playful reimagining and aesthetic blending. The Fourth World is neither a place for the glorification of traditional stories, nor a type of humanistic enterprise focused on domesticating children and youth. Instead, the Fourth World playfully fosters social interrogation and commentary while acknowledging the questing nature of such engagement.

My use of the term third space then weaves these strands together to:

- Redefine the cultural capacity of children and youth.
- Build field theory grounded in positive youth development, deliberative democratic principles, and CCD.
- Suggest grounds for ethical artistic and cultural engagement.

This text proposes a particular form of TFY, which functions as a space of play, of reflection, and as public acts of creating culture, or public-making, recognizing children and youth as civic assets and social actors. TFY third space *uses theatre and performance in partnership with young people and communities to consciously affect society in legitimate and measurable ways.*

> **KEY IDEAS**
>
> - TFY third space focuses on children and youth as artists and creators.
> - Theatre practices are particularly well suited to CCD.
> - TFY third space is interactive and purposeful.
> - My use of the term third space grows from the scholarship of Homi Bhabha, Harry Boyte, and Guillermo Gómez-Peña.

## 1.2 PUBLIC ART AND COMMUNITIES OF BELONGING AND LOCATION

I live in Tempe, Arizona, a small city of about 40 square miles, with a year-round population slightly under 200,000. Home to the main campus of Arizona State University (ASU), this dense, desert city holds a forward thinking aesthetic as well as a chip on its shoulder about its status in the Phoenix Metro area. In the late 1960s, architecture students at ASU developed an urban park design using the dry riverbed of the Salt River—which directly borders ASU's Tempe campus—focused on bringing water back into the low desert. Contained early in the twentieth century by the Roosevelt Dam, the Salt's dry bed then housed industrial landfills and unincorporated junkyards. Dubbed the Rio Salado Project, this vision grew—over a 30-year period—into a coalition of community, business, and civic partners, with continuing support from ASU. Originally conceived as a multicity project, the Rio Salado was ultimately funded almost entirely by the Tempe community, and the Tempe Town Lake opened in 1999, over 30 years after the idea's original inception as a class project.

Art and community have always been a part of the design of the Rio Salado. As of spring 2013, there are ten separate installations, featuring the work of ten professional artists. Incorporating practical structures and standalone art pieces, the vision of public art for the Rio Salado mirrors the concept as a whole—marrying public space for recreation and anchoring commercial enterprises—both gateway and destination. Randy Martin (2006: 3) points out that public art "can be considered a particular kind of social good that serves as a means to bring forth ideas about our lives together." Art here functions to cocreate meanings of place and community, building what Martin calls "the attachment to a location that encourages people to feel they belong together" (2006: 3). As a whole, the Rio Salado Project, with its 2-mile-long lake and 5-mile, 600-acre park system, represents how Knight and Schwarzman define *community-based art*: "any form or work of art that emerges from a community and consciously seeks to increase the social, economic and political power of that community" (2005: xvi). Projects in this vein, however, can be remarkably diverse. To illustrate how different public artwork can be, I want to share the stories of two of my favorite pieces at Tempe Town Lake, while further teasing out the different understandings of "public" contained within each.

## 1.2.1 Words over Water

"Words over Water" is the name of a 600-piece granite tile installation running along the south border of the Tempe Town Lake. The multidisciplinary team of poet, Alberto Álvaro Ríos, and visual artists, Karla Elling and Harry Reese, conceived of the project as an "abecedarium" or ABC book. As they point out on their original 2000 website,

> Our project is a search for meaning, which is intrinsically interesting. Rather than decoration, our *Abecedario* is a connection to the past and the future, to water and lack of water, to people and place. *Abecedario* is Spanish for abecedarium, which is a primer for learning the alphabet and for then using it to find and create meaning.
> (http://www.public.asu.edu/~aarios/abecedario/page4.html. Accessed 22 March 2013)

**Figure 1.1:** Tempe Town Lake, south-side boundary wall (photo by the author).

**Figure 1.2:** "Words over Water" detail (photo by the author).

**Figure 1.3:** "Words over Water" detail (photo by the author).

Etched with phrases, images, and glyphs, the tiles are installed on the small retaining wall around the edge of the lake and visitors encounter these tiles in various orders and in multiple ways. The ABCs of "Words over Water" is not linear (although it is cumulative), and one need not visit all 600 tiles to "find and create" meaning. Some of the phrases and images are evocative while others will make you smile. Elsewhere on their website, the artists refer to the installation as mapping the humanness of our experience with water, as well as acknowledging the millennial history of the Salt itself. In a very real manner, "Words over Water" fosters community, not audience. As perceivers, we are asked to contemplate a cultural landscape, not just a geographical one. In this way, the artists have created a virtual and kinetic space for perceivers to imagine and to reflect on the place in which they stand.

## 1.2.2 River Then, River Now, River Future

Located on the south wall of the 202 freeway along the north bank of the Tempe Town Lake, "River Then, River Now, River Future" is a 540 plus, square-foot mural consisting of over 16,000 handmade tiles. This participatory project was designed by artists Jeff East and Rebecca Ross and was constructed with the assistance of Michelle Lowe, Amy Rey, Cyndi Salter, and Rand Smith. It is composed of handmade tiles made by thousands of Tempe residents—the majority of whom were school-age children—in diverse residencies spanning four years. Both Jeff East and Rebecca Ross are teaching artists. East taught for many years at McKemy Middle School and Ross received the Scottsdale Cultural Council 2002 Art Educator of the Year award. Divided into three sections, the mural meditates on the Salt River through time using color to distinguish between past, present, and future. In a real way, "River Then, River Now, River Future" also creates community, albeit in a different manner than "Words over Water." Thousands of individuals contributed to the making of the mural.

While they did not all collaborate at the same time, of course, they did work in partnership within the larger vision of East and Ross. The mural too is composed of thousands of individual tiles and several collaborative pieces. Meaning, while the mural itself is collaborative, the mural includes smaller collective elements created in residency programs across Tempe and central Phoenix. In this way, the process of creation itself was shared across sites and socially constructed—as was the implementation of the residencies. The mural then, is an example of "community-based" or "participatory" art-making. As Jan Cohen-Cruz notes, "Community-based performance relies on artists guiding the creation of original work or material adapted to and

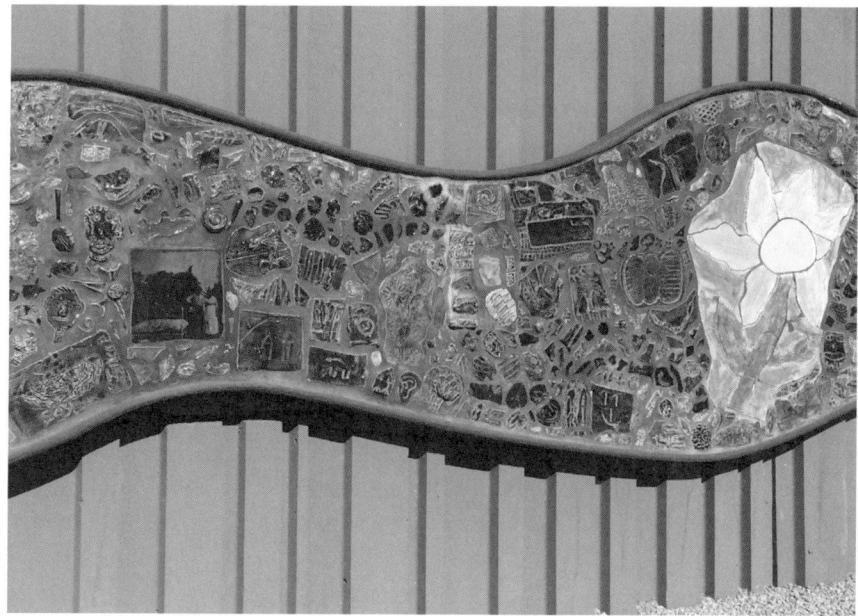

**Figure 1.4:** Section of "River Then, River Now, River Future" (photo by the author).

with, people with a primary relationship to the *content*, not necessarily to the *craft*" (2005: 2–3). Some of the differences then between the two pieces include *how* the works were made and *when* "public" was invoked.

Both of these marvelous art projects are "public art": that is, art in public space. "Public art" is a much broader category, of course, than one based on physical boundaries. Martin points out that public art "can be seen as a site or physical place, as a representation of civic ideas, or as an occasion for people to gather to engage in critical reflection—in short, a way of seeing, a way of knowing and a way of gathering" (2006: 2). Those of us from theatre understand how these categories overlap and flow, after all, *theatron* historically meant both "seeing" and "the place to see." To use Martin's words, seeing, knowing, and gathering are all essential elements of the theatrical experience. To be fair, Martin does not see these categories as mutually exclusive; rather, these categories ask us to contemplate the aesthetic relationships of social environments. Both "Words over Water" and "River Then, River Now, River Future" engage the public and in fact *actively build* "public" through evocative *place building*. Neither would exist without the Rio Salado and both are "local" in both literal and symbolic ways. In addition, these two examples are both participatory. The scale of participation is, however, quite different, as is the timing of that participation.

**Figure 1.5:** "River Then, River Now, River Future" detail (photo by the author).

"Words over Water" engages individuals who move through time and space in ways unknowable and uncontained by the art installation and the artists. Thousands of participants worked together to co-construct "River Then, River Now, River Future." Their participation collectively was structured and controlled by the artists' vision and by the material facts of the residency programs themselves.

This is a book about CCD theatre/performance with children and youth. I begin with stories about public art, however, to point out two important facts: (1) CCD theatre/performance is a form of public art (community-based practices engage in both ensemble building and placemaking—communities of belonging and location); (2) public art is neither new nor inherently radical. For millennia, artists have worked within civic environments to build monuments, tell stories, and create community. The Egyptian Sphinx and the Griots of West Africa spring from the same artistic well as "Words over Water" and "River Then, River Now, River Future." The large-scale military pageants of Nazi Germany and Stalinist Russia were also public art. In all cases, we see collisions between the social and the aesthetic. Community-based art also, is neither new nor inherently radical. In the United States, many historians date the explosion of community-engaged performance in particular to the period of transition between the nineteenth and twentieth centuries. Scholars highlight the pageant movement, settlement houses, and grassroots participatory art-making through university extension programs in particular (Bedard et al. 1989; Cohen-Cruz 2005; Jackson 2000; Kuftinec 2003), but public art and community-engaged performances have always been a part of human community and culture.

> **KEY IDEAS**
>
> - Public art is a collective process of seeing, knowing, and gathering.
> - Community-based theatre is a public art.
> - Community-based performance art is neither new nor radical.

## 1.3 CHILDREN AND YOUTH

Mainstream understandings of "childhood" typically revolve around an imagined childhood created through adult narratives, desires, and dreams. Recently, social media highlighted a Pinterest site called "My Imaginary Well-Dressed Toddler Daughter," run by Tiffany Beveridge (http://www.pinterest.com/tiffanywbwg/). Beveridge pins images of children's fashion as tongue-in-cheek representations of her imaginary daughter, Quinoa. Calling out the sometimes ridiculous nature of children's fashion, along with the manner in which commercial images frame youth, Beveridge captures adult imaginary landscapes with dry humor and snide commentary. "My Imaginary Well-Dressed Toddler Daughter" comments, of course, on a particular and extreme form of adult narrative around childhood. While the field of childhood studies generally conceptualizes *children* and *youth* as an anthropological organizing structure, I understand *childhood* and *youth* as cultural space as well. In other words, as Alan Prout points out, how we understand *childhood* and *youth* depends "on context rather than naturally unfolding processes" (2005: 1). Humans create multiple childhoods contextually and culturally, and young humans themselves are social actors within their milieus, not passive recipients or blank slates.

*Children* and *youth* are key words in Raymond Williams' sense. While the terms appear to simply reflect reality, in fact, the words map overlapping social and cultural ideologies. In *New Key Words: A Revised Vocabulary of Culture and Society* (2005: 380–383), the authors note that "youth," as a term, has a specific etymological meaning that has radically changed over the last 100 years. What was once a pejorative adjective used to describe an uncivilized young man has become a collective noun describing both an ideal marketing category and a social problem requiring specific institutions:

youth court, youth prison, youth clubs, and youth church groups. At heart in the United States, *youth* contains a contradiction, as the term describes both state apprehension of individuals seen as potential threats, and an ideal consumer culture energetically focused on pleasure, beauty, and playful self-indulgence. In their 2003 book, *Urban Nightscapes: Youth Cultures, Pleasure Spaces and Corporate Power*, sociologists Paul Chatterton and Robert Hollands highlight how mandatory schooling and child labor laws limit young people from forming identity through "traditional" adult avenues of career or work. Instead, young people draw on other realms—such as fashion, music, sports, leisure, and technology—as markers or sources of identity creation (73–74). Moreover, these realms not only focus youth away from public engagements and into private concerns, but they also position youth as cultural authorities. Internet marketing specialists now study youth's adoption or disdain for social media platforms in order to predict advertising revenue. So-called "cool hunters" find commercial potential by tracking brands, bands, and memes generated and circulated by young people.

The words *children* and *youth* do not just describe or mark physical bodies, time passed, or experience gained; these terms exist as complex theoretical concepts created and recreated ideologically and contextually. How youth workers (e.g., teachers, artists, ministers, and social workers) understand the conceptional categories of *childhood* influences how they interpret policies and build programs. Understanding *children* and *youth* as key words does not require subscribing to hard and fast rules; rather, youth workers of all stripes need to recognize that both our own and our communities' conceptual models limit our understandings of what and who young people are and/or should be.

Let me give you an example. A few weeks ago, my oldest daughter participated in a remarkable concert celebrating a local performing arts institution's 50th anniversary. The institution brought in an amazing composer/conductor to build an evening's performance with top high-school musicians from around Arizona. The concert explored classical music from the romantic to the avant-garde, and included spoken word and hip-hop influences. As I was waiting for my daughter in the lobby after the concert, I ran into a colleague who enthused about how wonderful the concert had been. She continued, "They handled John Cage so well! I mean who ever hears about young people playing such challenging pieces. I am so impressed with the work [Conductor's Name] did to build such a high level of skill with these youth." I was both struck and offended by how my friend assigned credit to the adult artists rather than recognizing the innate hard work and talents of the teenage musicians. Her understanding of childhood and youth constrained her ability to recognize young people as accomplished and skillful artists. In addition, these youth were the crème de la crème of high-school performers around the state. At my daughter's school, the top performers in band and orchestra spend over ten school hours a week honing their craft. Most too, work on their craft during out-of-school time, taking private lessons, practicing daily, playing in civic and/or commercial music groups, and attending intensives held around the country. Yet, in many an adult's mind, their age alone disqualifies them from being understood as accomplished and powerful.

In US American culture, adults automatically have more power and more rights than young people do. Adults may vote, but children and youth cannot. In fact, the legal voting age was not lowered to 18 until the early 1970s. While the United States understands citizenship as a birthright, there is no denying that young people are not citizens with all the rights and responsibilities therein. Legally, children and youth exist under a protectionist doctrine that functionally denies them some of the basic human rights guaranteed to adults. For example, the 1988 Supreme Court's Hazelwood decision determined that youth enrolled in schools do not have full rights of free speech. Youth curfews limit first amendment rights, including the right to peaceful assembly. Most people would have serious concerns if their city enacted a curfew for a small segment of the population. Imagine the outcry if say, Los Angeles or Phoenix created a law forbidding women, Asians, or Chicanos from traveling out of their homes after 10:30 pm. Yet, numerous municipalities have laws regulating young people's ability to access or travel across public and commercial space. Youth curfews reflect the social belief that young people are chaotic, dangerous, and need discipline because of their age. Structurally, a curfew preemptively assumes all young people have criminal intent if left to their own devices and that the natural habitat of young humans falls within the private domain—we literally exclude them from public. Children and youth then are understood through *potential*. High-school musicians might one day become artists, but as youth they currently only hold the potential to do so. In the United States, we provide no state or legal mechanism through which young people can collectively build social, cultural, and political power—or collective efficacy. The important take away from this discussion is an awareness of the complex power dynamics at play when working with children and youth. However, perhaps more importantly for our purposes, understanding *childhood* as something socially constructed by adults allows us to deliberatively redefine and reconstruct dominant narratives. TFY third space defines children and youth as a *public* that I define here as *collectives actively engaged in civic practices, public space, and social arenas.*

> **KEY IDEAS**
>
> - Childhood is socially constructed, not biologically innate.
> - TFY third space processes do not place artificial limits on the scope of the work or on the assumed abilities of the participants based on developmental determinations.
> - Children and youth are acknowledged experts on both being themselves and in charge of defining the meanings of their lives.
> - Children and youth are a civic public.

## 1.4 FURTHER DEFINING "PUBLIC"

*Public* is a difficult and slippery term. To define *public*, I pull from theories of the "public sphere," particularly Jürgen Habermas's text, *The Structural Transformation of the Public Sphere*, originally published in German in 1962. Here, "public sphere" means the communal space/place of discussion and action taking—moments of people coming together to build community, find meaning, and address local and specific needs or desires. The public sphere is the realm of public opinion and collective action. Habermas distinguishes the public sphere from both private space and the "sphere of public authority" or the realm of government, police, and the state. Habermas's public sphere functions both *locatively*—actual space with real people inside it—and *collectively*—people working together. Many theorists have taken issue with Habermas's original work. Some work to expand understandings of the public sphere to include individuals originally excluded by Habermas (e.g., women and laborers). Others question Habermas's underlying theoretical conceptualizations entirely (pointing out ways in which the original theories depend on industrialized economics). For our purposes, I define "public sphere" broadly to include *the act of coming together to create change*. While this coming together can occur virtually (e.g., Twitter, Facebook, and the Internet), humans still primarily understand *public* in the way Habermas explored—physical locations and communal creations.

To build a useful conceptual category for "public," I also lean heavily on the possibilities of *public* and *culture* explored by Boyte and Kari (1996), Boyte (2004), and Boyte and Shelby (2009). Boyte's work redefines civic place and political structure as creative and collective rather than reductive and authoritarian. He argues that "culture" is a verb—an act of coming together to create publics through everyday experience. Building from political theorists who focus on civic place understood through processes rather than innate states of being or static structures, Boyte and Kari expand *public* into a system,

"The loss of the idea that public affairs originates from the people means that we lose our stake in the nation" (1996: 15). Boyte and Kari go on to define citizenship not through birthright or voting privileges but as "visible effort on common tasks of importance to the community or nation, involving many different people" (1996: 21). Boyte calls the outcomes of these visible efforts "public work." Explaining his idea of public work through familiar uses of the term—sewers, bridges, dams, and energy grids—Boyte expands public work to include all vital aspects of placemaking, including public art, performance, museums, cultural and historical centers, et cetera. "Public work," he says, "is central to the idea of productive, everyday politics. Such politics means change in individuals' identities and practices as well as social change. It leads to people seeing themselves as the cocreators of democracy, not simply as customers or clients, voters, protestors, or volunteers" (2004: 5). Boyte's conception of *public* stands in direct opposition to the professionalization of institutional, political, and cultural life or understandings of citizenship that are defined by the ability to vote—practices which, by their nature, leave no room for children or youth. In this broad conception of culture, both large and small acts function as public-making, creating civic community through and in everyday, collective experiences. What excites me most about this understanding of culture and public work is the way in which Boyte focuses public communities into civic actions. Here, children can be powerful and create change. By building collaborations and creating art that speaks to others about issues important to them, youth engage in *public work*, civic and place-building. Boyte and Kari warn, however, against understanding public work only as products. They point out,

> When the emphasis is simply on the product, then regardless how grand the creation or how noble the aspiration, democracy is not part of the equation. The activity itself—those who do it and how it is done—remain hidden and in the background.
>
> (1996: 21)

Boyte's framing of culture as actively cocreated in the moment, and his emphasis on process and product, transforms community into collective agency and aligns well with TFY third space structures that value young people as active contributors to the health and successes of their communities. Boyte frames democracy as an everyday practice for which we are all equally responsible—even children and youth.

Finally, understanding culture as created in and by publics allows for the creation, development, and use of what Robert Sampson calls "collective efficacy." Collective efficacy addresses a group's understanding of their ability to collectively achieve intended outcomes. Sampson writes, "The concept of collective efficacy draws together two fundamental mechanisms—*social cohesion* (the 'collectively' part of the concept) and *shared expectations for control* (the 'efficacy' part of the concept)" (2012: 152, original emphasis). Communities and civic organizations rarely consider children and youth efficacious collectives or even as potential efficacious collectives. Instead, children and youth are either atomized (individualized through educational achievement paradigms) or civically organized through risk management (loitering laws, curfews, et cetera). However, culture is dynamic, creativity is a muscle, and children and youth *can* be collectively efficacious publics. This definition of public acknowledges a primary function of TFY third space: to build publics and places. We fold place, civic, and social publics into communities in such a way as to build social cohesion and shared expectations for control.

> **KEY IDEAS**
>
> - The public sphere is a collective and discursive space built on and around human environments.
> - Culture is action.
> - Public work is the act of coming together to create place.

## 1.5 PLACEMAKING AS A FUNCTION OF PUBLIC-MAKING

### 1.5.1 Physical Space and Social Place

Understanding the relationships between physical space and social place is more complex than it first appears. To ground my understanding of how physical environments and social/cultural environments relate, I use the work of Henri Lefebvre and Michel de Certeau. In his book, *The Production of Space*, Lefebvre argues that space is actually produced publicly, both through existing socially constructed power relationships (e.g., socioeconomic class) and through the everyday practices of social relationships. Space is a social product. I also build on Michel de Certeau's book, *The Practice of Everyday Life*. In this text, de Certeau explores the ways in which individuals use, adapt, and circumvent the givens of their lives. For example, in the chapter, "Walking through the City," de Certeau explores the differences between how city officials *produce* space, and the ways in which people actually *move* through a city. Using the term "strategy" to address how those in power structure space from above, for example, with a map or the view from a satellite, de Certeau points out that individuals at the street level move through locales in ways not predetermined by maps or the strategies of those in power. Rather, individuals use "tactics" to make the space their own, to modify place and their relationships to it. Largely responsible for the turn in social and cultural theory away from "consumers" toward "users," de Certeau's scholarship replaced passivity with conscious and unconscious activity. Everything from street shortcuts to guerrilla gardening to skateboarding to yarn bombing is an example of tactics used by individuals (and communities). Consider the different ways people move through a thoroughfare. How do men and women take up space differently? What are the different ways in which individuals walk down a sidewalk? I have three daughters and each of them moves through space in particular ways. As we four walk down our block to visit a neighbor, for example, Adele travels in a straight path down the middle of the walk only deviating from her walk when forced by a neighbor's overgrown bushes or the presence of one of her sisters. Maeve travels almost everywhere on her scooter or ripstick (a wasp-shaped, hinged skateboard with only two wheels). Maeve likes to go fast and will seek out the bumps and cracks in the walk to jump. She circles in people's driveways and travels the entire block multiple times while she waits for the slower walkers. Esmée (nicknamed Maisy) runs and walks with abandon. She peers closely at neighbor's yards, smelling flowers, picking stalks of grass, and using sticks to poke anthills. Maisy, ignoring distinctions between "public" and "private," considers the entire block her path. She runs around trees and bushes, walks over lawns, and sits on people's front porches. Of course, this is partially due to her age (3–4), but her behavior is also very much indicative of her unique personality. She is a social and happy child who strikes up conversations with people in their cars or inside their homes if their windows are open. In the act of walking down the street, my daughters collectively participate and create the *place* of my neighborhood. Streets and sidewalks are collective spaces, and anyone and everyone moves through them. *How* we move through them—our tactics—relate to who we are as people and to how the collective environment or place is defined and understood. In some neighborhoods, children tromping through your yard would be an affront—let alone kids tromping though your yard to shout in your windows. I define "place" as *the social production of space*. Place is both locative and cultural.

### 1.5.2 Placemaking

I need to spend a bit of time contextualizing my use of the term *placemaking*. In general, placemaking means thoughtful planning and building of *place* in geographical spaces. For example, the Project for Public Spaces (PPS) is a nonprofit organization founded in the mid-1970s, dedicated to building usable, public space. The PPS defines placemaking as "the planning, design, management and programming of public spaces. More than just creating better urban design of public spaces, placemaking facilitates creative patterns of activities and connections (cultural, economic, social, ecological) that define a place and support its ongoing evolution" (PPS 2011). Planners, urban architects, and governments also use "cultural placemaking" and "creative placemaking." In each case, they mean the leveraging of cultural and creative capital to build value. As Ann Markusen and Anne Gadwa write in their 2010 White Paper on creative placemaking,

> In creative placemaking, partners from public, private, nonprofit, and community sectors strategically shape the physical and social character of a neighborhood, town, city, or region around arts and cultural activities. Creative placemaking animates public and private spaces, rejuvenates structures and streetscapes, improves local business viability and public safety, and brings diverse people together to celebrate, inspire, and be inspired.
> (2010: 3)

Across the world, governments and communities use placemaking to address the "interaction between urban regeneration, economic development and social renewal in order to achieve more comprehensive development of the city" (Sepe 2009: 144). In the United States, most creative placemaking has been driven by the relationship between commercial and noncommercial enterprises to drive economic development and social enterprise. This effort builds from a cultural tourism model based on people choosing to experience rather than purchase durable goods. Economists and businesses refer to this as the "experience economy" (Pine and Gilmore 1999; Poulsson and Kale 2004). Greg Richards (2011) points out "creative resources are regularly employed to generate more distinctive identities, offering regions and cities a symbolic edge in an increasingly crowded marketplace" (1230). Across the world, the so-called "creative cities" focus on two general types of creative placemaking "clusters": (1) "created around activities such as fine arts, music, cinema, architecture, and design, and whose initiation is encouraged and planned by local administration" often built around the physical geography of arts buildings, and (2) "in the organization of great events or different kinds of recreational and cultural manifestations" or primarily time-based activities (Sepe 2009: 145). A city's "cultural district" would be an example of the first type of cluster, for example. The summer or winter Olympics would be an example of the second type of manifestation. In each case, creative placemaking revolves around economic development and city identity construction.

The above conceptualizations of placemaking depend on a rather narrow sense of capital and community wealth, and in my opinion do not adequately promote democratic publics or build webs of relationships. In fact, the Olympics are often accompanied by popular protest movements or characterized by urban "renewal" programs that displace poor families. As Roberto Bedoya explains,

> Much of the national discourse on creative placemaking is caged in an understanding of "place" as the built environment. Indeed physical places like artists' live-work spaces and cultural districts benefit from creative placemaking. But to understand the term—and the practice—solely in terms of the built landscape is to miss the complete picture. Creative placemaking is much more than what manifests physically within the built environment. Before you have places of belonging you must feel you belong—to a community, a locale, or a place.
> (Tucson Arts Council 2013: 7)

For the purposes of TFY third space, I define *placemaking* in a much larger sense than many urban planners and government officials. First, I understand placemaking as a function of public-making—building belonging. In other words, placemaking is a necessary but insufficient component of public-making. Placemaking is public work, claiming public space and building collective place for all peoples—including children, young people's inclusion is rare in the United States. Here, I define *place* as *settings for social action in which we build social efficacy*.

Children and youth experience marginalization in public *space* and *place*. Tracey Skelton and Katherine Gough edited a 2013 special issue of *Urban Studies* focused on children and youth. As they point out in their introduction, "Currently, in the majority of cities world-wide, young people are ignored and/or actively excluded from decisions that affect them" (457). Other theorists argue that children and youth are not just ignored, they are understood as actively disrupting the social order and peace of public spaces. "In short, young people are—sometimes simultaneously—portrayed as being both *at risk* in public space, and being *a risk* to the successful running of public space and the safety of its other users" (Brown 2013: 541, original emphasis). Understanding a group of youth congregating on the corner, for example, as active threats to community well-being, depends on implicit understandings of public space that exclude children and youth. Brown writes, "the very presence of young people in public space is now routinely used to justify punitive policies, which aim for their expulsion from those spaces" (2013: 551). Young people routinely are barred from both the public sphere and public space. The TFY practices I write about here attempt to bridge the divide between children and youth and civic, public environments. This is done through placemaking and public-making art actions.

> **KEY IDEAS**
>
> - People collectively create place inside and on-top of space—placemaking.
> - Placemaking, understood through narrow definitions, excludes particular populations from participation.
> - Place is the setting for social action.
> - Placemaking is part of public-making.
> - Placemaking is public work, claiming public space and building collective place for all peoples.

## 1.6 COMMUNITY CULTURAL DEVELOPMENT

Defining *place*, *placemaking*, and *public* in this fashion, places the TFY practices I argue into what is variously called *arts-based community development*, or *community cultural development*. I prefer the more inclusive term *community cultural development* (CCD) developed by Don Adams and Arlene Goldbard in *Creative Community: The Art of Cultural Development* (2001) and *Community, Culture and Globalization* (2002). In CCD, artists "collaborate with others to express identity, concerns and aspirations through the arts and communications media, while building cultural capacity and contributing to social change" (Adams and Goldbard 2001: 8). Many additionally consider CCD theatre to be a form of *applied theatre*. As Helen Nicholson writes in her 2005 text, *Applied Drama: The Gift of Theatre*, applied theatre is a loaded term. She points to both applied theatre's diverse locations "primarily […] outside conventional mainstream theatre institutions" and to the "interdisciplinary and hybrid practices" used by a variety of practitioners (2). James Thompson notes three definitional specifics of applied theatre practices or what he calls applied theatre's "visible components":

> Applied theatre projects always take place in communities, in institutions or with specific groups. They often include the practice of theatre where it is least expected; for example, in prisons, refugee camps, forgotten estates, hospitals, museums, centers for the disabled, old people's homes and under-served rural villages: sometimes in theatres. Applied theatre is a participatory theatre created by people who would not usually make theatre.
>
> (2006: 15)

I would add that another essential element of applied theatre is a mutable relationship between process and product.

I do not, however, consider TFY third space practices a form of applied theatre. While applied theatre practices, in general, can work equally well either in large groups or as focused consciousness raising for individuals (Taylor 2003; Thompson 2006), CCD focuses entirely on groups, institutions, and social processes. "The work is intrinsically community-focused: while there is great potential for individual learning and development within its scope, it is aimed at groups rather than individuals" (Adams and Goldbard 2002: 8–9). The practice of the dramatic/theatrical arts within the scope of public art or CCD does not ignore or negate individual concerns, but treats them within the context of shared awareness and group interests—collective efficacy. "Of the people, by the people, for the people," wrote community artist and scholar Richard Owen Greer (1994: n.p.). Indeed, Greer's use of Lincoln's Gettysburg Address further highlights the deep and abiding relationship of CCD to civic and collaborative principles. On a personal level, I resist the term "applied theatre" for reasons Cohen-Cruz effectively articulated in her text, *Engaging Performance: Theatre as Call and Response*: "I would argue that such theatre is not necessarily 'other,' but rather some of the voices they bring in have been othered and marginalized" (2010: 5). Judith Ackroyd-Cohen (2007) additionally highlights how the use of the term "applied" can pathologize communities and individuals by creating narratives of enlightened individuals using their superior knowledge and skills to solve the "community's" problems through the application of specialized and monocultural processes. The term applied theatre can hide marginalizing strategies under the veil of doing good (Cohen-Cruz 2010: 5–7). In an essay posted on HowlRound, Michael Rohd (8 July 2012: n.p.) writes,

> The challenge of the trending term "applied" is that it suggests those who "use" theatre tactics for something other than (though perhaps inclusive of) the creation and presenting of performance are in the "service" game, while those who "make and show" are in the "art" game."

In theatre by, with, and for young audiences, we already have to actively resist missionary narratives of theatre "saving the day" as well as narratives of "service." Thus, I much prefer community-based theatre and CCD to applied theatre. Labels, of course, are shorthand indicators of larger cultural and personal values. My use of the terms community-based and CCD place my value system into a collective and public practice, rather than at individual levels.

Contextually, creative activities focused on "public work" place a premium on people's abilities to communicate effectively within all symbol structures, and posits TFY third space as a social good that functions to establish political agency and collective efficacy rather than being oriented toward individual self-esteem or achievement. Which is not to say of course that performances highlighting individual achievement are not still necessary and enjoyable. One of my daughters is an accomplished musician and I invariable enjoy showcases of her hard work. Nevertheless, I position the work of a TFY third space as socially, aesthetically, and culturally different. This philosophical approach emphasizes performance functioning as a form of creative capacity building oriented specifically toward engagement in public and civic institutions and structures. Under the principles of everyday politics, work within TFY third space does not *give* youth power, but rather models for them how to navigate and practice power.

**KEY IDEAS**

- TFY third space practices are a form of CCD.
- TFY third space builds publics and is a practice of power.
- CCD pays attention to community and public spheres not individual achievement.

## 1.7 DELIBERATIVE DEMOCRACY AND THE POLITICS OF REPRESENTATION

To understand children and youth as a public highlights the need to define and structure third space interactions within a model building the "social, economic and political power of that community" (Knight et al. 2005: xvi). Toward that end, I root TFY third space practices in principles of *deliberative democracy*. In a nutshell, deliberative democracy is a system of political decision making that places reasoned, pluralistic discussion front and center in the process. Deliberative democracy rejects the idea that participation in the public sphere is a form of personal, private consumer choice (between political party A and political party B). Additionally, deliberative democracy recognizes and articulates the existence of both formal publics (the realm of public authority à la Habermas) and informal public spheres. McBride compares informal public spheres to the ancient Greek understanding of the *agora* or marketplace (2005: 508). Political theorist and president of the University of Pennsylvania, Amy Gutmann calls for social and cultural connections based on deliberative democratic principles among all peoples. Deliberative democracy fundamentally depends upon fostering mutual respect as well as the ability to make reasoned judgments based on context and perspective, not individual interest. Deliberative democracy places dialogue front and center in the democratic process, and conversation/deliberation legitimizes laws. (Laws are not legitimated because they are laws, but because after reasoned conversation the people decided there *should* be laws.) At the most basic level, deliberative democracy "affirms the need to justify decisions made by citizens and their representatives" (Gutmann and Thompson 2004: 3). Principles of deliberative democracy applied in community settings means paying attention to transparency, project goals not personal goals, fostering mutual respect and reciprocity, and learning how to negotiate conflict. Deliberative democracy is compatible with both direct and representative democratic forms but derives legitimacy not from majority rule, but rather from reasoned judgment. In an environment in which political decision making more often devolves into brinkmanship, sound-bite arguments, or demonizing opponents, reasoned judgment seems to take a back seat to political posturing—to the detriment of the public sphere, public work, and culture as a whole. "Deliberation is not a single skill or virtue," Gutmann writes, "it calls upon skills of literacy, numeracy and critical thinking, as well as contextual knowledge, understanding and appreciation of other people's perspectives. The virtues that deliberation encompass include veracity, nonviolence, practical judgment, civic integrity and magnanimity" (1999: xiii). Primary to the deliberative democratic principle is the understanding that while only rarely do all people agree on what constitutes a "good" idea, people coming together in a spirit of collective goodwill and critical generosity *can* make the world a better place. The moral foundations of deliberative democracy build on the belief that people are not objects to be governed (or risks to be managed); instead, people are self-directed agents collaborating in their own governance. Rather than being understood as a fight between opposing viewpoints then, deliberative democracy functions as a method of coming together to create (1) accessibly reasoned, (2) binding decisions, (3) bridging informal and formal publics, and (4) that remain fluid and open to change in the future. In effect, deliberative democracy "contains a set of principles that prescribe fair terms of cooperation" (Gutmann and Thompson 2004: 125).

I place principles of deliberative democracy in direct contrast with a US American educational and assessment system highlighting young people's competency through competitiveness, or being the best—winning. This keen concentration on individual exceptionalism has been codified at the policy level in multiple ways including "at-risk" discourses and the Federal No Child Left Behind Act (2001). Even popular culture entertainments such as Disney's *High School Musical* and television programs such as *Glee* and *America's Got Talent* depend on a value system, defining people rooted in individual achievement through the focused exploration and training of innate and individual "talents." However, the heart of the arts practice I explore here can be found in a radically different place from the traditional US American paradigm of singular achievement and meritocratic individualism. As Nicholson notes,

> The idea that drama can take people beyond themselves and into the world of others is deeply rooted in the values of applied drama and this chimes particularly well with a vision of social citizenship as a collective and communitarian undertaking.
>
> (2005: 24)

Theatre's soul rests in the belief that one person can step into another person's life with honesty and truthfulness and that the time spent within another's life can help us all see their "truths." Gutmann adds, "Public institutions should manifest and cultivate mutual respect among individuals as free and equal citizens. This aim is basic to almost every democratic ideal" (1999: 303). I argue for a practice that nurtures a communal space of fairness in which all voices have value (even the voices in disagreement with the majority).

Deliberative democracy structures cooperation and collaboration; its natural counterpoint is the politics of recognition (Laden 2001; McBride 2005; Valdez 2001). Necessary in a pluralistic society, the politics of recognition functions as a system of justice based in freedom to participate in moral and public spheres. The politics of recognition in particular addresses structures that unfairly restrict certain individuals from the freedom to participate in social, cultural, and political publics. Originally articulated by Charles Taylor (1992), the politics of recognition builds from Hegel's conceptualization of human identity as dialogically constructed in social ways. Humans do not come to consciousness alone; our many communities acculturate us into being-ness. In other words, you are more than just your thinking. Taylor argues humans are harmed both psychologically and politically/socially when their identity structures are denied mutual respect and dignity—African Americans during the Jim Crow era, for example. I follow the path of Nancy Fraser, however, who argues that rather than being a function of identity (or identity politics), the politics of recognition rests in status relationships. Fraser writes, "misrecognition, accordingly, does not mean the depreciation and deformation of group identity, but social subordination—in the sense of being prevented from participation as a peer in social life" (2000: 113). When political, cultural or social structures exclude some humans or designate others as inferior, those humans are denied the freedom of full participation in social and public life. Using the justice model of politics of recognition means paying attention to who is at the deliberative democratic table, who has to eat in the kitchen and who is denied food altogether. Fraser writes, misrecognition arises when institutions structure interaction according to cultural norms that impede parity of participation. Examples include marriage laws that exclude same-sex partnerships as illegitimate and perverse, social-welfare policies that stigmatize single mothers as sexually irresponsible scroungers, and policing practices such as "racial profiling" that associate racialized persons with criminality.

(Fraser 2001: 24–25)

The goals of the politics of recognition are to seek out systems that impede parity of participation and replace them with processes that foster participation.

TFY third space recognizes parity of participation as a principle goal. TFY third space practice also highlights the importance of cultural and social relationships. While citizenship can be considered a birthright, citizens are made not born. As a facilitator, I structure collaborative and participatory work to promote the principles inherent in the concepts of deliberative democracy and to create a space for complex and thoughtful disagreement and communal exploration of relevant topics. Redefining cultural understandings of children and youth, focusing on collective accomplishments, and fostering mutual respect as well as the ability to make judgments based on context and perspective are all key parameters of the third space. Additionally, using the politics of participation or parity and freedom as foundational moral systems allows TFY third space to pay attention to structures that unfairly prohibit individuals and groups from participating equally in cultural, social, and civic publics.

**KEY IDEAS**

- Facilitation structures are based on principles of deliberative democracy including transparency, cooperative decision making, mutual respect, reciprocity, and deliberation.
- Freedom to participate equally in social, civic, cultural, and political publics is the moral imperative of TFY third space.

## 1.8 DEFINING COMMUNITY

*Community* can be a difficult word to parse. Social scientists use the word in particular ways, whereas politicians use the term to mean something quite different. For our purposes, I build off the work of Anthony Cohen (1985) and David Studdert (2005). Cohen points out two highly pertinent ideas to artists working in CCD. First, at a basic level, community defines a group of people who have something in common while separating them from others (Cohen 1985: 12). As a lifelong Cowboys fan, I have a system of beliefs and desires in common with other Cowboys fans. We can bond over whatever odd thing Jerry Jones has done or who is the best all-time quarterback—Roger Staubach, of course. Cowboys fans also are *not* Steelers fans. Therefore, community fundamentally defines and distinguishes. Second, "People construct community symbolically, making it a resource and repository of meaning, and a referent of their identity" (Cohen 1985: 118). Community fundamentally defines how we understand *and perform* our multiple overlapping selves. Symbol, however, does not have a one-to-one meaning; symbol has no fixed referent. Take a moment and ponder how powerful this fact renders artists who deeply understand and can manipulate symbol systems. In short, symbols are the stuff of people's lives. Cohen notes, "Symbolism owes its versatility to the fact that it does not carry meaning inherently. A corollary of this is that it can be highly responsive to change" (Cohen 1985: 91). Of course, manipulating symbol systems does not equal change, particularly social change. Cohen points out that different members of any particular community attach different meanings to how they understand that community.

> In the face of this variability of meaning, the consciousness of community has to be kept alive through manipulation of its symbols. The reality and efficacy of the community's boundary—and therefore, of the community itself—depends upon its symbolic constructions and embellishment.
> (Cohen 1985: 15)

When I Google, "Cowboys fan pages" I receive 26 million results. If I were to page through those millions of sites, I could categorize the different ways people understand the Cowboys, football, and fandom itself. For example, fans manipulate symbolic boundaries to change distinguishing aspects of community. Say, a non-Cowboy football team seems to be doing well. Many fans will begin to target that team and its fans as different (not as good) as the Cowboys. Such manipulation might include ridiculing particular players, positions, or demonizing whole cities. To summarize Cohen, community both defines and separates through the manipulation of symbol.

Sociologist David Studdert's 2005 text, *Conceptualizing Community: Beyond the State and Individual*, illuminates philosophical conceptualizations of the word, "community." In particular, Studdert advances a unique read of Hannah Arendt's concept of "space of appearance" as "the everyday arena where human being-ness and sociality take place on an ongoing and daily basis" (Studdert 2005: 154). For our purposes, however, his list of "common sense" understandings of "community" is most useful. Studdert's four facets of community:

1. We all belong to multiple, overlapping communities.
2. […] community is never a fixed state, rightly it should be considered a verb not a noun, and it is always the outcome of sociality as an action—be that action or speech—and it is therefore impossible to perform without the presence of other people.
3. And because it is an outcome of a series of actions community is never an abstraction like 'history' or 'mankind.'
4. […] my membership of a community depends on something beyond myself—it depends on others recognizing me and allowing me—just as I recognize and allow them.

(Studdert 2005: 2–3)

I want to tease out some of the more subtle ramifications of Studdert's definitions. First, we never belong to just one community, rather our communities reflect the various aspects of our being. I remember the first time I had to walk a fussy baby around during a large athletic event. As I roamed the halls of the arena, I noticed other caregivers shuffling their cranky children through the circular halls, patting backs, and rolling strollers back and forth. We acknowledged one another with winces and smiles depending on the volume of our respective charges. I remember thinking to myself, "Oh, my goodness, we're a club—a club of people who never get to enjoy the game." Prior to having a child, I never even noticed parents with grumpy children.

Another important point, we cannot belong to a community of one. Community depends on the mutual and relational recognition of others as well as in the ongoing specific actions taken by "members." Like status and reputation, "community" exists in other people's minds and actions and comes into being through social interaction. "Community" occurs in the back and forth between people. In fact, Studdert argues community *only* happens with others; we act community. In addition, Studdert posits community as specific and of the moment rather than a loose abstraction. Which is not to say that community does not function symbolically but rather points to the specificity of the social actions causing community to come into being. This last point is particularly relevant to performance-oriented CCD. Studdert highlights action—speech acts and performance acts—as the natural environment of community—like water around a fish. In fact, community cannot exist without such acts. Think about that fact for a moment.

As I write this section, there have been multiple blogs, presentations, and books exploring theatre, performance, and efficacy. Many polarize efficacy/utility and aesthetics, and question whether something can be both useful and artistic. For example, on an August 2013 blog post on HowlRound, Caridad Svich writes,

> What is art's efficacy?
> I am of a conflicted mind about the nature of art and whether it has true efficacy, especially when it is not necessarily made with the direct and immediate goal to affect a change in a law or is somehow related to matters of governance in a village, town, or city. I believe in theater and social action. I believe in applied theater. But I also believe that art is not merely an instrument of social change. In fact, I am wary of art being put to utilitarian uses and being asked to fit a "useful" application in society.
>
> Art is. And often is outside matters of written law. It delves into the chaotic, strange, odd, and unresolved aspects of humanity and being. It dives into the complications of love. It battles for a country's soul through poetic means. It wrestles the spirit. It questions, sometimes, the meaning of religion. It embraces faith.
>
> Art is unruly. It resists governance.
> It is by nature transgressive. Artistic truth is resistant to consensus.
> To write is an act of intervention.
> "Here," Art says, "is difference. Look."
>
> (n.p.)

If we take the theoretical implications of Studdert's argument to their logical conclusion, the art-for-art's-sake/art-for-utility binary becomes white noise. Yes, Art *is*. Moreover, in that "is-ness," in that chaotic, strange and unresolved being, Art *does*. Performance—social action—is always *already* doing something.

This discussion also reminds me of the manner in which performance philosophers understand gender as cultural performance enacted on and through the body: "the body is not a "being," but a variable boundary, a surface whose permeability is politically regulated, a signifying practice within a cultural field of gender hierarchy and compulsory heterosexuality" (Butler 1990: 189). Community, like the body, is fundamentally unstable and defined by boundaries. Community appears in social action, understood both as a symbol and through a symbol. Perceiving community in this fashion has far-reaching ramifications and explains much about our current world. For example, think about the vicious internal battles characteristic of identity politics or between conservative and liberal branches of particular religions or political parties. Who counts as Black, Asian, Mexican, Christian, Republican, or Catholic? Community is always a priori about "us" and "them." With fluid and unstable boundaries, people emotionally and intellectually invest in regulating and maintaining a community's symbolic and ideological membranes.

Like bodies, communities are regulated internally and externally. Importantly, however, Studdert argues à la Hannah Arendt, "a person in isolation is not a person […], it is also clear that a person talking to themselves is also not a person; speech for Arendt is action; it personifies action" (Studdert 2005: 149–150). In her 1958 text, *The Human Condition*, Arendt outlines a philosophical definition of human action located in the symbolic realm and sustained by communal conversation. Unlike traditional western philosophy then with its clear mind-body split, Arendt's approach decenters identity and being-ness from atomized human thinking—I think therefore I am. Arendt relocates our humanness to the web of relations or as Studdert explains, "everything that relates and ties human being-ness together; everything, every interest object, relationships we establish with objects, all manifestations of culture, language, law, custom, habits, the materiality of buildings, discourse, idealism, spiritualities and ultimately what is often termed species consciousness" (Studdert 2005: 159). We become human through social interaction. At a fundamental level, we can only *be* human through social interaction. The ramifications of such a statement are profound. First, I find this understanding of humanness much more engaging than Nietzsche's, or biologists' self-interest theory, or pop psychology definitions captured in songs such as Simon & Garfunkel's "I am a Rock." Second, the "web of relations" only comes into being through social action—not internal, atomized thought—but because all humans conceptualize meaning and symbol differently, the web of relations can only be apprehended partially. Our understandings will always be composite and partial. In addition, that concisely is the brilliance of theatre and performance—theatre symbolically represents the "web of relations" in three dimensions, through social interaction and time. In fact, I would argue theatre and performance uniquely capture the web of relations or the symbolic and social space of humanness and community.

> **KEY IDEAS**
>
> - Community defines and distinguishes.
> - We all belong to multiple communities.
> - Community is the social and symbolic space of humanness.
> - People construct community symbolically attaching diverse meanings to those symbols.
> - However, community is not generalized abstraction.
> - Fluid and partial, community appears only in social action.
> - We internally and externally regulate community.
> - Communities depend on mutuality and interdependent recognition.
> - The "web of relations" equals everything that relates and ties humans together.
> - Theatre/performance expresses the web of relations.

## 1.9 A PAUSE TO BUILD FIELD THEORY IN CCD WITH CHILDREN AND YOUTH

Fundamental to TFY third space is an exchange in which artists partner with publics in a mutually beneficial and satisfying relationship to create change. Here, I explore a process of co-constructing artistic work with children and youth—public work, public art, good work/s—functioning to advance both complex understandings of reality and the collective good. In particular, TFY third space focuses on building spaces of exchange and reciprocity valuing young humans as contributing members of society, not merely as potential contributors. This text takes as a given that all people are fundamentally creative but that creativity is a practice (not an inherent quality) some have developed further than others. A system of communication, art allows us to step outside of lived experience and consider the totality—the overall shapes of lives—and the diverse ways people make meaning. Building collective efficacy within communitarian arenas and through principles of deliberative democracy and the politics of recognition automatically positions young people in ways outside of the traditional locations usually allowed to young humans (e.g., school, private homes, and sports clubs). Foundational principles of community-based theatre and CCD with children and youth discussed already in this section include:

- Culture is action.
- Children and youth are competent cultural producers.
- Children and youth are acknowledged experts on both being themselves and the meanings of their lives.
- Childhood is understood as socially constructed, not biologically innate; and thus, processes do not place artificial limits on the scope of the work or on the assumed abilities of the participants.
- Primary unit of concern is the community and public-making not individual achievement.
- The work consciously builds the social, political, economic, and/or cultural power of the communities involved.
- Facilitation and participatory techniques are understood through principles of deliberative democracy rather than pedagogy, consensus, or traditional directorial relationships.
- Participants have express relationships to the content of the work developed.
- Children and youth are civic publics.
- The public sphere is a collective and discursive space built on and around human environments.

I want to compare and contrast the ten principles developed here with Goldbard's seven unifying principles for CCD. She posits these not as rigid structures but rather with a "multitude of different expressions in practice":

1. Active participation in cultural life is an essential goal of CCD.
2. Diversity is a social asset, part of the cultural commonwealth, requiring protection and nourishment.
3. All cultures are essentially equal and society should not promote any one as superior to the others.
4. Culture is an effective crucible for social transformation, one that can be less polarizing and create deeper connections than other social-change arenas.
5. Cultural expression is a means of emancipation, not the primary end in itself; the process is as important as the product.
6. Culture is a dynamic, protean whole, and there is no value in creating artificial boundaries within it.
7. Artists have roles as agents of transformation that are more socially valuable than mainstream art world roles—and certainly equal in legitimacy.

(2006: 43)

Goldbard (2006) and Cohen-Cruz (2005) point to the social justice and civil rights movements of the 1960s and 1970s as rooting the current iteration and development of community-based arts in the present moment, so you should not find Goldbard's strong social justice bent surprising. Many of the principles I advocate are similar, of course, to the ones Goldbard lists. Indeed, I am indebted in my thinking to the germinal work she and Adams produced. While my list builds from theoretical underpinnings of the practices and primary participants, her list incorporates both the "why" of community engagement and expands artist/facilitators' role definitions. Goldbard's numbers six and seven pull from the realities of visual artists more than children's theatre specialists but have direct implications for how CCD specialists understand their relationships to their particularized art field. Here, Goldbard reacts to the boundaries between elite and popular cultures and the diverse aesthetic vocabularies of each.

A market economy depends on both scarcity and specialness in order to increase pricing structures—for example, an artist's paintings are worth more after the artist has died. Many then would rank an abstract oil painting as both more scarce and more special than a quilt. Community-cultural development processes and products turn this economic relationship on its head. Of course, the reality of theatre with children and youth has been traditionally defined as external to market economies. Culturally, TFY has been understood (by its practitioners) as more socially valuable or "honorable" particularly for upper-middle-class women. The difficulty of this bifurcated system has been, however, a belief in "virtue" as its own reward. This is why a glut of women graduating from university theatre programs in the 1930s, 1940s, and into the 1950s found themselves in volunteer or below-living-wage positions across the United States, producing and touring theatre shows for school children (van de Water 2012: 12–19). To work for pay, especially as a woman, was not only class bound but also children's theatre was seen as less threatening to the nascent, dispersed commercial theatre structures that just so happened to be headed almost uniformly by men. I do not wish to rehearse arguments for or against value judgments. Instead, I point out that the challenge of helping others move outside narrow, professional definitional boundaries is part and parcel of both children's theatre and working in community environments.

Another reality of artistic role-making Goldbard signals toward in points six and seven is the manner in which community-based art practices integrate abilities and practices from multiple fields. There are those who have been invested in building barriers between practices and labeling functions outside of the traditional as not-art. Likewise, there are those invested in expanding understandings of *artist* and *culture*. In the competitive granting world, access to funding often hinges on artists' abilities to successfully defend their roles as an artist (rather than teacher, community organizer, or social activist). Nevertheless, community-based processes do depend on balancing multiple roles in context: artist/citizen/teacher; parent/maker/activist; chef/performance artist/food justice activist. There are many who find the rather dizzying needs of various roles difficult to balance or perhaps even disturbing. Nevertheless, such code switching persists as a hallmark of how artists self-define within community engagement processes.

I need to unpack understandings of *activist* and *social change* within this context however. Goldbard's list and the practice of CCD as a whole have a strong activist and social justice bent. I too have strongly held political and social views, but I consider third space facilitation incompatible with my personal political platform. This does not mean that I do not have a platform. Frankly, to position young people as socially competent cultural producers who consciously build the social, political, economic, and cultural power of their communities takes a strong social change stance. My primary function as facilitator, however, hinges on building space for youth to claim power and public-making in ways they understand as culturally powerful. I never hide my own beliefs but I do not view CCD with youth as equivalent to theatre for social change. I am not training young people for Boal's revolution, but rather to engage as full and equal citizens within a democratic society in the present. There are those who will interpret this stance as a cop-out, but I

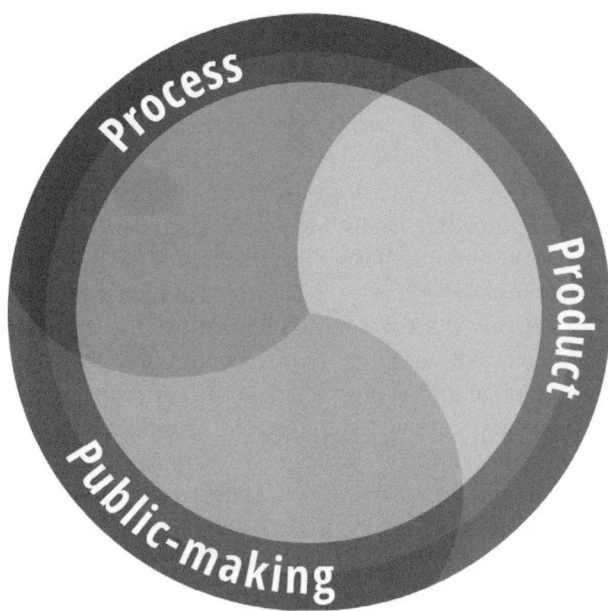

**Figure 1.6:** TFY third space.

understand my role as aesthetic specialist and symbolic languages expert not the content specialist. The primary unit of concern is the community and community participants should directly connect to the stories, not to me. My political stances should not then be imposed or take precedent over the stances of the participants. To work in this manner then is at once both populist and detached. For TFY third space, activism structures the engagement and the messages/stories and themes and "actos"[1] are developed by the participants. Cohen-Cruz points out, "Theatre reproduces the same hierarchies that plague the world at large, the same assumptions about who can speak, who must listen and who is not even invited into the conversation" (2010: 5). Facilitators must take immense care not to impose the adult voice over the values and energies of the youth. Our responsibilities rest in understanding the ramifications of the choices, not in making those choices for the children and youth with whom we work.

Pragmatically, I divide the practices of TFY third space or CCD with children and youth into three fluid categories: *Process*, *Product*, and *Public-making*. I include a graphic representation here so that you can see the ways in which these categories deeply intertwine. Process and product relate reflexively of course, while public-making occurs throughout the range of activities and in the form itself. I discuss all three of these categories extensively in this text, but I wish to briefly mark the way in which I define them. *Process* here means the progressive creation of embodied narrative and spectacular material, including sound/music and gesture while also developing practical and symbolic ensemble within a deliberative context. *Product* is an event produced within a specific duration and locality, which reenacts intangible originals (not real, but not not-real) developed and refined in the processes of devising or adapting work intended to contribute to change. *Public-making* acknowledges that culture is socially created, collaborative, and fundamentally creative. Public-making is a visionary process that reconfigures the strategies of community givens through acknowledging the tactics already in use and leveraging and adapting them in inspirational ways. Public-making can also highlight givens within a community or groups and build ensemble tactics through cultural and symbolic forms. In all cases, public-making is community-driven, context sensitive, and fluid. In many ways, public-making *is* the public work performed by CCD with children and youth. CCD creates art actions oriented toward change—but change in what? In the next several sections, I elaborate on how art actions can intervene in political, social, and economic systems to create good.

## 1.10 A BRIEF INTRODUCTION TO CAPITAL AND CULTURAL ECONOMIES

*Liberty cannot be preserved without a general knowledge among the people …. And the preservation of the means of knowledge among the lowest ranks, is of more importance to the public than all the property of all the rich men in the country.*

– John Adams

We live in a highly economized world oriented toward labor, consumption, and the circulation of different kinds of capital. Our US American worldview government and society is rooted primarily in material culture and capitalistic structures. Economics and the ways in which economic systems and social/cultural systems collide can be particularly fruitful avenues for investigation and manipulation. The epigraph opening this section highlights the triangle relationship between economics, freedom, and knowledge. In John Adams's 1765 essay from which I pulled the quote, he points out historic ways the wealthy have attempted to control access to knowledge in order to control freedom and preserve their own wealth. Adams claims close connections between liberty, information, and material success. In order to consciously increase the cultural, social, economic, and/or political power of a particular community and claim publics with youth, we have to pay attention to freedom, knowledge, and economics.

In this section, I explore a couple of related concepts offering models of how art and theatre intervenes within material social systems—cultures and economies. Pierre Bourdieu's theories root my understandings of theatre and art here. A French sociologist and public intellectual, Bourdieu's work expanded on materialist conceptions of social structures and sociological reproduction. He particularly explored class and repressive social systems. Bourdieu (1977, 1984, 1993) argued different forms of capital, in particular *social, economic,* and *cultural,* could be turned into one another. Bourdieu's theory of capital transference radically increased the philosophical and material importance of individuals' lived experiences—which inculcate taste, patterns of consumption, and social connections—to unpacking complex economic systems. People's lives matter, what they make, what they consume, and how they interact in physical and social environments. Bourdieu explored how repressive structures continue to marginalize particular categories of people through class distinctions built on embodied practices internalized over time. He coined the term *habitus* to refer to the conscious and unconscious patterns of experience and internal schema through which people construct meaning and perform social and cultural patterns. One's habitus provides differentiated access to cultural capital (e.g., knowledge, language, skills, patterns of dress, values, and aesthetics). Readers trained in pedagogy likely are familiar with how cultural capital influences educational attainment. Bourdieu's 1977 book, *Reproduction in Education, Society and Culture*, explored the ways in which the class distinctions of students and teachers constructed evaluation and assessment of youth as intelligent or stupid, capable or incapable. He argued that privileged youth inherit the cultural capital and the social capital (social networks and connections) of their parents that allow them to leverage economic capital. Bourdieu's theories continue to ground a large portion of constructivist educational philosophies and analysis of educational disparities. One's habitus instills schema that structure evaluation and assessment. What counts as "success," "intelligence," and "ability" depend on one's schema. I grew up in a working-class environment, my habitus as a child was constrained by the habitus inhabited by my parents. I inherited their class and I learned particular skills, behaviors, and patterns of being in the world. Unlike my middle-class children, for example, I did not participate in sports as a child. In my habitus, not only did girls not participate in team sports, youth did not participate in structured leisure time. I watched television, rode my bike, explored the storm sewer system, and played in the local creeks. I roamed all over the neighborhood and was responsible entirely for myself until after my parents arrived home from work. By the time I was 13 or 14, I worked several jobs. As a high-school student, I was expected to perform well in school and to contribute to our family economy by purchasing my own clothing and leisure activities. My children participate in structured leisure time, primarily team sports and arts enrichment programs. Their highly competitive scholastic/artistic environment (they attend a performing arts school) hangs on my ability to financially and culturally secure private lessons, additional tutoring, and private access to advanced technology and material. In this way, I "invest" my access to social, creative, and cultural capital in my children. I share this personal information to highlight the different ways habitus informs and constrains one's access and ability. I learned a strong work ethic in my family; I learned what to do with my free time. I learned how to recover from economic setbacks, how to manage money, and how work-for-pay functions. My children have learned advanced skills in music and dance, teamwork, and physical and intellectual achievement.

Within economics, "capital" means "a commodity itself used in the production of other goods and services. It is a human-made input, such as plant or equipment, created to permit increased production in the future" (Smithson 1982: 111). Physical or real capital (such as Smithson's example of a manufacturing plant) represents the ability to transform inputs into outputs. This definition remains valid when we discuss human capital. For example, many people promote university education as an investment in human capital. Arguments based on economics understand the money spent on educational attainment as buying human capital (e.g., skills, knowledge, and credentials) that will allow individuals to make more money over their life span. This theory grounds arguments concerning how much states should invest in higher education. Increased human capital raises the long-term economic success factors for entire economic ecosystems. In this understanding of capital, too, inputs change into outputs. Lindon Robison, Allen Schmid, and Marcelo Siles define social capital as "a person's or groups' sympathy toward another person or group that may produce a potential benefit, advantage, and preferential treatment for another person or group of persons beyond that expected in an exchange relationship" (2002: 6). Here, they define "sympathy" as "an affinity, association, or relationship between persons or things wherein whatever affects one similarly affects the other" (2002: 6). We build social capital in the networks of friendships, colleagues, and affinities grown over our life spans. For example, here at the ASU, graduates across the 40 years of TFY MA, MFA, and PhD programs continue to interact. Conversations among ASU TFY alums meeting for the first time cover when they graduated and who was in their cohorts, allowing them to map their relationships to one another—building and maintaining social capital. Social capital can be understood in non-economic terms as well. Many consider social capital to be the literal glue that maintains America as a vibrant national community of belonging. In *Bowling Alone* Robert Putnam (2000) famously argued that decreases in social connectivity and the bonds created through affinity threaten democracy itself.

> **KEY IDEAS**
>
> - Different kinds of capital can be turned into one another.
> - Children and youth inherit their habitus from their parents and their communities.
> - Social economic status has a great impact on the ways in which individuals and communities define and understand wealth and success.

## 1.11 EXPANDING CAPITAL SYSTEMS

To understand how art actions can intervene in economic systems, however, I need both a wider and more specific definition of "capital" than the one offered in the previous section. Community development and community organizing understand capital both as "a means" and as "a means to an end." In other words, we build capital toward goals, but stronger capital itself often is the goal. Community organizing and development literature expands understandings of capital to include more diverse constructs than industrial economics does. For the purposes of expanding my use of capital systems, I depend on the work of Anthony Bebbington (1999), Partha Dasgupta and Ismail Serageldin (1999), Mary Emory and Cornelia Flora (2006), Mary Flora (1995, 2004), Suzanne Morse (2004), Rhonda Phillips and Gordon Shockley (2010), and David Throsby (2001) to ground my terminology and theoretical concepts. To explore how community-based performance practices can intervene in community ecologies, I adapted the Community Capitals Framework (CCF) developed by the National Rural Funders Collaborative as "an analytical tool to determine the effectiveness of its investments in addressing structural conditions of rural poverty [...] (Emory and Flora 2006: 20). The CCF model understands the complex economic and cultural/social environment of any given community as a system of seven overlapping domains that intricately and complexly interact with one another. I have expanded the CCF model into nine domains that fluidly overlap and intertwine:

1. Built capital
2. Civic capital

3. Creative capital
4. Cultural capital
5. Environmental capital
6. Financial capital
7. Human capital
8. Political capital
9. Social capital

*Built Capital* includes community infrastructure and built environments. My family's built capital would include our house, carport, patios, and shed. Additionally, my family participates in my city's water, sewer, natural gas, irrigation, and electric systems.

*Civic capital* "refers to those places and institutions that bring people together. It can cross over other forms of capital, but generally these are investments in place, such as parks, cultural centers, and theaters" (Morse 2004: 24). Civic capital could also include libraries, meet-ups and festivals, indeed any type of location, or event bringing community members together in the same place and time. I particularly enjoy Morse's emphasis on "place" here.

*Cultural capital* includes language, skills, patterns of dress, and value systems. Cultural capital can be particularly complex as individuals belong to multiple, overlapping cultures with diverse values and beliefs. Cohen-Cruz (2010) points out, "Cultural capital constitutes a set of resources: the particular music, performance, poetry, folk wisdom, customs, food and dress that are frequently sources of collective strength and pride and a way to bring people together" (126).

*Creative capital* includes aesthetic structures and creative abilities, adaptive reuse, creative expression, and capacity for creative problem solving along with divergent thinking patterns.

*Environmental capital* includes a community's natural resources, these resources can be geographical (e.g., the Salt River anchoring the Rio Salado Project mentioned in 1.2) or ecological. The environmental capital for communities participating in Second Life or online immersive role-playing games includes virtual landscapes and technological ones, such as software interfaces and graphics processors.

*Financial capital* means money and credit markets. Financial capital can be both formal and informal.

I have already discussed *Human capital*, but would include here one's singular and collective capacities. Formal and informal education and implicit and explicit knowledge systems would also go in this domain. Morse points to a larger understanding of human capital investment too, including

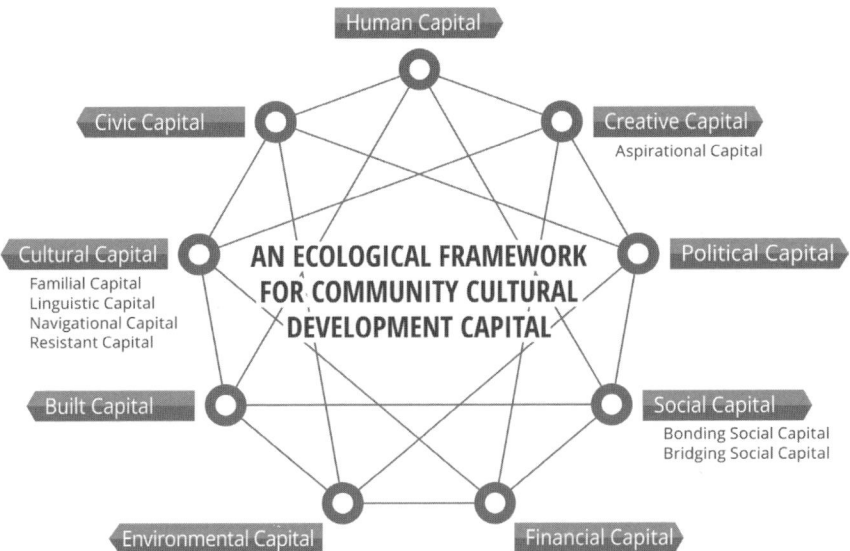

**Figure 1.7:** An ecological framework of CCD Capital.

"secondary investments that enhance [people's] ability to participate better in society" (2004: 24).

*Political capital* includes access to and influence over decision makers and policy crafters. In my neighborhood, my neighbors include several city employees, two elected officials (a state representative and a city council member), and neighbors who serve on influential citizen councils and working groups. For a small neighborhood with under 100 homes, my neighborhood has strong political capital.

Finally, *social capital* can be considered one's specific and collective social networks. To complicate matters further, theorists divide social capital into two particular forms: bridging and bonding. *Bonding social capital* strengthens ties within social networks. *Bridging social capital* functions as baggy networks bridging one social network with another.

Of course, the elaborate capital system I sketch out here fluidly connects across categories and many of my delineations are somewhat arbitrary. For example, we could easily combine civic capital into bonding and bridging social capital. I believe, however, the specificity inherent in the above nine domains allows for deeply considered planning, evaluation, process, product, and public-making. In other words, while we could quibble over the inclusion of civic capital in social capital for example, I include civic capital as a singular category in order to pay specific attention to fostering connections among community members to strengthen civic capacities and public-making. I am interested here in leveraging capital to build a community's internal resources at both the macro and micro levels.

A further helpful expression of *resistant* capital was articulated by Tara J. Yosso and David G. Garcia in their 2007 article, "'This is No Slum!' A critical race theory analysis of community cultural wealth in Culture Clash's *Chavez Ravine*." Across the globe, theorists and economists underline the diverse ways communities understand and constitute community "wealth." Marginalized communities, in particular, adapt to environments limiting their freedoms. These communities then build particularized skills and abilities navigating the realities of their worlds or what I have labeled as creative capital. Yosso and Garcia illuminate the ways diversity and marginalization builds particular cultural skills that should be considered as key components of community wealth. They criticize deficit planning and analysis that focuses on what communities lack and suggest instead asset development as a useful lens through which to understand and critique theatre and community-based performance. "We further assert that community cultural wealth comprises at least six forms of capital: aspirational, linguistic, social, navigational, familial, and resistant" (Yosso and Garcia 2007: 154). In the bullet list below, I define Yosso and Garcia's delineations:

- *Aspirational capital* concerns the ability of a community to set hopeful goals for the future even in the face of trauma or difficulty. "This resiliency is evident in those who allow themselves and their children to dream of possibilities beyond their present circumstances…" (Yosso and Garcia 2007: 158). I would locate aspirational capital as a subset of creative capital.
- *Linguistic capital* builds from the ability to speak multiple languages and navigate multiple cultural codes. In particular, the ability to code switch and navigate what are sometimes conflicting environments. Yosso and Garcia also include narrative style and orality in this form. "Linguistic capital also refers to the ability to communicate through visual art, music, or poetry" (Yosso and Garcia 2007: 161). I would locate linguistic capital as a subset of cultural capital.
- *Navigational capital* "refers to skills in maneuvering through social institutions. Historically, this implies the ability to maneuver through institutions not created with Communities of Color in mind" (Yosso and Garcia 2007: 162). I place navigational capital as a subset of cultural capital.
- Yosso and Garcia separate *familial capital* from social capital and use the term to expand kin networks to family of choice as well as genetic relationships. Familial relationships nurture history, memory, and social

connections, building networks of obligation and tradition. Unlike Yosso and Garcia, I locate familial capital as a subset of cultural capital rather than social capital. Although, it could logically fit in either location. Yosso and Garcia use familial capital to label particularized cultural constructions of family, which is why I believe familial capital slots most logically into cultural capital.

- Finally, "resistant capital refers to those knowledges and skills fostered through oppositional behavior that challenges inequality" (Yosso and Garcia 2007: 166). I would locate resistant capital as a particular brand of political capital. Young people often develop highly refined resistant capital. Youth growing up in state care, for example, often assert agency primarily through resistant capital. I include resistant capital as a subset of cultural capital.

Yosso and Garcia's descriptions helpfully articulate and strengthen the capital systems for community engagements. Additionally, I second their call for asset development protocols rather than risk management. In my experience, an asset development approach refocuses participants' understandings of their own skills and attributes. This is particularly relevant to working with children and youth who are trained by the dominant educational system to understand themselves in relationship (perhaps competition) to a symbolic "normal" child or youth. Mapping community wealth—as defined by the community—is a key part of the community engagement process itself.

TFY CCD practices seek to build a community's political, social, economic, and cultural power. In effect, we seek to strengthen—to invest—in the capital network of the community with whom we work. We build value. Using an economic lens, we can understand TFY CCD as a process of analyzing existing resources and leveraging them to frame and build value in particular capital domains. So what does this mean on a practical level? In TFY CCD processes, we build social connections, both internal to our ensemble and externally through our partnerships. We map the cultural and civic assets of our community and use these connections to build and strengthen community capital with craft and aesthetic skills in meaningful public art actions. On the individual level, we build both creative capacity and particular skills for our participants—human capital—but we also build civic capital in our focus on collaboration, claiming publics. The products themselves highlight cultural and creative capital while the aesthetic frame heightens meaningfulness. In other words, by learning how to understand the ideological frames of our participants and the ways in which power circulates, our projects and programs can frame meaning, identity, and value in ways speaking to both the internal community and to outsiders.

An expanded understanding of capital networks allows TFY CCD artists to argue for the use of TFY CCD as *a literal investment into a community as well as tangentially supporting civic sustainability and cultural wealth.*

For example, my first long-term digital storytelling residency was on the Gila River Indian Community in District 5 at a local high school. We worked the entire school year to build a digital story exploring the youths' perceptions of who they were, how they fit into their community, and sources of pride and challenge. We leveraged

1. Cultural and environmental capital: the landscape of the community, the rhythms of speech, a gentler sense of time, visual symbols of the Akimel O'odham as well as the tribe's relationship to water/Gila River.
2. Social capital: the extended family connections of the youth, the skills of their immediate family members, the families' networks within traditional music, dance, and storytelling.
3. Human and creative capital: the skills of the youth, their creative capacity to articulate personal meaning, and their storytelling skills.

Through our processes, we trained the youth in photography and digital video, nonlinear editing, theatrical performance, design skills, public speaking, narrative, creative writing, and provided extended time to focus on personal growth and ensemble engagement. The project situated the youth as experts in their culture: teachers and explorers. The final product created space for the youth to speak back to both the larger culture of Arizona, but also to their community leaders and spiritual elders—civic capital and public-making. The youth presented their work multiple times to district councils, held talk back sessions, gave public presentations, and functioned within the civic space of their tribe. In the multiple public sessions, youth responded to both positive and negative feedback; their abilities to communicate, to engage in deliberation and democratic dialogue—as well as their resistant capital—circulated and strengthened public-making and placemaking. However, I used an educational and sociopsychological framework to justify, plan, and evaluate "The River People" project that limited my (and my partners') understandings of the possibilities. Looking back, I understand that my philosophical frame limited the CCD possibilities I could have accomplished.

Given this elaborate capital system how can it be useful in CCD? Lionel Beaulieu of the Southern Rural Development Center states, "community development should begin with a systematic assessment of the assets that exist in the community" (Beaulieu 2002: 3). The Southern Rural Development Center publishes several asset-mapping resources including individual skill assessment worksheets and organization asset worksheets at http://srdc.

msstate.edu/trainings/educurricula/asset_mapping/. I have found their worksheets a useful starting point for building my own worksheets adapted to particular projects and partnership parameters. Understanding the diversity of capital assets in general is a useful skill for TFY CCD practitioners. Below is a worksheet I use either for myself or with community partners to map capital assets. Of course, comprehensive asset mapping involves huge resources of time and people. Sometimes, such mapping can itself be a lovely project. For example, we once did an asset map with youth through photography and creative writing. The below chart is only a start.

| Community Asset Mapping  Date:  Define the physical/community boundaries (include map if possible) | |
|---|---|
| **BUILT CAPITAL:** *What is the physical human-made environment? What buildings or places does the community have or have access to? Use maps and photographs if possible.* | |
| **CIVIC CAPITAL:** *What institutions/events/organizations bring people together? What brings people together in the same place and time? These can be locations (like a library or a park or a school), event specific (like a festival, a play or a free breakfast), organizational (like a chamber of commerce or a religious institution), and associational (like a culture club or athletic teams).* | |
| **CREATIVE CAPITAL:** *What creative skills, crafts and talents does the community possess or can leverage? Think broadly: e.g., visual arts, music, singing, dance, quilting, photography, pottery, cooking, recipes, writing, poetry, spoken word, rapping, gymnastics, comedy and joke telling, coaching and sports achievements, acting, preaching, design. If you are listing specific people, include how they connect within the community and contact information if appropriate. What are the primary aesthetic and symbolic symbol systems of the community?* | |

*(continued)*

| | |
|---|---|
| **Aspirational capital:** *How does the community define life time success and achievement? Who are the community's heroes? How does the community define happiness?* | |
| **CULTURAL CAPITAL:** *What are the languages, skills, patterns of dress and value systems of the community? What do people have pride in? How do they express and perform their pride?* | |
| **Linguistic capital:** *What codes does the community have to switch between? Who performs and teaches others how to code switch?* | |
| **Navigational capital:** *What institutions does the community navigate? How do they perform these navigations? Who knows how to do these best? Who teaches others?* | |
| **Familial capital:** *What kin networks are part of the community? What are the diverse ways "family" is defined?* | |
| **Resistant capital:** *How does the community perform resistance externally? Resistance to what and whom? What forms does this resistance take? How does the community perform resistance internally?* | |
| **ENVIRONMENTAL CAPITAL:** *What are the environmental/natural features within the physical/community boundary? Lakes, creeks, nature walks, bat habitats, canals, et cetera. Use photographs and maps if possible.* | |
| **FINANCIAL CAPITAL:** *What access to funds does the community have? What funds will be necessary?* | |
| **HUMAN CAPITAL:** *What formal and informal methods of investing in people does the community use? What kinds of skills can be found in the community? Think broadly: care giving (elders, children, ill, mental health), executive skills (budgeting, human resource management, planning and evaluating),* | |

*(continued)*

| | |
|---|---|
| *construction and renovation (carpentry, welding, plumbing, dry walling, painting), cleaning, gardening, et cetera. List names and contact information if relevant.* | |
| **POLITICAL CAPITAL:** *What access to and influence over decision makers and policy crafters does the community have? List names and contact information if relevant. How many community members have written a letter or called their representative over an issue? How many have been involved in protests? What issues galvanize the community?* | |
| **SOCIAL CAPITAL**: *What are the collective social networks of the community? If the community is small enough you can create a map/visual representation of relationships.*<br><br>**Bonding Social capital:** *What formal and informal events strengthen ties within the community? Who in particular brings people together and how? Include names and contact information if relevant.*<br><br>**Bridging Social capital:** *With what other communities and networks does the community interface? Who in particular builds bridges into other communities and networks? How? Include names and contact information if relevant. What formal and informal ties does the community maintain?* | |

## KEY IDEAS

- Communities define and value "wealth" in disparate ways.
- Capital functions as an interlocking system and I present an articulated and complex TFY third space model allowing nuanced and specific planning and evaluation.
- Capital can be both a means and a means to an end.
- Overall community well-being and a community's ecology depend on complex, interaction of capital (among other things).
- Asset mapping allows TFY CCD practitioners and their participants to take a snap shot of community wealth.

## 1.12 DEFINING DEVELOPMENT

In this section, I define *development* in two separate albeit somewhat overlapping ways: positive youth development and the capabilities approach. Work within particular communities may depend on one or the other paradigms or fluidly shift between the two. However, anyone interested in TFY third space should understand each of the approaches as well as their potential benefits and/or challenges. In particular, keen understanding of these paradigms can help set the stage for answering *what* interventions do theatre and performance make in social, political, cultural, educational, and spiritual structures.

### 1.12.1 Positive Youth Development

Youth-focused socially engaged arts practices blur the boundaries between public and private, work and home in unique and powerful ways. In US culture as a whole, children and youth have limited access to public spaces and to democratic dialogues. Again, children do not vote, youth do not have access to as many capital domains as adults, they are kept on the margins of public and policy culture and so have inadequate means to acquire the many social, cultural, and capital skills needed to negotiate the public sphere. However, children- and youth-focused CCD provides opportunities for young people to embody and perform their beliefs about themselves and others while public-making, contributing to their communities. Understanding culture as action allows for positive and productive civic engagement, highlighting children and youth as community assets not niche markets, risks, or potential humans.

In the 2001 edited volume, *Trends in Youth Development: Visions, Realities, Challenges*, authors Gary MacDonald and Rafael Valdivieso point out that a perspective in youth development starts with three questions: "What kinds of human beings do we want all of our children to be? What skills do we want them to possess? What do we want them to be able to do to succeed in adolescence as well as adulthood?" (172). *Development* is a difficult word dragging a chain of neocolonial baggage and neoliberal connotations. When used casually, *development* in conjunction with *child* or *youth* generally refers to the biological processes of physical maturation. We cannot, of course, divorce physical processes from ideological conceptualizations of those processes, so development models can position young people as incomplete adults—what Danish sociologist Jens Qvortrup (1994) refers to as "Adult Beings" and "Child Becomings." Notably, the first question MacDonald and

Valdivieso ask is not, "What kinds of human beings are our children already?" *Development* needs to be unpacked on multiple levels. Here, I am interested particularly in deconstructing the common ways we understand *development* with children and youth—growth, maturation, skill-building, and unfolding— with the ways *development* can be parsed in socioeconomic understandings and cultural organizing practices. Youth development models firmly root in developmental psychology but have been influenced by community development philosophies. Thus, they do not automatically assume a binary construction of adult/child, complete/incomplete, and being/becoming. I use *development* as part of a lifelong journey; competence, for example, has no fixed upper limit. A youth development model understood in this manner does not place information or knowledge out there and separate from the individual. We do not *get* developed nor do we *have* development. Rather, we develop. *Development* can be understood to be an organic structure, innate to the human condition rather than an imposed or mechanical one.

Philosophically, I prefer positively oriented youth development models— programs focusing on young people's strengths rather than their deficits. In 1990, the Search Institute (http://www.search-institute.org/assets/) created a list of 40 internal and external assets critical for young humans to thrive. These divided equally between internal and external assets. The Search Institute has continued to refine their lists and the most recent iteration was published in 2006. This list included twenty external assets divided into sections including: support; empowerment; boundaries and expectations; and constructive use of time. The list also includes twenty internal assets divided into sections including: commitment to learning; positive values; social competencies and positive identities. Over the many years that the Search Institute has been using and refining their list of the 40 assets the list has aligned more and more closely with developmental psychology. Their list incorporates research from multiple platforms but represents particular orientations to who and what young people should be. For example, Asset 20 "Time at Home", under constructive use of time, reflects dominant conceptions driving research designs and interpretations of research findings positing the private domain as the most appropriate and positive space for children and youth, as well as traditional middle-class cultural capital investment strategies. This assumption rests on a class-oriented and protective conception of private space and the home. As a middle-class parent who adores her children, yes, my home *is* the safest environment for them. However, not all homes are equally safe, nor are all all parents equally able to invest in their children in the same manner. I point this out not to quibble with the Search Institute's work but to highlight the ways in which dominant understandings frame discourse and that includes scientific/research discourse.

In 2002, the National Research Council (NRC) and the Institute of Medicine of the National Academy of Sciences (NAS) issued a report summarizing the critical domains of youth development that used the terms "personal" and "social assets" (Eccles and Gootman 2002). The NRC/NAS divides personal and social assets into four distinct domains: physical development; intellectual development; psychological and emotional development; and social development. The report suggests that the more assets a young person has, the more likely that person will experience future or current well-being (2002: 73). They also note that, "it is beneficial to have assets in each of the four general categories" and "within each general category, one can do quite well with only a subset of the many characteristics listed" (2002: 73). The full list of personal and social assets includes:

*Physical development*
- Good health habits
- Good health risk-management skills

*Intellectual development*
- Knowledge of essential life skills
- Knowledge of essential vocational skills
- School success
- Rational habits of mind—critical thinking and reasoning skills
- In-depth knowledge of more than one culture
- Good decision-making skills
- Knowledge of skills needed to navigate through multiple cultural contexts

*Psychological and emotional development*
- Good mental health, including positive self-regard
- Good emotional self-regulation skills
- Good coping skills
- Good conflict-resolution skills
- Mastery motivation and positive achievement motivation
- Confidence in one's personal efficacy
- "Planfulness"—planning for the future and future life events
- Sense of personal autonomy/responsibility for self
- Optimism coupled with realism
- Coherent and positive personal and social identity
- Prosocial and culturally sensitive values
- Spirituality or a sense of a "larger" purpose in life
- Strong moral character
- A commitment to good use of time

*Social development*
- Connectedness—perceived good relationships and trust with parents, peers, and some other adults
- Sense of social place/integration—being connected and valued by larger social networks
- Attachment to prosocial/conventional institutions, such as school, church, non-school youth programs
- Ability to navigate in multiple cultural contexts
- Commitment to civic engagement

(73–74)

The NRC/NAS asset list more closely aligns with educational philosophies and Bloom's Revised Taxonomy (Anderson et al. 2001)—which names and classifies learning processes into knowledge dimensions and cognitive dimensions—while also reflecting developmental psychology and strong epidemiological ideas of community health and welfare. In general, I prefer the NRC/NAS model as it more accurately reflects my own focus on deliberation and the politics of representation and communitarian systems. Nevertheless, both asset taxonomies can be helpful for planning and evaluation purposes and many youth development organizations already use one or the other. Additionally and importantly, both the Search Institute model and the NRC/NAS place young humans in contexts. While both classifications focus primarily on individuals, each recognizes social models of identity and belonging. Finally, the Family and Youth Services Bureau of the US American federal government identifies four key components research links to young people's lifelong successes: competence; usefulness; power; and belonging (2007: 3). These components, combined with the above asset catalogues, structure how I understand positive youth development (summarized in the below chart). In this chart, I combine the NRC/NAS taxonomy with the four key components. Of course, the personal and social assets categorized by the NRC/NAS slot into more than one component. This chart then reflects my mental model of positive youth development within TFY CCD practices.

In "A Theory of Human Motivation," a 1943 article published in the journal *Psychological Review*, Abraham Maslow posited that all humans have basic survival and growth needs. Maslow ranked these needs into two basic categories: deficiency needs and growth needs. While later researchers and theorists have quibbled with Maslow's hierarchical rankings, they remain useful categorizations. Deficiency needs include those basic requirements that all organisms must meet to survive: physiological (e.g., food, water, shelter, and air) and safety (e.g., security of body, of resources, and of health). In addition, Maslow posits that humans have two other deficiency needs: love/belonging (e.g., friendship, family, social relationship, and cultural affiliations) and self-esteem (e.g., self-esteem, confidence, and respect of others) or again, what the Family and Youth Services Bureau labels "competence usefulness, power, and belonging" (2007: 3). Maslow points out that without these basic needs, humans cannot progress and grow. If a person's basic needs are not met (e.g., food), then the need for food will occupy that person's thoughts to the exclusion of all else. If an individual's basic needs for food, shelter, safety, belonging, and esteem *are met* then those needs cease to motivate behavior. Maslow's hierarchy of needs is a useful structure to remember as it highlights a primary difference between social welfare delivery (programs that help youth meet their most basic deficiency needs) and positive youth development programs, which tend to focus on competence, usefulness, power, and belonging at the collective level. I believe that unless a child or youth's basic needs for food, water, shelter, and safety have been met, TFY CCD practices are both inappropriate and ineffective.

Strength orientations share several characteristics influencing relational structures. For one, asset development models do not inevitably correlate with young people's age. In general, youth development programs do not automatically separate young people into age categories but tend to allow young people to self-segregate and skill segregate. This decouples power and status from age. That is not to say that power and hierarchy are not present, as all groups of people use power and position to organize themselves. Status, however, is less automatic and power flows more freely within a youth development paradigm. This flux allows a more complex awareness of the circulation of power among the youth themselves and this can reinforce deliberative democratic principles, although not necessarily, of course. TFY third space CCD processes support explorations of power beyond the hierarchical control structures most youth experience in school settings. In my experience, generally, adults and young people share power in asset development paradigms. For example, a process solidly grounded in positive youth development asks youth to be a part of any planning, evaluation, and assessment processes. Youth also often design their own programs and/or provide substantive governance in youth development programs. Furthermore, this lateral control structure highlights the importance of deliberative dialogue techniques, shared leadership approaches, and skills in facilitation as well as access to adequate time for processing. Another influential component of youth development models rests in the primacy of relationships and the energy needed to build ethical and authentic engagement. In most cases, young people connect in youth development processes because they wish to engage, not because they

| | Physical development | Intellectual development | Psychological and emotional development | Social development |
|---|---|---|---|---|
| **COMPETENCE** | Good health habits<br>Good health risk-management skills | Knowledge of essential life skills<br>Knowledge of essential vocational skills<br>School success<br>Rational habits of mind—critical thinking and reasoning skills<br>In-depth knowledge of more than one culture<br>Good decision-making skills<br>Knowledge of skills needed to navigate through multiple cultural contexts | Good mental health, including positive self-regard<br>Good emotional self-regulation skills<br>Good coping skills<br>Good conflict-resolution skills<br>Mastery motivation and positive achievement motivation<br>Confidence in one's personal efficacy<br>"Planfulness"—planning for the future and future life events<br>Sense of personal autonomy/responsibility for self<br>Optimism coupled with realism<br>Prosocial and culturally sensitive values<br>A commitment to appropriate use of time | Ability to navigate in multiple cultural contexts<br>Commitment to civic engagement |
| **USEFULNESS** | | Knowledge of essential vocational skills<br>Good decision-making skills<br>School success | Good coping skills<br>Good conflict-resolution skills<br>Mastery motivation and positive achievement motivation | Sense of social place/integration—being connected and valued by larger social networks |

TFY CCD Youth development matrix

*(continued)*

| Physical development | Intellectual development | Psychological and emotional development | Social development |
|---|---|---|---|
| | | Confidence in one's personal efficacy<br>"Planfulness"—planning for the future and future life events<br>Sense of personal autonomy/responsibility for self<br>Optimism coupled with realism<br>Coherent and positive personal and social identity<br>Prosocial and culturally sensitive values<br>Spirituality or a sense of a "larger" purpose in life<br>Strong moral character | Ability to navigate in multiple cultural contexts<br>Commitment to civic engagement<br>Attachment to prosocial/conventional institutions, such as school, church, non-school youth programs |
| **POWER** | Knowledge of essential life skills<br>School success<br>Rational habits of mind—critical thinking and reasoning skills<br>Knowledge of skills needed to navigate through multiple cultural contexts<br>In-depth knowledge of more than one culture | Good emotional self-regulation skills<br>Strong moral character<br>Good coping skills<br>Good conflict-resolution skills<br>Mastery motivation and positive achievement motivation<br>Confidence in one's personal efficacy | Connectedness—perceived good relationships and trust with parents, peers and some other adults<br>Sense of social place/integration—being connected and valued by larger social networks<br>Commitment to civic engagement |

| Physical development | Intellectual development | Psychological and emotional development | Social development |
|---|---|---|---|
| | | "Planfulness"—planning for the future and future life events<br>Sense of personal autonomy/responsibility for self<br>Optimism coupled with realism<br>Coherent and positive personal and social identity<br>Prosocial and culturally sensitive values | Ability to navigate in multiple cultural contexts<br>Attachment to prosocial/conventional institutions, such as school, church, non-school youth programs |
| **BELONGING** | School success<br>Knowledge of skills needed to navigate through multiple cultural contexts | Good mental health, including positive self-regard<br>Good conflict-resolution skills<br>Confidence in one's personal efficacy<br>Sense of personal autonomy/responsibility for self<br>Optimism coupled with realism<br>Coherent and positive personal and social identity<br>Prosocial and culturally sensitive values<br>Spirituality or a sense of a "larger" purpose in life<br>Strong moral character | Connectedness—perceived good relationships and trust with parents, peers and some other adults<br>Sense of social place/integration—being connected and valued by larger social networks<br>Ability to navigate in multiple cultural contexts<br>Attachment to prosocial/conventional institutions, such as school, church, non-school youth programs |

are compelled to do so. This can create space for more evenly balanced relationships between adults and young people; as well as highlighting the need for adult facilitators to skillfully and ethically build relationships with and among young people. Like all relationships, lateral adult–youth relationships depend on honesty and mutual respect. Reciprocity then becomes key within this paradigm. We all learn from one another.

Positive youth development provides a particular framework useful in TFY CCD practices with children and youth; however, the TFY CCD positive youth development matrix does not quite capture the communitarian and present-oriented approach of CCD as a whole, nor directly address democratic principles. Additionally, while positive youth development models appreciate children and youth as social beings, the approach still orients heavily toward future (adult) capacities and abilities rather than appreciating children and youth as children and youth in the moment. To expand the theoretical center of *development* then, I turn in the next section to the work of Harvard professor Amartya Kumar Sen, winner of the 1998 Nobel Prize in Economics.

> **KEY IDEAS**
>
> - Positive youth development focuses on asset development.
> - Asset development understands youth as social beings.
> - Asset development focuses on individuals first, communities secondly.
> - Assets can be defined differently, but I use the NRC/NAS taxonomy.
> - A focus on assets can transform traditional power dynamics.

## 1.12.2 Defining Development within the Capabilities Approach

Amartya Kumar Sen and political philosopher Martha Nussbaum are best known for their philosophical and political framework known as the Capabilities Approach. This theory bridges economics, moral philosophy, and politics, and links freedom and well-being in a normative model. Sen works in welfare economics and global development, so his theoretical model focuses on macro and micro-systems, in particular by analyzing individual human capacities and capabilities. The capabilities approach contrasts with other development systems that might focus, for example, on gross national products, infrastructure industrialization and/or modernization, advances in social transformation, or a rise in personal incomes (Sen 1999: 3). Sen points out that freedom to achieve well-being depends on what people can be and do—their capabilities—and therefore development practices should promote freedom along multiple axes: "Freedoms of different kinds can strengthen one another"

(1999: 11). Sen's system addresses the fallacy of using so-called "healthy economic structures" as proxy measures for social and cultural achievement—after all repressive states can create effectively functioning economies without advancing human capacity or citizen well-being in any appreciable manner. By positioning people's ability to make choices in support of their own well-being as a moral imperative, Sen argues utilitarian economic theories that do not support freedom are unjust. As most advanced states transitioned out of an industrial economics, advancing and building human capital began to be *the* central state welfare policy. But as Sen states, "The acknowledgment of the role of human qualities in promoting and sustaining economic growth—momentous as it is—tells us nothing about why economic growth is sought in the first place" (1999: 295). *Economic growth supports human freedom not the other way round.* States exist only to secure common welfare and human well-being. Nussbaum cogently points out, "The purpose of global development, like the purpose of a good domestic national policy, is to enable people to live full creative lives, developing their potential and fashioning a meaningful existence commensurate with their equal human dignity" (2011: 185). In this way, the capabilities approach roots development in maximizing human freedom to live a full and complete life. The moral argument of the capabilities approach aligns nicely with the moral philosophy of the politics of representation, in that both focus on capacity, equality, and human dignity. Capabilities approach uses three terms in particular ways: functionings; capabilities; and agency.

*Functionings*: activities or states comprising well-being. "Functionings are related to goods and income but they describe what a person is able to do or be as a result. When people's basic need for food (a commodity) is met, they enjoy the functioning of being well-nourished" (Human Development and Capabilities Association 2005: 1). Functionings connect to well-being so these can be quite simple (nourishment, clean water, and personal safety) or complex (being able to dance on pointe, adequate time to exercise, and sitting down to dinner as a family). In both cases, functionings support human fulfillment.

*Capabilities*: express what people are able to do and be. Capabilities are the possible combinations of functionings to craft a meaningful life. For example, capabilities have been compared to having money in your pocket. With money in your metaphorical pocket, you can buy lunch, donate to another human, or buy a play ticket. Capabilities function in a like manner. Capabilities express freedom of possibility. Capabilities are positive functions expressing individual values. I do not value the possibility of donating money to the Klu Klux Klan and therefore the capacity to donate to the KKK cannot be considered one of my capabilities. In other words, activities or states people do not value are not capabilities. Capabilities leverage functionings in order to craft possibility.

*Agency*: the capabilities approach is highly similar to the manner I define agency throughout this book: the ability to act and contribute to change. On an individual level, agency means the ability to pursue and realize objectives. The opposite of agency is oppression, coercion, and apathy. "Agency is related to other approaches that stress *self-determination, authentic self-direction, autonomy* and so on. The concern for agency means that participation, public debate, democratic practice, and empowerment are to be fostered alongside well-being" (Human Development and Capabilities Association 2005: 3). To put this in context then, a focus on agency means that although my daughters have advanced capabilities to be and do almost anything, I cannot require them to be a veterinarian or civil engineer—even though I believe either of these career paths would be satisfying to them. As agents, my children will pursue their own values and goals—even if those goals bear no resemblance to goals I wish they would pursue.

Capabilities approach places freedom at the center of development processes and anchors CCD protocols in well-being *as defined by* the community itself. Capabilities approach contrasts utilitarian philosophies, in that it focuses on "the ability—the substantive freedom—of people to lead the lives they have reason to value and to enhance the real choices they have" (Sen 1999: 293). The capabilities approach tackles development through individuals' agentic freedom to leverage funtionings into lives of meaning and value. To return for a moment to my early discussion around community capital and community wealth, the capability approach grounds how we begin conversations about development. Questions we need to ask include: grow what and toward what end? The moral imperative beneath TFY CCD is the advancement of human freedom and dignity.

Sen explicitly links the capabilities approach with theories of deliberative democracy (Crocker 2007; Drèze and Sen 2006). He connects agency and freedom to democratic societies addressing democracy in three dimensions: depth; breadth; and range. All dimensions rate participation. *Depth* addresses both the *how* and the *quality* of citizen participation in civic publics. Citizen participation in community affairs and decision making include what I have defined here as the public sphere and civic engagement. *Breadth* refers to the numbers of individuals affected by a decision and who participates in the decision. Voter turnout is one measure of democratic depth. *Range* addresses the kinds of decisions in which citizens participate and decide. For example, budgets, hiring practices, policy, and laws would be kinds of decisions as, of course, would be the decision to go to war. What decisions do citizens actually have the ability to make? Like Gutmann and Boyte, Sen agrees democracy equals more than just voting and majority rule. Sen reiterates the relationship of the public sphere and deliberative methodologies with vigorous methods of participation. Again, democracy incorporates political self-determination—agency—not simply majority rule or consumer forms of representation/identification. Strong democracies protect freedom and exhibit *depth*, *breadth*, and *range*. Sen writes, "Democracy has complex demands, which certainly include voting and respect for human rights, but also [...] the protection of liberties and freedoms, respect for legal entitlements, and the guaranteeing of free discussion and uncensored distribution of news and fair comment." (1999: 10). Sen understands democracy as valuable in and of itself, but also highlights a robust democracy's ability to protect freedom, promote agency, and foster well-being.

The capabilities approach functions particularly well with CCD with children and youth. In fact, Mario Biggeri, Jerome Ballet, and Flavio Comim (2011) point out that a focus on children and youth theoretically speaks to the capabilities approach as well as being morally important to the present and future functioning of societies. "When children are acknowledged as subjects of respect and agency in society, a new vision of development can be achieved. Children also have an active role to play in promoting human development" (4). In other words, children and youth, like all humans, have capabilities and should be understood *as agents*. The Biggeri, Ballet, and Comin book argues comprehensively for the need to include children and youth as participatory members of their societies. They write,

> The term "social participation," as it is generally used, implies something more than mere action: it implies that action is public, that it is visible in the whole society (or community), as well as in particular interactive systems (like families or classes). In other words, social means (potentially) visible for everybody, not only for a few specialized persons or roles (like parents, teachers, experts). Social participation is a visible action in public (societal) contexts. For this reason, social participation is a clear manifestation of citizenship, intended as inclusion in a society, with full rights and opportunities.
>
> (2011: 12)

Sen argues that democracy depends on multiple axis of participation (Crocker 2007; Drèze and Sen 2006) and notes that a democratic society's primary aim should be to nurture capable agents. In other words, a culture that excludes entire segments of its population from social participation is not a strong democracy, nor fostering well-being and freedom. TFY third space takes as a moral imperative the fostering of capable agents while positioning children and youth as full participants of their communities, states, and nations. Across the globe over 25% of the world's population is fifteen or under. Policies that do not grant children and youth full participatory rights marginalize over a quarter of all humanity. Such societies foster impoverished modes of being and constrain individuals' ability to live lives of personal meaning and value. A focus on capabilities rather than only assets understands that diverse functionings can be transformed differently. Different people and communities will understand and transform functionings contextually.

Sen resists creating taxonomies of central human capacities for multiple reasons; however, other theorists and philosophers have created such lists. Unlike the asset classification for youth development, capabilities approach taxonomies revolve around fundamental human rights or what Nussbaum calls freedoms so vital that their absence makes life not worth living (2011: 33). Sabina Alkire (2002, 2005) suggests using these lists to jump start capabilities planning and assessment conversations with communities rather than using them as normative values. Alkire bases her model in the human values scholarship of philosopher John Finnis and postulates seven dimensions of human development (2002, 2005). She notes these seven are each of intrinsic value, irreducible, specific, yet general enough to allow cultural diversity and geopolitical expression, "critical and complete: taken together they should encompass any human value" (2002: 193), not drawn from any one philosophical, moral, or value system but rather expressive of general human flourishing and nonhierarchical. Alkire's seven dimensions are drawn from Grisez, Boyle, and Finnis (1987) and include:

1. *Life itself*—its maintenance and transmission—health, and safety.
2. *Knowledge and aesthetic experience*. Knowing the world.
3. Some degree of excellence in *Work and Play*. "Human persons can transform the natural world by using realities, beginning with their own bodily selves, to express meanings and serve purposes. Such meaning-giving and value-creation can be realized in diverse degrees."
4. *Friendship*. "Various forms of harmony between and among individuals and groups of persons—living at peace with others, neighborliness, friendship."
5. *Self-integration*. "Within individuals and their personal lives, similar goods can be realized. For feelings can conflict among themselves and be at odds with one's judgments and choices. The harmony opposed to such inner disturbance is inner peace."
6. *Self-expression, or Practical Reasonableness*. "One's choices can conflict with one's judgments and one's behavior can fail to express one's inner self. The corresponding good is harmony among one's judgments, choices, and performances—peace of conscience and consistency between one's self and its expression."

7. *Religion.* "Most persons experience tension with the wider reaches of reality. Attempts to gain or improve harmony with some more-than-human source of meaning and value take many forms, depending on people's worldviews."

(Alkire 2002: 186; Alkire 2005: 48)

Martha Nussbaum builds her more comprehensive list of ten central capabilities from her background in global women's rights as well as via a focus on social justice. Nussbaum offers,

1. *Life.* Being able to live to the end of a human life of normal length; not dying prematurely, or before one's life is so reduced as to be not worth living.
2. *Bodily health.* Being able to have good health, including reproductive health; to be adequately nourished; to have adequate shelter.
3. *Bodily integrity.* Being able to move freely from place to place; to be secure against violent assault, including sexual assault and domestic violence; having opportunities for sexual satisfaction and for choice in matters of reproduction.
4. *Senses, imagination, and thought.* Being able to use the senses, to imagine, think, and reason—and to do these things in a "truly human" way, a way informed and cultivated by an adequate education, including, but by no means limited to, literacy and basic mathematical and scientific training. Being able to use imagination and thought in connection with experiencing and producing works and events of one's own choice, religious, literary, musical, and so forth. Being able to use one's mind in ways protected by guarantees of freedom of expression with respect to both political and artistic speech, and freedom of religious exercise. Being able to have pleasurable experiences and to avoid non-beneficial pain.
5. *Emotions.* Being able to have attachments to things and people outside ourselves; to love those who love and care for us, to grieve at their absence; in general, to love, to grieve, to experience longing, gratitude, and justified anger. Not having one's emotional development blighted by fear and anxiety. (Supporting this capability means supporting forms of human association that can be shown to be crucial in their development.)
6. *Practical reason.* Being able to form a conception of the good and to engage in critical reflection about the planning of one's life. (This entails protection for the liberty of conscience and religious observance.)

7. *Affiliation.*
    a. Being able to live with and toward others, to recognize and show concern for other humans, to engage in various forms of social interaction; to be able to imagine the situation of another. (Protecting this capability means protecting institutions that constitute and nourish such forms of affiliation, and also protecting the freedom of assembly and political speech.)
    b. Having the social bases of self-respect and non-humiliation; being able to be treated as a dignified being whose worth is equal to that of others. This entails provisions of non-discrimination on the basis of race, sex, sexual orientation, ethnicity, caste, religion, national origin and species.
8. *Other species.* Being able to live with concern for and in relation to animals, plants and the world of nature.
9. *Play.* Being able to laugh, to play, to enjoy recreational activities.
10. *Control over one's environment.*
    a. Political. Being able to participate effectively in political choices that govern one's life; having the right of political participation, protections of free speech and association.
    b. Material. Being able to hold property (both land and movable goods), and having property rights on an equal basis with others; having the right to seek employment on an equal basis with others; having the freedom from unwarranted search and seizure. In work, being able to work as a human, exercising practical reason and entering into meaningful relationships of mutual recognition with other workers.

(2011: 33–34)

While overlapping quite a bit, these lists of central human capacities or freedoms can create a ground from which to engage, plan, and conduct TFY CCD practices. Together they offer a comprehensive understanding of well-being along multiple axis of development. Much like positive youth development models, the above lists help jump-start conversations with community partners to build and design art actions addressing human capabilities and well-being within a positive or growth framework rather than deficit models.

This text grows out of both my own practices as a community-engaged artist working with children and youth and as a scholar teaching in an MFA and PhD theatre program. My students devote themselves to theatre for youth because they have a deep and passionate belief that they can make a difference in the lives of young people and in the health of their communities.

TFY, in general, tends toward utopian practices. In addition, my students can point to the performing arts as a defining force in their own lives. As such, my students bring deep enthusiasm to TFY CCD. Unfortunately, however, enthusiasm and good intentions are not sufficient to creating work advancing human freedom and the public good. A primary goal for TFY CCD practices is to advance the social, cultural, economic power, and well-being of particular communities while claiming publics for children and youth. Understanding multiple articulations of wealth, assets, human freedom, and human capabilities builds underlying theory to ground the process, production, and public-making involved in TFY third space. Combining the individualistic orientation of positive youth development with the capabilities approach's more macro understandings of human freedom and value can help build field theory and an empirical root for TFY CCD practices while also promoting pragmatic incorporation of a community's values and desires. For example, using the above lists, I create work sheets and value statements for individuals to process for themselves. After such processing, we come together as a group to decide upon a central capability we would like to address together. The capabilities approach then functions like a frame to build development capacity in the group and in the community.

**KEY IDEAS**

- Capabilities approach concerns individual freedom and human dignity.
- Functionings are activities or states comprising well-being.
- Capabilities express what people are able to be and do.
- Agency is the ability to act and contribute to social change.
- Capabilities approach aligns with deliberative democracy and participatory publics.
- Public-making is part and parcel of the capabilities approach.
- Society should nurture capable agents able to effectively engage in the public sphere and civic environments.
- Capabilities approach focuses on fostering capable agents, addressing well-being and justice.
- Capabilities approach focuses on individuals first, communities secondly.

## 1.13 GOOD WORK

What do I mean when I say make good work or to live a good life? The Harvard Graduate School of Education's research group, Project Zero, began investigating the concept of "good work" in 1996. I find their definition a helpful starting point to frame *good* TFY third space art actions. Project Zero defines good work as work that fits two criteria: (1) the work itself [is] innovative (or creative); (2) innovative individuals or institutions [see] it as part of their mission to assume some responsibility for the implications of their work (Gardner, Csikszentmihalyi, and William 2001: 1). In other words, good work touches upon both the quality of the work *and* the moral or ethical implications of the processes and conclusions of the art, or, as the Imagining America Consortium (www.imaginingamerica.org/index.html) points out, acts that uphold a "commitment to public practice and public consequence." I cannot emphasize this point too much: community-based artists create a web of mutual connection and community but these ethical responsibilities are not merely relational—to the stakeholders and participants—but also include domain/field accountability. I discuss these ideas separately below.

The term "good work" addresses both the social awareness of the art process, product, and public-making *and* the quality of the art itself. CCD practices cannot be divorced from the traditional art worlds/homes of their artists. While diverse artists fall into diverse aesthetic camps as Goldbard points out in her 2006 text, "The community/quality dichotomy invites posturing and polarization, supported by a thin reed of substance that almost topples under the weight of rhetoric it is made to carry. I see it as a false choice. No one sets out to make bad art" (55). In this case, I agree absolutely and further maintain that CCD artists not only have an ethical responsibility to the communities with whom they work, but also an *ethical* responsibility to their art form—that is, in fact, what can make the TFY third space practices a form of public art. In fact, the quality of CCD practices must be high or the practice does not fully qualify as creative nor take part in the symbolic economy of the art form itself and thus claim public space. Which is not to say that the aesthetics of community-engaged art with children and youth are not fraught with tension, complexity, and competing understandings of what makes a performance "good." For one, participatory art practices honor the cultural and aesthetic competencies of children and youth—rather than depending 100% on adult/facilitator aesthetic beliefs. We leverage community wealth, as defined by the community and the children and youth. Community-based artists work with communities not for them.

The history of US American TFY emphasizes ways in which both the field as a whole and professional TFY companies themselves have been undervalued as theatre. Personally, I no longer believe this to be across-the-board true. Residual, however, are deep concerns as to the aesthetic practices of "educational theatre," "children's theatre," or "kiddy shows" by theatre professionals in the

United States. A quick glance at Equity contracts for children's theatre actors or blog reviews of certain TFY performances highlights my point. Underlying conversations of the "goodness" or "badness" of performance aesthetics with and by children and youth are two philosophical concepts relating less to actual practices and more to conceptions of young humans themselves.

1. Dismissal of children's aesthetic competencies in favor of adult-defined "sophistication" related to being/becoming models (adult aesthetics are better than children's aesthetics).
2. Concern with technical precision (classical values of order and balance) versus disorder and chaos. Chaos/control is already deeply embedded in the manner in which we understand children and youth, connected literally to their bodies. Children are chaotic and should be controlled—"unattended children will be sold to the circus" reads a sign at an outdoor local restaurant in Phoenix.

In addition, classic aesthetic philosophies contain more than a little moralizing wherein what we customarily call "production values" becomes conflated with "good" and "bad" reinforcing the order/chaos distinction. Nevertheless, there is real distinction between production values/presentational skills and lack thereof. I adored watching one of my daughters "play" the letter "V" as a kindergartener, but there is no doubt that the performance was terrible theatre. Defining the aesthetic vocabularies in use in any given residency with a focus toward clearly and effectively manipulating them is part of accomplishing good work. Mapping these vocabularies also deeply relates to how artists understand community assets/wealth.

Project Zero's definition of good work highlights for me the importance of the deliberate and accomplished manipulation of aesthetic symbol systems toward specific social change. The aesthetic has always been part of cultural spheres but has become ubiquitous in the twenty-first century US market economy—design rules. Young people's interactions within the world are saturated with multiple kinds of media and material objects. Children and youth have advanced understandings of form, function, and the way aesthetic qualities foster emotional resonances—our responsibility is to bring this knowledge into awareness in order to foster capability. In addition, I believe art-making is key to navigating and understanding public representations and mediated space as constructed and therefore open for reconstruction. Complex conversations about aesthetics are part and parcel of TFY third space in order to advance capabilities.

In 1998, Howard Gardner identified three historical factors limiting the misuse of professional work like science, scholarship, and art:

First of all, there have been the values of the community, in particular religious values. For example, in principle a scientist could conduct experiments in which prisoners are exposed to certain toxic agents. But religion counsels the sanctity of all human life. A second balancing force has been the law. In many nations, prisoners are protected against unusual forms of treatment or punishment. Third, there is the sense of calling, or ethical standards, of professionals. For example, a scientist might take the position that a contribution to knowledge should not be secured at the expense of human or animal welfare; indeed, some scientists have refused to make use of findings obtained by the Nazis as a result of immoral experiments.

(4)

According to Gardner, community values, the law, and an individual's personal and professional moral code are the primary limiting factors for creating immoral or even evil work. In an increasingly expanding practice such as youth-focused community-engaged arts, the ethics of the practice and in-depth exploration of facilitators' own moral codes and value systems must be an ongoing component of any process. This is so important that I need to say it again: *community-based practitioners must commit to an ongoing and in-depth exploration of their own moral codes and value systems.* We live in a society driven by market forces, so we cannot depend upon a centralized "community value" to promote social justice and ethical practices. Likewise, the law hardly touches upon CCD practices unless we involve human subject review boards or copyright clauses. Not to mention, as a wise colleague pointed out recently, "What is legal is not always ethical and what is ethical is not always legal." We are therefore left almost utterly dependent upon what I would characterize as a barely coherent professional moral code and individual artists' belief systems for guidance in "good work" practices.

The stakes within the realm of the arts, of course, are quite a bit different than, say, medicine or the biological sciences. I do believe, however, that unethical CCD practices can cause spiritual and community harm. One danger is the misuse of community-engaged residencies to alleviate stresses caused by structural or systemic inequalities. Such a use can short-circuit the transformation of inequalities or structural deficits by temporarily reducing the need for change without actually addressing the problems. For example, I once worked with an Arizona state division of social workers primarily focused on child-abuse intake and investigation. My course-based team and I created a piece of theatre growing from the experiences and emotional sacrifices of these frontline social workers. We used intensive interviewing and oral-history techniques, shadowing, story circles, and participant creative-writing activities to build the piece. After a successful showcase of the performance piece, Child Protective Services (CPS) administration approached me about continuing the residency on a semi-permanent basis and as a continuing part of my students' field experiences. The administration viewed the project as a cost-effective method (we were volunteers) of building team spirit and addressing retention issues. At the time, the latest round of state budget cuts had almost doubled each worker's caseload while eliminating counseling and mental-health services for unit workers. After discussing the matter further with unit workers and my students, we concluded that CPS administrators had their hearts in the right place, but were using the project as a band-aid to cover what was effectively a mortal wound. Such a situation could only prevent "good work."

Alternatively, CCD practices also can promote youth identity practices that collaborating institutions feel are antithetical to their own needs and values, which would also prevent "good work" in its fullest sense. I have written elsewhere about my fraught relationship with an alternative school on the Gila River Indian Community (Etheridge Woodson 2003). I viewed my community partners as the indigenous youth and their families but neglected the school and its teachers. The schoolteachers understood themselves as the last chance opportunity for youth to "make it" and earn a high-school diploma. They cared deeply about their students and promoted rigid discipline and self-control as the primary means of success. Youth were allowed to perform only in narrowly understood ways. The lateral facilitation strategies and perhaps flamboyant performances of self I promoted (and performed) in my work undermined the schools' systems and hierarchical controls. The moral code of the residency was compromised and its "good work" short-circuited by my mistakes and misunderstandings. While I may not agree with the choices made by school administrators, nevertheless I had an obligation to ethically practice a residency to maximize the good work, an obligation in which I failed.

The field of theatre in the United States is driven by a bizarre mix of the commercial and the nonprofit, with an unequal balance between the traditional values of the art form and the market forces driving play production, ticket prices, training programs, and new-work development. The diverse practices of CCD are also inherently inconsistent, enfolding unbalanced forces that could include funder restrictions and/or expectations, diverse understandings of "partnership" including government and private enterprise, contradictory conceptions of success, religious restrictions and/or conflicts, incompatible understandings of childhood, distrust toward adolescents as community representatives, and incoherent aesthetic values. Yet, despite these inherent difficulties, I believe strongly in this type of creative practice. One of the only ways I know how to prepare practitioners to navigate the fluid nature of TFY third space practices is rooted in deep, engaged, and ongoing mapping of the structures and philosophies of CCD practices with children and youth. A principle I live through the structure of this text.

> **KEY IDEAS**
>
> - Good work means paying attention to practice, product, and public-making.
> - Participatory art practices honor the cultural and aesthetic competencies of children and youth.
> - Theatre practices designed toward social change manipulate aesthetic symbol systems.

## 1.14 FIELD THEORY IN CCD WITH CHILDREN AND YOUTH, PART 2: LINKING CAPITAL AND DEVELOPMENT

I wish to return now to explicitly articulating TFY CCD foundational principles, particularly integrating the above. In section 1.9, I offered this list of key ideas:

- Culture is action.
- Children and youth are competent cultural producers.
- Children and youth are acknowledged experts on both being themselves and the meanings of their lives.
- Childhood is understood as socially constructed not biologically innate, and thus processes do not place artificial limits on the scope of the work or on the assumed abilities of the participants.
- Primary unit of concern is the community and public-making not individual achievement.
- The work consciously builds the social, political, economic, and/or cultural power of the communities involved.
- Facilitation and participatory techniques are understood through principles of deliberative democracy rather than pedagogy, consensus, or traditional directorial relationships.
- Participants have express relationships to the content of the work developed.
- Children and youth are civic publics.
- The public sphere is a collective and discursive space built on and around human environments.

# Field Building—or—the Twenty Principles of TFY Third Space

I want to expand this list to include principles discussed in sections 1.10–1.13, particularly oriented toward how CCD with children and youth can intervene in social systems.

- Children and youth are participatory publics.
- TFY third space understands children and youth as social beings with human capabilities.
- Overall community well-being and ecology depends on interdependent and complex flows of capital, collective placemaking, and human agency.
- TFY third space claims publics with children and youth.
- TFY third space nurtures children and youth as capable agents, able to collectively engage in the public sphere and civic environments.
- Good work in TFY CCD pays equal attention to practice, product and public-making.
- TFY CCD builds community wealth and well-being through asset development and human capabilities development.
- Deliberative democratic and communitarian principles guide all aspects of TFY third space.
- TFY third space works toward change.
- Children and youth are agents and assets within their communities.

These twenty theoretical concepts ground my construction of TFY third space and CCD with children and youth. Is this an educational practice? Yes. Is this a development practice? Yes. Is this a democratic process? Yes. How does TFY CCD work then? Figure 1.8 is my attempt to graphically represent the conceptual processes of TFY CCD.

This graphic attempts to define the complex iterations of TFY third space by mapping key decision areas. In the placemaking section, the question is *what* approach? This segment locates the general TFY CCD goal. Will the focus be on:

- Building effective connections and shared values (knowledge and attitudes).
- Intensifying civic participation and engagement (democratic participation and capacity building).
- Solving a particular problem.
- Problem-finding (engaging diverse communities in unpacking difficulties or understandings from lateral perspectives, for example: why do youth not use current resources; why has there been a rise in violence at local skate parks; and what do foster youth see as the primary barrier to future success?).

**Figure 1.8:** Public-Making: Theatre for young audiences third space.

- Visioning for the future and/building sustainable long-term community capabilities. Gary Green and Anna Haines write, "Visioning focuses on what strengths must be developed to reach a desired end state. It expands the notion of public participation beyond the other models and suggests that the community can design and create its own future" (Green and Haines 2002: 41).

The CCD section locates TFY CCD objectives. Questions needing an answer include:

- Grow what power in what ways?
- Which capabilities? How?
- How will the project claim publics? Who needs to be included in the process? What Public? How will we perform public? What is the public-making strategy?
- What resources and capital will the project leverage? What capital systems will the project interact with? How will the project build value?

- What individual assets will be developed? What assets will be deployed?

Figure 1.8 does not of course list *all* the possible placemaking goals, but organizes thematic and structural considerations within a gestalt theoretical model. Understanding the placemaking approach grounds the project's public-making while addressing how TFY CCD projects add value and define success. I will return to Figure 1.8 in Section 3 in order to show how to use it to structure partnering, planning, and evaluating but for now I turn my attention to ethics, leadership, and facilitation within TFY third space.

> **KEY IDEAS**
>
> - The twenty principles of TFY CCD are:
>
>   1. Culture is action.
>   2. Children and youth are competent cultural producers.
>   3. Children and youth are acknowledged experts on both being themselves and the meanings of their lives.
>   4. Childhood is understood as socially constructed not biologically innate, and thus processes do not place artificial limits on the scope of the work or on the assumed abilities of the participants.
>   5. Primary unit of concern is the community and public-making not individual achievement.
>   6. The work consciously builds the social, political, economic, and/or cultural power of the communities involved.
>   7. Facilitation and participatory techniques are understood through principles of deliberative democracy rather than pedagogy, consensus, or traditional directorial relationships.
>   8. Participants have express relationships to the content of the work developed.
>   9. Children and youth are civic publics.
>   10. The public sphere is a collective and discursive space built on and around human environments.
>   11. Children and youth are participatory publics.
>   12. TFY third space understands children and youth as social beings with human capabilities.
>   13. Overall community well-being and ecology depends on interdependent and complex flows of capital, collective placemaking, and human agency.
>   14. TFY third space claims publics with children and youth.

15. TFY third space nurtures children and youth as capable agents, able to collectively engage in the public sphere and civic environments.
16. Good work in TFY CCD pays equal attention to practice, product and public-making.
17. TFY CCD builds community wealth and well-being through asset development and human capabilities development.
18. Deliberative democratic and communitarian principles guide all aspects of TFY third space.
19. TFY third space works toward change.
20. Children and youth are agents and assets within their communities.

# NOTE

1  Spanish-language word used by farm workers/theatre-makers, now used cross-culturally.

# Section 2

Ethics, Leadership, and Facilitation

*A leader is best when people barely know he exists, when his work is done, his aim fulfilled, they will say: we did it ourselves.*

*– Lao Tzu*

In order to work ethically in communities, community cultural development artists need highly developed understandings of pluralism, power, and status to effectively ground their practices. In Sections 2.1 through 2.6, I explore key ideas for principled and thoughtful engagement with others while offering a short primer on concepts drawn from cultural studies and performance studies. Next, I explore authentic leadership practices, healthy ensembles, and what research can tell us about nurturing/facilitating creativity and creative teams. Finally, I offer my particular method of spiral devising, performance generation, and compositional practice.

## INTRODUCTION

Three givens of TFY third space facilitation take us back to ideas from the introduction to this book:

- Children and youth are artists.
- Children and youth are citizens.
- Children and youth are community assets.

TFY third space recognizes youthful participants as valuable, creative artists, and as knowledgeable citizens of their communities and ensembles. These ideas place great emphasis on reciprocity and sideways power structures as well as intrinsic motivation. "According to [self-determination] theory, the preconditions of being intrinsically motivated for a certain job are autonomy, feelings of competence, and social relatedness" (Osterloh 2007: 166). Adult facilitators walk into the studio with specific knowledge of benefit to the ensemble, but everyone in the room holds knowledge and ability—capital—no matter their age. By nurturing feelings of independence, ability, and social connection, CCD artists leverage community capital and wealth. TFY third space facilitation structures function differently from traditional director–actor relationships as well as from skill-based, teaching-artist residencies. Over the years, I have begun starting each of my residencies with two activities to get all individuals on the same page: (1) Give/Gain, which I learned from the innovative theatre company, Phakama, and (2) three rounds of musical chairs—winner take all, team play, and everybody wins. I will return to the ways to use musical chairs later, but Phakama's Give/Gain philosophy effectively captures the essence of the facilitation structures I discuss in this section.

With membership spread across the globe, Phakama emphasizes diversity and democracy. Their philosophy roots in a "process that we call Give and Gain, learning becomes two-way; everyone has something they can give to the project and everyone has something to gain. And through this interchange of skills, knowledge, information and ideas, everyone becomes both student and teacher" (2012: n.p.). Asking individuals what they have to give and what they hope to gain helps foster mutuality. Give/Gain places emphasis on the skills and knowledge diversity of an ensemble while nurturing an environment centered on mutual benefit and responsibility. Moreover, creativity research shows that the most effective creative teams build a common language and they value one another's diverse skills and knowledge (Sawyer 2006: 121). Give/Gain foregrounds variety and the value of being responsible for one another.

TFY third space facilitation roots in principles of deliberative democracy, emphasizing dialogue, thoughtful analysis, and choice making. Amy Gutmann and Dennis Thompson define deliberative democracy as

> a form of government in which free and equal citizens (and their representatives), justify decisions in a process in which they give one another reasons that are mutually acceptable and generally accessible, with the aim of reaching conclusions that are binding in the present on all citizens but open to challenge in the future.
>
> (2004: 7)

Within systems of scarce resources, hard decisions have to be made. Decisions can be made by fiat; decisions can be made through consensus; unknown parties for unknown reasons can make decisions behind the scenes; or opposing parties can bargain *quid pro quo* style to arrive at decisions. Deliberative democracy emphasizes discussion, building common language and the fluid processes of decision making. In addition, decisions must be justified in an accessible form—"To justify imposing their will on you, your fellow citizens must give reasons that are comprehensible to you" (Gutmann and Thompson 2004: 4). As an ensemble organizing principle, deliberative democracy emphasizes group transparency, collaborative discussion, and reflective leadership.

I once participated in a workshop in which the facilitator hid the structure for effect. We devised material in an incomprehensible sequence, which she then slotted into a set structure. Hiding the machinery worked in this particular instance to heighten some participants' emotional engagement. For others, the secretive structure allowed them to bypass their expectations and beliefs concerning their creative capacity. In particular, the moment the performance came together created delight for self-avowed noncreatives—an a-ha or structural catharsis. As an artist, however, I felt limited by her structure and experienced her control as disrespectful to my own creative processes. My particular aesthetic skills were ancillary to the facilitator's mastery of the presentational form. The experience did not grow me in my own practice or value me as a collaborative equal.

Rather than imposing structure or hiding the machinery, community-based theatre with children and youth facilitation begins from the premise: all participants are artists—even if they do not self-identify as such. Starting from ground zero, TFY third space explicitly and transparently treats participants as co-learners, co-artists, and fundamentally creative individuals. Principles of deliberative democracy do not, however, embrace naiveté or Kumbaya-philosophy—can't we just hold hands and all get along? Decisions do not have to be consensual: "[d]eliberative democrats do not expect deliberation always or even usually to yield agreement" (Gutmann and Thompson 2004: 7). However, when decisions are made, all understand the reasons behind the choice and practice what Gutmann and Thompson call the "economy of moral disagreement" (2004: 7). Moral disagreement trades in mutual respect, opponents are not vilified; bridges are not burned. In the economy of moral disagreement, opponents recognize the necessity of working together in the future—we maintain social investments for future good. As a now retired colleague once said, "We can disagree without being disagreeable."

Deliberative democratic principles structure facilitation as collaborative with all equally responsible for the long-term health of the partnerships created. When conflict occurs—because conflict will occur—principles of deliberative democracy dictate respectful, open negotiation with mutual consideration for all positions. Deliberative democracy precepts leave room for future negotiations while also allowing time to explore multiple views and perspectives. As studies of participation in community and business cultures point out "being treated with dignity and respect" as well as building understanding of how individual participation contributes to the common good is of "high importance" (Osterloh 2007: 169). While such principles extend the time necessary for residencies and do not eliminate hurt feelings or minority discrimination, they promote complex thinking, mutual respect among persons, and disagreeing without being disagreeable (or trolling). Deliberative democratic principles value participants as mutually building the creative process/product while fostering noncompetitive understandings of community and publics. As a TFY CCD facilitator, I understand deliberative democracy methods as a key contributor to public-making.

> **KEY IDEAS**
>
> - TFY third space recognizes children and youth as valuable, creative artists and as knowledgeable citizens.
> - TFY third space facilitation uses principles of deliberative democracy emphasizing dialogue, thoughtful analysis, and choice making.

## 2.1 STARTING FROM WHERE YOU ARE: ETHICS AND PLURALISM

Theatre, indeed art in general, is not value-neutral. The project of entering into relationships with communities to whom we do not belong is also not a neutral activity. This section explores philosophical structures to support ethical strategies for engagement as well as exploring the potential structural possibilities of community-based theatre with children and youth. Here, I use theory to illuminate the frameworks—or the systems of beliefs governing action—within which community cultural development with children and youth function. In order to make ethical choices within community engagements and partnerships, we need clear understanding of how the structures governing our complex lives operate. Beverly Naidus points out that theory is "an articulation of an understanding that comes from lived experiences. Without that comprehension, people would continually live with a fragmented misunderstanding of what surrounds them daily" (2009: 6). Practitioners need to build conceptual models of their lived experiences. We also need to develop and refine skills navigating those structures in order to create powerful and relevant art. In addition, power and status map all human relationships in overt and covert ways. We cannot just unpack the social structures in other words, but also need to explore the ways in which power and status organize hierarchies within our conceptual models. Finally, community-based theatre with children and youth is grounded in facilitating artists in civic places working with communities organized by conscious and unconscious systems of beliefs. Adult facilitating artists enter into primary relationships within a community with radically different power constructs—

adult–child/being–becoming. We are always "other" than our participants. Ethically and aesthetically negotiating these social and cultural dynamics demands deep understanding of how cultures, communities, and power operate at the organizational level. I explore these ideological structures so that facilitating artists can maximize their good work while minimizing potential harm or unethical engagement strategies.

In order to work constructively in the fraught circumstance of community cultural development, artists need to understand ideology, both their own and that of others. For the purposes of this text, I define ideology as *systems of beliefs and values*. Artists must also learn to notice the ways in which ideology and power become embodied and performed. Theatre artists have a head start in this process as theatre, in fact, depends on ideology for intelligibility as Baz Kershaw points out,

> performance can be most usefully described as an ideological transaction between a company of performers and the community of their audience. Ideology is the source of the collective ability of performers and audience to make more or less common sense of the signs used in performance, the means by which the aims and intentions of theatre companies connect with the responses and interpretations of their audiences. Thus, ideology provides the framework within which companies encode and audiences decode the signifiers of performance.
>
> (1992: 16)

All people live in a soup of beliefs and values, or what Clifford Geertz (1973) calls our "cultural DNA." These include what counts as "polite" behavior and what it means to be "feminine" or "masculine." Sometimes these values are so commonplace they become invisible and naturalized. For hundreds of years, western societies believed that due to female biology, women were incapable of learning. Today, we know that a uterus has nothing to do with an individual's innate intelligence. Nevertheless, many societies around the globe still restrict girls' and women's educational opportunities. Pakistani student, Malala Yousafzai, survived a 2012 assassination attempt and still lives under a Taliban death threat because of her passionate advocacy for girls' rights to an education. Socially, people communally construct how we meaningfully move through the world in ways both mundane and sublime.

A mundane example: I grew up understanding that dinner always had to include two vegetables and meat followed by a sweet treat. My partner believes meat and bread must be involved with every evening meal to be considered "dinner" but is pretty flexible with regard to vegetables. Sweets to him are a luxury and should only be consumed on special occasions. We separately define "dinner" in related yet different ways connected to the systems of values in which we were raised. Neither one of us, for example, would consider dog-meat as an acceptable "meat" dish. My partner's father is a dentist and has a strong bias against desserts and candies of all kinds. My father was raised in Central America and believes that sugar should be a part of every meal. Both of us live in a larger culture that considers dogs as pets, not food. In addition, we were both raised in the United States where food is plentiful and generally affordable. Neither of us ever went hungry. In college, I quit eating red meat altogether for moral and ecological reasons not for financial ones. All these cultural, geographical, and individual beliefs come into play during something as simple as meal planning. When my partner and I blended our families, we had to negotiate multiple belief structures. What evening meals "should" contain was a minor segment of our larger cultural negotiations and performances.

Sections 2.2 through 2.6 explore several specific concepts (e.g., culture, values, beliefs, diversity, power, status, hegemony, and symbolic capital) that I believe necessary to building general understandings of the ways in which cultures and communities function as well as how art can intervene in that functioning. While undoubtedly intricate, this philosophical model should help practitioners navigate the complex waters of aesthetics, identity, and community. Like all explorers, we need to build as accurate a map as possible before we begin our journeys into other people's territory. You should know, however, that as with all maps, the model I lay out will be incomplete, highlighting certain aspects while ignoring others. This theoretical partialness reflects not only the complexity of the subject but also my views on the relative importance of the ideas explored.

> **KEY IDEAS**
>
> - Theatre, indeed art in general, is not value-neutral.
> - TFY CCD artists need to understand their own as well as their partners' ideologies—systems of beliefs and values.
> - People communally construct how we meaningfully move through the world.

## 2.2 CULTURE, VALUES, AND BELIEFS

All people live inside of culture—indeed within multiple intersecting cultures. Yet, I have had young white students tell me that they had no culture. Indeed, they felt envious of their peers who performed obvious cultural affiliations. Instead of not having a culture, these white middle-class youth have a culture so naturalized that its identity structures have become invisible to them—

universalized as "normal." In a similar manner, I have noticed a refrain in my work with preservice and young teachers and teaching artists. When I first begin to discuss power and difference, some teachers will tell me that they do not "see color" in their classrooms or workshops but instead understand all of their students as individuals. While this rhetorical strategy has become less common in the last five years or so, I have to point out some difficulties here. First, only Whites ever make this assertion. To claim to not "see" color in our environments is an untruth. Second, to see difference does not make one a racist. I believe these undergraduates, young teachers, and teaching artists struggle with how to engage difference when they have never been trained how to do so, *nor has their own practice of daily living forced them to learn*. Without engagement strategies and deep understandings of how difference operates in diverse environments, discussions of status and power can be frightening. Third, our ideological beliefs are highly structured by our identity locations (e.g., ethnicity, skin color, appearance, gender, country or region of origin, ability/disability, sexual orientation, class, and religion) and certain groups and communities (e.g., people of color and Mexican immigrants) have not been allowed to understand themselves as universal in contemporary US America. But, *difference factors into all human relations* both at the individual level and at the collective. In addition, because theatre and performance are ideological transactions as well as cultural productions, community-engaged artists need deep understandings of how ideology structures human meaning and being. This is both an ethical obligation and an *aesthetic* need. After all, aesthetic perception depends on subtle interactions between intellectual ideas surrounded by emotional landscapes. We need to map our community partners' social and cultural performances and tactics within their lived experiences to make collaborative art—to engage their aesthetic structures deeply.

I adapted Figure 2.1 from a health care cultural competency and literacy training manual (2005) commissioned by the Health Resources and Services Administration of the US Department of Health and Human Services. Created to address ongoing and systemic treatment disparities provided to people of color, this graphic conceptualizes the pervasiveness of cultural difference. Articulated by Edward Hall in the 1970s, the iceberg analogy has long been used in intercultural communication programs. The analogy works in this context for multiple reasons not the least of which is that icebergs, like culture, primarily exist on levels invisible to the eye. Notice how many beliefs relate to cultural assumptions—leadership, child-raising, friendship, and decision-making processes. In a similar manner, notice how surface-level cultural artifacts stand in for "culture" writ large. In the 1980s and early 1990s, K-12 schools often negotiated multiculturalism through artifacts rather than deeper engagement with cultural literacies. I have a colleague who calls artifact-based programs,

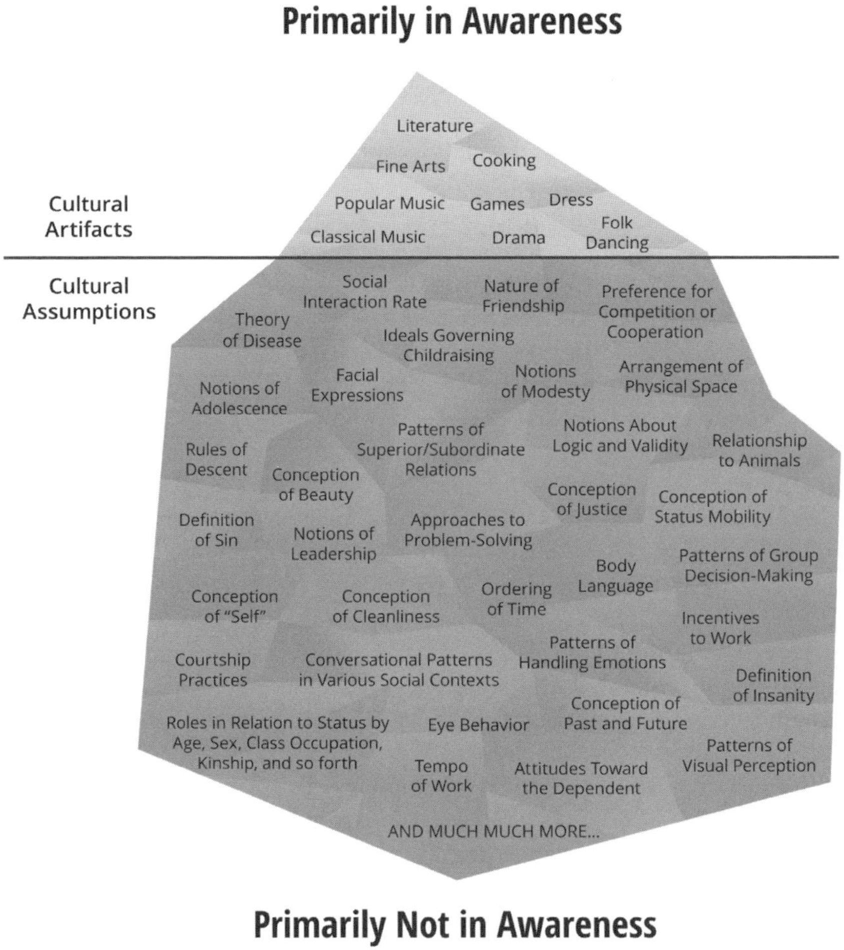

## Primarily in Awareness

**Cultural Artifacts**

Literature
Fine Arts    Cooking
Popular Music    Games    Dress
Classical Music    Drama    Folk Dancing

**Cultural Assumptions**

Social Interaction Rate    Nature of Friendship    Preference for Competition or Cooperation
Theory of Disease    Ideals Governing Childraising
Facial Expressions    Notions of Modesty    Arrangement of Physical Space
Notions of Adolescence
Patterns of Superior/Subordinate Relations    Notions About Logic and Validity    Relationship to Animals
Rules of Descent    Conception of Beauty
Definition of Sin    Notions of Leadership    Approaches to Problem-Solving    Conception of Justice    Conception of Status Mobility
Body Language    Patterns of Group Decision-Making
Conception of "Self"    Conception of Cleanliness    Ordering of Time
Incentives to Work
Courtship Practices    Conversational Patterns in Various Social Contexts    Patterns of Handling Emotions
Conception of Past and Future    Definition of Insanity
Roles in Relation to Status by Age, Sex, Class Occupation, Kinship, and so forth    Eye Behavior
Tempo of Work    Attitudes Toward the Dependent    Patterns of Visual Perception

AND MUCH MUCH MORE...

## Primarily Not in Awareness

**Figure 2.1:** Iceberg Analogy.

"food and fiesta." Third space theatre for children and youth demands more complex understandings of culture than food and fiesta. While artifacts can be useful in structuring or devising prompts for performative events and can point toward aesthetic vocabularies, they cannot stand in for deep understanding of cultural beliefs and ideological systems. Artifacts do not equal culture.

Take a moment and think about your own cultural beliefs. How (or if) do you begin conversations with people you do not know? Is that conversation different if the other person is above you in power? Below you in power? How do you understand time? What is your preferred manner of handling conflict? What counts as "conflict" to you? What cultural beliefs order your notions of friendship and respect? How do you perform leadership or dependency? In what ways did your family cultures reinforce mutuality and respect? How do you and your family express grief and sadness? How do you understand belonging? Privacy? How are your values reflections or rejections of the deeper cultural belief systems in which you were raised?

Reflective practice is important not only for long-term personal satisfaction but also for engaged, ethical facilitation. A simple way to begin processing your own culturally influenced beliefs and values is to think of your death—how would you want to be remembered? What epitaph will be written on your grave, and what five key qualities will your eulogy relate? Another method to chart your values is to map yourself within a continuum (while noting that binaries are in and of themselves limiting). For example, where would you place yourself on the following spectrums?

```
HONESTY-----------------------------------SPARE SOMEONE'S FEELINGS
COMMUNITY----------------------------------------INDIVIDUALITY
SAVE MONEY-----------------------------------BUY THINGS I WANT
RATIONAL DECISIONS--------------------EMOTIONAL ENGAGEMENT
NATURE-------------------------------------------------------------NURTURE
REPRESENTATIONAL ART---------------------------------SYMBOLIC ART
```

Again, binaries are both self-limiting and culturally constructed, but the process of mapping binaries can help to illuminate both conscious and unconscious cultural values. What binaries would you have included here that I did not? How do you understand oppositionality?

Ranking is another artificial construct that can be helpful in limited quantities. Take the below list of qualities for example, and rank them in order of importance to yourself.

Wisdom
Wealth
Recognition
Spirituality
Loyalty
Knowledge and skill
Integrity
Authenticity
Personal appearance
Self-discipline

Alternatively, list what you believe are your ten top characteristics. Characteristics and personality traits are not of course the same as beliefs.

Noting what characteristics you value on the other hand can help you to align your professional practices with your personal beliefs while providing insight into your own ideological perspectives. Another suggestion would be to note your three most negative personal characteristics—with what do you struggle the most? Why? Values mapping is an important component to ethical engagement with others. As Krista Lawlor (2008: 338) points out, "we know what we believe only with effort." In addition, beliefs are not static, they transform and grow and adapt. Reflective practice depends on continuous engagement with your deep-level self.

Social and developmental psychologists as well as moral philosophers discuss beliefs by noting: (1) some beliefs are more powerful than others, and (2) beliefs are nested. Beliefs are not singular in other words, but scaffolds. My beliefs about what colors look attractive together does not carry the same weight as my belief in how one should care for and nurture mental and physical health. However, all of these beliefs connect to deeper ones I hold about beauty and self-discipline. In practical terms, my children wear clothes that they love (that I do not particularly like), but I do not let them skip brushing their teeth and I regulate their exercise-to-screen-time ratios. Daryl Bem writes, "every belief can be pushed back until it is seen to rest ultimately upon a basic belief in the credibility of one's own sensory experience or upon a basic belief in the credibility of some external authority" (1970: 5). Our belief structures root in both our embodied existence and our social/cultural settings. To go back to teeth and wellness, I have personal physical experience of clean teeth versus furry teeth. My empirical data too combine with knowledge of cavities and plaque derived from experts that I respect. At an almost unconscious level, I hold deep beliefs in the validity of science and medicine as a way of knowing the world, and my own capacity to map the world through personal sensual experience. Bem refers to mostly unconscious beliefs as "zero-order beliefs" noting, "our most fundamental primitive beliefs are so taken for granted that we are apt not to notice that we hold them at all […]" (1970: 5). Another example, I believe I am a person named "Stephani" and tomorrow my name will still be "Stephani." I do not verbalize this as a belief; however, I simply introduce myself as "Stephani." As I write this, my almost three-year-old daughter struggles with her concurrent desires to be both "big" and "little." Last week she moved into the next age grouping in her preschool and has pushed back at home. She told me the other night that she would "grow up big" in her new class, but then she was going to "grow little again" and be my "baby." Zero-order beliefs ground other beliefs; they are central within our intellectual and emotional structures. Milton Rokeach (1969: 5) defines zero-order beliefs through connection noting, "the more a given belief is functionally connected or in communication with other beliefs, the more implications and consequences it has for other beliefs […]."

Here, my toddler has a different zero-level belief than I do. I understand time to only move forward and human growth to be physically progressive. A lifetime of empirical data convinces me that we cannot age backwards. My three-year-old will always be my baby, but she will never again *be* a baby. As a toddler, however, Maisy's identity structures revolve around her status as the youngest child in a house full of children. Rokeach also observes, "the more central a belief, the more it will resist change" (1969: 3). We have tried to explain growing up to Maisy, but she resists our understandings in preference for her own empirical data. She is now and has always been the *Baby*. Her baby-ness connects deeply to other beliefs she holds and roots her own understandings of her self and how she interacts in the family culture. While zero-level beliefs are not synonymous with cultural assumptions from the iceberg image, both represent interactions between individuals' personal experiences and cultural environments and the ways in which our internal landscapes relate to and reflect our social and embodied practices. I do not share my daughter's story to highlight differences between "correct" and "incorrect" understandings of reality. Rather, I highlight how our fundamental—and often invisible—beliefs structure our understandings of the world and our place within it. In a real way, both my belief structure and Maisy's are *true* and construct profound personal meaning.

> **KEY IDEAS**
>
> - All people live inside culture—indeed within multiple intersecting cultures.
> - Ideology structures human meaning and being.
> - Beliefs structure our understandings of the world and our place within it.
> - Constant and recursive self-reflection is one of the only ways to maintain an ethical practice.

## 2.3 DIVERSITY AND DIFFERENCE

I understand "diversity" as the wide and glorious range of human difference. An asset in any creative project, community, or culture, diversity—understood broadly—contributes to robust creative and social structures. Contemporary understandings of diversity have moved beyond demographics (e.g., ethnicity, primary language, gender, and sexual orientation) to include broader ranges of difference. Which is not to say that all differences are equal in US American culture. For example, many states do not protect gay, lesbian, or transgender people from employment discrimination; queer people can be legally fired in 29 states simply because of their sexual orientation. Difference functions as a key component of all human interaction, of course, as Sharon Grady (2000: 5) points out,

> Our own self-definition grows and changes as we interact with or measure self against "others." We actively differentiate and order the world accordingly, often separating out the foreign from the familiar. The initial scale of difference is often a visual one.

As physical beings, we depend on our senses to provide empirical data about the world and our relationship therein, so visual data easily can elide into difference as a whole. However, diversity has many more complex components than skin color, body shape, and hair texture. I explore specific components below, but first a quick note about the word, "race." You most likely have noticed that I do not use "race" as a term. "Race" grew from the historical period of conquest and colonialism and philosophically roots in Plato's Great Chain of Being filtered through medieval Christian world views. The Great Chain of Being strictly organizes all of reality within a hierarchical structure understood to be ordained by God. As used by Colonial Europeans, "race" served to separate and distinguish non-whites as a predetermined lower order of beings under the guise of scientific explanation. Contemporary understandings of genetics have proven without a doubt that there is no such thing as "race." Humans do not have separate species. Quantitative genetic research and the mapping of the human genome show that at a genetic level any two members of a so-called "race" are as biologically different from one another as they are from individuals outside of their racial frame. The American Anthropology Association statement (1996) on race points out,

> "Race" thus evolved as a world view, a body of prejudgments that distorts our ideas about human differences and group behavior. Racial beliefs constitute myths about the diversity in the human species and about the abilities and behavior of people homogenized into "racial" categories. The myths fused behavior and physical features together in the public mind, impeding our comprehension of both biological variations and cultural behavior, implying that both are genetically determined. Racial myths bear no relationship to the reality of human capabilities or behavior. Scientists today find that reliance on such folk beliefs about human differences in research has led to countless errors.
> 
> (Smedley 1996: n.p.)

"Race" conflates biology and culture together into a strange mix reliant on nineteenth century understandings of heritage and blood—the "one drop rule" and blood quantum in example. I acknowledge that "race" serves sociological and cultural functions. However, given the term's unsavory past (including eugenics and the Holocaust) and unavoidable quasi-biological orientation, I use "ethnicity," "ethnic group," or "ancestry." A research study conducted by Ruth McKay and Manuel de la Puenta (1995) noted that respondents did not really distinguish between "ethnicity" and "race" understanding these terms to be interchangeable. In McKay and de la Puenta's work, individuals most often defaulted to "race" while *meaning* "ethnicity." Words have power though and I believe the biological implications of "race" to be a particularly fraught misrepresentation of humanness. In addition, the conflation of "race-biology" strangely elides into culture so that individuals will tell you that they are 25% German or ask "how much" Irish I am. Culture of course does not equal genetic ancestry, but in common idiom people speak as if it does—and such commentary quickly becomes problematic. Thus, I chose not to use the term, "race" at all. This choice will not be a choice everyone will—or can—make; nevertheless, as we move forward, we need to pay particular attention to how words drag unintentional meanings along behind them.

Diversity, of course, addresses more than the color of one's skin or ancestral geographic region, encompassing multiple human differences. Like our beliefs, differences nest in unequal relationships and complex intersections. In a 2010 article, published in the *Journal of Psychological Issues in Organizational Culture*, Lee Gardenswartz, Jorge Cherbosque, and Ruth Rowe adapted a diversity wheel graphic originally proposed by Marilyn Loden and Judy Rosner (1991). Used extensively in business and consciousness-raising trainings, the diversity wheel conceptualizes the many and complex facets of diversity both among groups and for individuals. I too have adapted this graphic (see Figure 2.2) to more accurately reflect my focus on community-based theatre and performance rather than human resource training (as well as my focus on communitarian identity structures).

The diversity wheel graphic acknowledges our nested identity locations. Core is personality. While personalities are not necessarily entirely stable, many traits do remain relatively constant for our entire life span. The internal dimension ring includes those elements that remain fixed through most of our lives and have continuing impact on identities. Components on the internal dimension are the default characteristics that most individual include when they ponder pluralism. Diversity should be conceptualized much more expansively however. The external dimension incorporates components that morph and shift through our life spans. I note, however, how "physical ability"

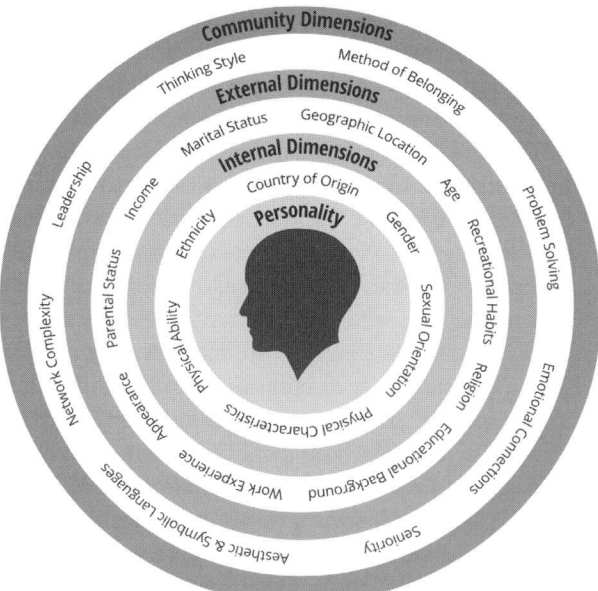

**Figure 2.2:** TFY CCD adapted diversity wheel.

functions on both the internal and external dimension. For example, illness, age, injury, and pregnancy affect (sometime temporarily) physical abilities. Community dimensions may be less self-explanatory than the other layers, and I explain each component in detail as follows.

Community dimensions map elements contributing to the diverse ways of being (and engaging) in our different communities. While I explore working with/in community in depth later, for our purposes here community is as much about who does not belong as who does—community exists to contain and to exclude—boundaries of belonging. Communities can be formed from ethnic identities, geographical proximity, religious affiliation, or groups of like-minded individuals; Cornerstone company member, Paula Donnelly once shared, "I belong to the community of dark beer drinkers." Some communities have more permeable boundaries than others, or membership might be transitory, like childhood.

*Method of belonging* addresses how one belongs to a group. One can be born into a community or move into a community. People voluntarily can join communities or be forced into one, for example incarcerated populations or some gang memberships. The methods through which people fit into community create different capacity for interaction and engagement. To use myself as an example, I belong to the community of Arizona State University's School of Film, Dance and Theatre (SOFDT). Composed of faculty, staff, students, and alumni, the SOFDT community adheres around location, interest, and experience—and a love for acronyms. I belong to this community as a member of the faculty *and* as an alum of the program that structures my "fit" in the community in unique ways.

*Problem solving* refers to the diverse ways in which individuals handle challenges or conflict. Some individuals negotiate problems behind the scenes. Others form coalitions or collectives to address challenges. Diverse individuals solve problems differently. In addition, individuals may solve conflict differently in different contexts. I solve problems within my family in a manner I do not within SOFDT. I solve structural difficulties (university bureaucracy) in a different manner than personality conflicts among faculty or students. Some individuals react slowly to challenges, others respond immediately and passionately. In any group of people working together toward a common goal, challenges will occur. Understanding the preferred problem-solving languages of a group (and individuals) can go a long way toward minimizing disruption while allowing challenges to move groups creatively.

*Emotional connections* maps two related aspects of diversity in community membership:

1. Emotional investment in the community as a whole.
2. Emotional connections to different members of that community.

How passionately people support their community speaks of the different ways in which they will engage. We all know individuals who are passionate advocates for their church or synagogue or perhaps their yoga studio, local library, or children's school. Other community members may be more casual in their affection or engagement. In a similar manner, different individuals within a community create diverse emotional connections. I have colleagues in the SOFDT with whom I maintain deep emotional investments; we propose projects together, plan and assess curriculum, and coauthor articles. Other colleagues are "hall friends." We wave to one another and shoot the breeze periodically but do not socialize outside of SOFDT nor work as closely together. Many undergraduates in the SOFDT have graduated without ever having taken a course from me, but there are graduate students who see me every day. The social and emotional bonds connecting individuals to the group and to others are diverse and adaptable.

*Seniority* refers to the longevity of an individual within a community. In my close-knit neighborhood, several families have lived here for over twenty years. One elderly neighbor has resided in her home since the 1940s and serves as the neighborhood historian. She remembers when my, now rather urban, neighborhood housed a dairy and a pig farm. In a school setting like SOFDT, we literally have "seniors" as well as emeritus faculty, brand new staff plus first-semester freshmen. Seniority functions differently in different environments of course, but remains a point of diverse engagement and institutional knowledge. Seniority does not always run parallel with power relationships but often can. Mapping who counts as community "seniors", as well as how the community understands those people, can tell partnering artists quite a bit about how a community understands itself. It is not uncommon, for example, for different "generations" within a community to conceptualize community identity differently.

*Aesthetic and symbolic languages* refers to two components:

1. The distinctive symbol systems of a community.
2. Individuals' unique use of aesthetic and symbolic representations.

Communities reinforce belonging through the circulation of singular collaborative symbols and shared narrative structures. Families, for example, can speak in codes built on years of experiences together. In my family, holidays center around particular recipes passed down through multiple generations. To explain that one "feels like Aunt Loetta's jello salad" or to describe someone as having an "Uncle Carl moment" communicates volumes among my sisters. At my daughters' school, youth can affiliate into clubs built around shared narratives, for example the Harry Potter club organizes itself through the different houses from that series and the youth meet to play Quidditch. I find combining the iceberg illustration's "cultural artifacts" section with "aesthetic and symbolic languages" a useful starting point when assessing a community's aesthetic and symbolic languages. Cultural artifacts can point to—although they are not the same as—a community's aesthetic structures. Youth who identify as "hip-hop," for example, share specific rhythmic structures and particular performance styles. This component also addresses individual's unique adaptations of their community's aesthetic structures. How different people adapt and perform the codes and symbols of their group/s speaks to the creative natures of those inside the same community. This diversity is an amazing social and cultural asset particularly relevant to community-based theatre and performance. Partnering performance artists should pay particular attention to the aesthetic and symbolic languages of a community. In general, I have found that only some of these languages will be explicit, but a whole range of symbolic communication will occur implicitly in the everyday performances of community partners and members. As theatre artists, our primary tools are the essential elements of theatrical performance: embodiment; ensemble;

text/narrative; theme/idea; time/duration; spectacle; situated place; sound/music; and reenactment of an elusive original. Paying attention to the way a community understands and uses "time," for example, creates a rich and contextualized aesthetic palette. Additionally, theatre artists bring advanced skills in dramaturgy to the table, and these skills help community artists map aesthetic and symbolic language structures in play.

*Network complexity* concerns the different connections within a community as well as that community's external ties. Some communities can be highly structured environments with different kinds of scaffolding ordering relationships. Within communities, too, individuals create diverse kinds of connections with one another that further structure interactions. The SOFDT is a highly structured and complex community. Connections inside SOFDT develop first through methods of belonging (e.g., students, graduate students, faculty, and staff) and longevity within the community. Complexity grows quickly, however, when you add primary art form (e.g., film, dance, and theatre), degree programs within the arts (the school has twenty degrees, including two minors), specialty within the arts (e.g., acting, ballet, lighting design, and pedagogy), and the emotional connections between individuals built through their common experiences. Smaller communities can be just as complex however. We all know families with complex arrangements of spouses, siblings, second and third marriages, grandparents, and children. Other communities may have little complexity and perhaps more temporary or fluid membership. Fandoms and online environments, for example, might have passionate members who never connect except within bulletin boards or Twitter. A temporary community built through performance attendance or workshops generally has little network complexity. Additionally, individuals within a community might be more or less connected to others. When a colleague retired several years ago, hundreds of individuals from around the globe sent best wishes and favorite memories with many traveling long distances to celebrate with him. He de facto served as a center of community complexity and his retirement had consequences for the community's network (and social capital) after he left.

*Leadership* speaks about two aspects of diversity of communities and within communities:

1. Leadership status for the community as a whole.
2. Individuals within the community and the roles they perform on a continuum from follower to leader.

The community itself might have a leadership role within larger social or cultural affiliations. For example, the National Association for the Advancement of Colored People (NAACP) exists as a membership organization dedicated to social justice and the elimination of discrimination. As an organization, they played a large role during the civil rights movement of the 1950s and 1960s and continue as leaders today. People can also be leaders within a community informally or formally. Diversity within leadership exists as well. Some leaders rule through fiat and others through consensus. Some individuals lead from the side through their own considerable personal charisma or social standing. The acknowledged matriarch of my large extended family, my grandmother exercised her leadership through storytelling. No matter what the situation, she had a parable, bible verse, or story from her life narrating both how we should address the issue and how we should understand it.

*Thinking style* seems at first as if it should belong to the personality core but I am interested in teasing out subtle aspects of diversity within a community and among communities themselves. While acknowledging that individuals have unique preferences and tendencies for how they process and respond to information, like that suggested by Carl Jung and codified by instruments like the Myers-Briggs, here I am more interested in the patterns of thought emphasized by particular communities. If you page back to the iceberg analogy and revisit some of the many cultural assumptions deeply related to thinking and belief patterns, you will recognize how contextually dependent mental processing can be. Diverse communities process information in diverse manners. This segment in effect functions as the information analogue to the aesthetic and symbolic languages segment. For example, at the university level, individual courses function as fluid, temporary learning communities. Courses can be required (forced membership) or elective (affinity memberships), but particular courses enforce and reify particular thinking patterns. A class in linear equations will emphasize logic and patterning while defining *variability* and *constants* in particular ways. Compare that to a class in solo performance. Solo performance will emphasize symbolic thinking, abstraction, and the physical embodiment of narrative. Solo performance will define *variability* and *constants* in quite different ways than the course in linear equations. Individuals will bring diversity to each of the classes, of course, but the courses themselves emphasize and require different patterns of thought. As an artist, I find the task of teasing out the subtle performance distinctions of different communities immensely satisfying. I use my artist's eye to "see" the differences and bring them into conscious awareness so that collectively we can recreate, recast, and play with the performance languages. These aesthetic structures can be particularly complex, but manipulating them allows us to collectively create and recreate life's patterns. Thinking styles affect narrative structures, dialogue and textual poetry while also reinforcing the web of relations.

Using the diversity wheel, I wish to highlight how nested and complex differences function. People are never just one thing—black, white, middle class, poor, gay, Mexican, teen—we all pull from multiple aspects of our identities and life paths. Additionally, groups are never monolithic entities composed of carbon copy people. The default for most conversations on diversity starts and ends with internal components understood through sensual data, but diversity can be understood as vastly more complex. Nonetheless, US America as a whole still aligns status differences along primarily visual clues (e.g., skin color, hair texture, and body shapes). We live in an unbalanced society. Some have status and wealth, whereas others live in desperate poverty. In fact, according to the 2010 US Census, one in five children live in poverty. While income disparity has grown rapidly in the United States among all groups, people of color represent a disproportionate number of the poor. Historically, ethnicity and skin color has been used to contain people's identities within narrow boundaries. Racism, sexism, classism, and identity stereotyping continue to regulate social interactions and legitimize oppression. The next section explores two related concepts, power and status, to further ground discussion around ethical community-based engagement.

> **KEY IDEAS**
>
> - Diversity is the wide and glorious range of human difference.
> - The diversity wheel can be a useful tool to widen understandings of pluralism beyond sense data while also unpacking community's particular performances of belonging.
> - We live in a world unfortunately characterized by racism, sexism, classism, and identity stereotyping, which regulates social interactions and legitimizes oppression. CCD TFY practices pay particular attention to oppression of all kinds.

## 2.4 POWER AND STATUS

Power is not a simple concept for political philosophers nor social historians. Probably readers will be most familiar with sociologist Max Weber's (1968) understanding of power as the ability to do what one wishes even in the face of resistance or disapproval. Weber's broad and individualized definition makes absolute sense functionally but philosophically works too generally for our exploration in aesthetic engagements. For the purposes of this text on community cultural development with children and youth, I find Bertrand Russell's definition more useful, "Power may be defined as the production of intended effects" (1938: 25). Additionally, Hannah Arendt (1969: 64) points to the communal nature of power in complex social systems, "power corresponds to the human ability to not just act but to act in concert. Power is never the property of an individual […]." Arendt points to ways in which power, like meaning, flows system wide. For our purposes, *power* in community-based theatre with children and youth *is the* ability to act in concert to achieve intended effects. People often conflate power with agency but they are not the same. Sociologist Murray Milner points out, "power is not simply the episodic exercise of agency. It is also the accumulated residues of past actions, which provide the largely taken-for-granted structural context of subsequent actions" (1994: 27). Here, Milner refers to the accretion or hardening of power relationships into sociological and cultural structures regulating human relationships (discussed further in the next section). Within our definition, power is not a static "thing" but a system phenomenon. An example might be helpful here. For much of western history, men accumulated more power than women. In the United States, women legally were not allowed to have credit cards or buy a home in their own name until 1974. Such a structure constrained relationships between men and women and structured social power in particular ways. Until women could access financial tools equal to their male counterparts, men maintained not only more power but also "power over" women's choices. *Power over* is often written in a continuum from influence to control. Culturally in the United States, adults have more power than children, but adults also have power over children. This "power over" can work in one of two ways: power can prevent actions or it can promote them, but in both directions "power over" places limits on freedoms. These two meanings of "power,"

- Power = the ability to act in concert to achieve intended effects
- Power over = continuum of influence-to-control that limits the freedom of others to achieve their will.

have direct relevancy to community-based theatre with children and youth. Remembering that the goal of community cultural development is grounded in building the social, political, economic, spiritual, and/or cultural strength of the communities involved, power becomes a key field. To put this in acting terms, TFY CCD residencies will have a super objective. Participating artists must foster an environment in which they and their collaborators can act in concert to achieve the residency super objective, a focus on social change, human development, freedom, and justice.

In addition, key to ethically accomplishing residency super objectives is a clear understanding of "status." One of those words everyone understands, "status" means one's relative importance. Unpacking the term, however, makes clear how complex "status" and status relationships really are. First, while status can be understood to "belong" to an individual (honor or reputation, for example), status locates within the minds of others. No matter how I understand my own status within a hierarchical system, others' opinions about me form the basis for my prestige. Much like power, status functions within social systems but remains individualized and connected intrinsically to individuals. People who misread, misunderstand, or remain convinced of their own high status despite contrary evidence have difficulty interacting in social environments. We have specific words to recognize individuals like this, for example, *megalomaniac, prima donna.* Status also exists in limited form. If everyone had the same social standing, then status would cease to be a comparative organizing characteristic. In other words, status appears only in limited quantities within hierarchies. For one person to move up the hierarchy, another must be displaced or removed entirely. An example of how status works as a limited commodity can be seen in so-called "star athletes" on sports teams. Only one or perhaps two individuals can be the "star" of a sports team. To occupy this position too places the individual within a realm of passionate love and passionate hate, for example, basketball player LeBron James. Anthropologists call the social and cultural methods of reducing status—like those to which LeBron James is subject—social leveling mechanisms. I have a friend who explains social leveling mechanisms as a bucket of crabs. "As soon as you think you are climbing up and out," he says, "they pull you back down." Status flows in systems and people unpack these structures easily. When we were in graduate school together Johanna Smith—now a professor at California State University, San Bernadino—taught me a status game played with a deck of cards. Participants are dealt a card but not allowed to look at it. Instead, players hold the card face out on their foreheads. Then players mingle as if they were all at a party. Players interact with others using their card status—Kings are high and Aces low. After the facilitator calls time, players are asked to line up according to their understanding of their perceived status. In all the many times I have played this game with multiple age groups, players only rarely mistake their relative status and generally even mistakes are within a card or two of their actual numerical placement. Humans use status.

Status and prestige function as a social resource (a form of capital) and in this manner also concern power. While money and income have come to be understood as an almost universal method through which one can achieve status and prestige in the United States, you must be careful not to conflate the two. Social status derives from any number of social or cultural characteristics valued by the group. Community cultural development specialists will be called on to work with multiple communities. Each of these communities will define status slightly differently and the methods through which they determine status will be radically diverse. Status could derive from knowledge, from ability, from location, from access to particular resources, from clothing, from musical taste, physical beauty, et cetera. There are concurrent sociological status relationships, however, which operate on most US Americans. For example, in general, white men have more social capital than do Native American women. Native English speakers have more social status than do those with English as a second language.

TFY CCD artists need to understand how status operates within the general culture of the United States while also acknowledging the contextual nature in communities. The ability to reflect openly on difference, power, and prestige will be a vital component of ethical engagement in communities. In a similar manner, being able to map the ways in which communities practice power and social prestige will be a useful skill. In order to practice both of these skills, I suggest TFY CCD artists reflect candidly on their own social honor as related to their diverse identity locations. Again, prestige and power flow in contextual social systems so context is particularly important. For example, age within a family context will be understood differently than age within a school or work context, as would the status of ninth graders in a junior high (oldest youth) versus in a high school (youngest youth).

The worksheet opposite uses the first two rings of the diversity wheel to ascribe status. I offer this activity to readers and suggest ranking status as *high*, *mid*, and *low* for simplicity. To determine status, first decide the default setting for the specific cultural context. For example, in the United States as a whole, the default for physical ability is a fully able-bodied adult. Individuals with physical disabilities, then, automatically have lower general prestige because they do not match the default. With the Disabilities Act of 1990, US Americans attempted to reset this default. Likewise, those individuals with exceptional physical abilities have higher status than most able-bodied adults, as they can accomplish more than the default. Remember context remains particularly relevant however. For example, Parental Status: I have three children. Within the general context of US American culture, three children in a heterosexual partnership equals high prestige. I would argue, in fact, that being a parent at my age is understood as default. Within a university setting however, being a parent confers a lower status as parenting and academia still conflict in multiple ways—particularly, parenting more than one or two children. On the other hand, as a theatre for youth specialist, having children confers specific prestige within the narrow confines of the culture of theatre for youth specialists. Context matters. In the Table opposite, choose a particular context then rank your status. How is status performed in the context you have chosen? For example, I identify as gendered female. Growing up in Dallas,

Texas, "female" meant a particular kind of behavior: long-hair, make-up, and nicely manicured nails equaled higher status than short-hair, doc martins, and un-plucked eyebrows. Paying attention to how communities perform status fosters more nuanced understandings of pluralism.

**CONTEXT:**

| Component | Status | How is Status Determined and/or Performed? |
|---|---|---|
| Country of Origin | | |
| Gender | | |
| Sexual Orientation | | |
| Physical Ability | | |
| Ethnicity | | |
| Physical Characteristics | | |
| Geographic Location | | |
| Income | | |
| Age | | |
| Recreational Habits | | |
| Religion | | |
| Educational Background | | |
| Work Experience | | |
| Appearance | | |
| Parental Status | | |
| Marital Status | | |

> **KEY IDEAS**
>
> - I define power:
>   1. Power = the ability to act in concert to achieve intended effects
>   2. Power over = continuum of influence-to-control that limits the freedom of others to achieve their will
> - Status is one's relative importance in a closed system.

## 2.5 HEGEMONY

Oppression, particularly structural oppression, relates intimately to status, diversity, and difference. People can oppress one another, of course, but more insidious forms of oppression grow in social structures that systemically support and strengthen inequity. Such structures become accepted over time—universalized—marginalizing whole categories of people and ways of living. I have great suspicion whenever individuals invoke "universal." Humans are so amazingly complex, brilliantly creative, and sublimely diverse that I have difficulty with the term when applied to cultural and behavioral contexts. "Universal" becomes code for naturalized, dominant cultural practices.

As community-based theatre specialists with children and youth, we have to learn to question everything—how stories are told, whose stories are told, even, what counts as a story. In Elin Diamond's *Unmaking Mimesis*, she reminds us that representational theatre is "conservative and patriarchal" and can function as "a symptomatic cultural site that ruthlessly maps out normative spectatorial positions by occluding its own means of production" (1997: iii). Meaning, theatre, like public art in general, is not inherently progressive, alternative, or even ethical—theatre and performance is not, in other words, self-evidently good. Ric Knowles (2004: 17) points out that "the shared assumption underlying all of this work is that cultural productions neither contain meaning nor uni-dimensionally shape behavior and belief; rather they produce meaning through the lived everyday relationships of people with texts and performances." Knowles and Diamond both point to the constructed nature of theatre and performance and to the manner in which individuals decode and understand art. Both, in essence, reinforce Kershaw's point that theatre is an ideological transaction. Returning for a moment to my definition of public-making—*socially constructed through lived and embodied practices*—highlights TFY CCD artists need to understand how the strategies and the multiple tactics of lived experience interact and operate in any given environment. How does power flow? How do people perform belonging or not? How do individuals move through social spaces? Who is not allowed within a community and why? How is status accrued?

Knowles' thesis is particularly important to our discussion here because theatre does not contain meaning, rather meaning grows from lived experiences in social environments within the constant ebb and flow of material oppression and unequal power relationships. As artists, we cannot make public art without understanding the landscape and performances of power and oppression in any given environment *if for no other reason than the aesthetic need to construct work in which we shape the potential meanings circulated*. Craft demands control. However, community cultural development in general, let alone with children and youth, intervenes in status quos in order to build, foster, and/or strengthen a community's social, political, spiritual, economic, and/or cultural power. Therefore, both the form and content of the work and the purpose of the work demand that we understand power and oppression in ways both subtle and overt. TFY third space is inspirational and utopian at heart—we produce participatory publics in our processes and through our products—this is our placemaking. Third space TFY's purpose unapologetically is to do good. This, coupled with a core value understanding diversity as social, cultural, aesthetic, and civic assets, makes it imperative that facilitating artists learn to recognize and understand power and oppression. Because ultimately neither public art, in general, nor community-based theatre is inherently good work. We must make it so.

In April of 2013, one of my daughters participated in a school event conducted by Junior Achievement called, BizTown. This curriculum and culminating immersive experience teaches elementary-aged youth the common beliefs and terms of a consumer economy. For example, lesson two focuses on "free enterprise" as a central concept and lesson. Lesson fifteen centers around area businesses—that support BizTown—using them as case studies to teach "quality" business practices. For example, my daughter mentioned Papa John's, US Airways, Bank of America, and the Diamondbacks Baseball team as fundamental in her experience. The culminating event is a daylong participatory "performance" in which young people take on job roles with accompanying tasks and scenarios. Youth list several job possibilities they would like to explore and then are assigned their roles. These roles within the simulated economy/town include mayor, police officers, bank tellers, yoga instructors, CEOs, pharmacists, construction workers, et cetera. My daughter was a radio reporter. BizTown, indeed public schooling in general, is an ideological apparatus educating individuals while naturalizing conceptual practices.

Junior Achievement's stated mission, as listed on their website, is to "inspire and prepare young people to succeed in the global economy." This inspiration takes the form of training for a free market economy. BizTown curriculum and young people's embodied participation within this curriculum resides within a particular US American ideology of how markets should work. Additionally, the ways in which the event structures participation are also influenced by the ideological belief structures of teachers, parents and BizTown leaders. My daughter attends a public, performing arts school with much less demographic diversity than the surrounding community. The school is predominantly white and predominantly female. As she chatted with us over dinner about her day at BizTown, Maeve told us how her friend (a Native American male) was cast as a construction worker, but that everyone thought he was a crossing guard because of his orange vest (this caused the young man frustration). Additionally, we discovered in conversation that this same young man was cast as the "criminal" for the staged crime (a stolen teddy bear) solved by the "police." In a school with few boys and fewer indigenous youth, the collision of manual labor and crime in one brown body troubles me greatly.

I do not share this story to call out BizTown or my daughter's teachers as racist but rather to highlight the ways in which social systems are inherently unbalanced as well as the manner in which meanings form contextually. Facilitators need to practice awareness and critical thinking around the circulation of symbols. Sharon Grady points out, "Now more than ever there is a need for a pluralistic perspective in our drama and theatre work. By this I mean a more in-depth understanding of and respect for the identity locations that mark us as different from one another" (2000: xiii). I would add the need to understand how difference is also always understood within hierarchical structures of status relationships and material oppressions. Whether or not this fifth grade, brown-skinned young man "chose" to perform the roles of manual laborer and criminal does not change the nature of how meanings circulate and are understood. Arizona has a long and complicated relationship to indigenous peoples as well as Mexican immigrants—the young man identifies as Azteca. To not understand how this contextual status works on young men of color shows a supreme lack of understanding of power and representation on the part of the adults involved. To be a young man of color in this particular environment is to be subject to an unbalanced power dynamic with a narrow ideological structure. This young man does not have the same inherent representational power that my white daughter does by virtue of the larger culture in which they both live.

Antonio Gramsci (1973) named the (mostly unconscious) acceptance and circulation of dominant belief structures—or what Murray Milner (1994: 27) calls the "taken-for-granted structural context"—*hegemony*. Imprisoned by Mussolini for almost ten years, Gramsci divided nation states into two separate spheres: political society and civil society. In the political realm, the state rules by force (e.g., secret police, army death squads, gulags, and prisons). In Gramsci's civic realm, the state rules through more subtly coercive means including the circulation of ideas and beliefs. Gramsci's work especially explores "power over." Gramsci particularly was invested in understanding fascist Italy, so I further depend on the work of Raymond Williams to ground my use of *hegemony* within the cultural realm. Williams writes, "the concept of 'hegemony' goes beyond 'ideology.' What is decisive is not only the conscious system of ideas and beliefs, but the whole lived social process as practically organized by specific and dominant meanings and values" (1977: 109). Key here is an understanding of the unbalanced nature of our social worlds. There are dominant beliefs and subordinate beliefs. There are dominant people and subordinate people. Williams writes,

> Hegemony is then not only the articulate upper level of 'ideology', nor are its forms of control only those ordinarily seen as 'manipulation' or 'indoctrination'. It is a whole body of practices and expectations, over the whole of living: our senses and assignments of energy, our shaping

perceptions of ourselves and our world. It is a lived system of meanings and values—constitutive and constituting—which as they are experienced as practices appear as reciprocally confirming. It thus constitutes a sense of reality for most people in the society [...].

(1977: 110)

A useful term "hegemony" helps us to unpack the unconscious and invisible ways unbalanced systems replicate and reproduce, and most systems lack balance. Williams goes on to point out, "Any process of socialization of course includes things that all human beings have to learn, but any specific process ties this necessary learning to a selected range of meanings, values, and practices [...]" (1977: 117). BizTown's function as an economic educational structure narrows the feasibility of certain choices while also naturalizing their absence. For example, mother is not an option within BizTown and neither is superhero. Hegemony reifies the status quo by naturalizing the belief structures necessary to maintain unequal power relationships. Thus, the invisibility of such a system naturalizes the absence of "mother" as an option for BizTown while maintaining the continuing separation of civic practices and "private" practices. The concept of hegemony asks us to question our own paradigmatic assumptions about the world and how we move through it.

**KEY IDEAS**

- "Universal" is code for naturalized, dominant cultural practices.
- Neither theatre nor community cultural development is inherently a "good" practice, artists must consciously make it so.
- Social systems are inherently unbalanced and meanings form contextually inside them.
- Difference should be understood within hierarchical structures of status relationships and material oppression.
- Hegemony is a lived system of meanings and values that circulate and maintain unequal social relations through lived experience.
- TFY CCD practitioners need to questions their own paradigmatic assumptions about the world and treat "universals" with suspicion.

## 2.6 PUTTING ETHICS AND PLURALISM TOGETHER

So, how can you take all this information on culture, power, status, difference, hegemony, and capital and distill it into workable parameters for yourself? Jill Dolan's marvelous 2005 book, *Utopia in Performance: Finding Hope at the Theater*, explores the ways in which theatre creates shared moments of utopia understood as fleeting moments of "what if" rather than polemic commands or sugary fairytales. Theatre "that can experiment with the possibilities of the future in ways that shine back usefully on a present that's always, itself, in process (13). Dolan articulates a theatre praxis both strengthening and questioning communities' *structure of feelings*. Raymond Williams explained "structure of feelings" as,

> a particular sense of life, a particular community of experience hardly needing expression, through which the characteristics of our way of life [...] are in some way passed, giving them a particular and characteristic color [...] a particular and native style [...] it is as firm as "structure" suggests, yet it operates in the most delicate and least tangible parts of our activity.
> (1961: 64)

Theatre can intervene in daily existence to frame relationships and highlight hegemonic structures limiting possibilities. Theatre can also reify and strengthen unequal relationships and material oppression, of course. Regardless, theatre created through community cultural development processes will be understood, decoded, and interpreted through a community's structure of feeling. Again, theatre is an ideological transaction. Dolan asks,

> How can we take the space opened in performance and imagination and actively encourage utopian performatives? Isn't this what any group of actors and directors tries to do each time they set out to create a performance?
> (2005: 169)

Our task in third space theatre with children and youth remains thinking through the possibilities and inherent cultural, social, and human wealth in communities collaboratively, to devise breathtaking theatre that speaks to and enriches both the community itself as well as larger US American culture. In my experience, focusing on positives, building assets, and deploying the wealth of the community (understood broadly) allows for more holistic and potentially utopian possibilities than polemics about unfairness or disparity. TFY CCD practices engage in inherently unbalanced systems as children and youth are marginalized within civic and public space. However, the potential functionality of TFY CCD framing children and youth as communitarian assets creates space for a-ha moments and for joy. Which is not to say that groups should not focus their art actions on exposing the underbelly of their community but we should do so with clear-eyed understandings as well as imbedding that art action in processes promoting change.

TFY CCD artists' ability to successfully and ethically engage communities depends on craft competency as well as grounded philosophical understanding of the ways in which material culture functions. Equally important, however, will be their own integrity. Individuals of integrity live their values and belief systems—they practice what they preach. Having integrity means we also engage in recursive self-examination—judging our own actions. I do not mean to say, of course, that we should paralyze ourselves or become narcissistic. I have had a quote taped inside my bathroom cabinet for many years reminding me:

> The person of integrity is not superman; he will be, from time to time, defeated, frustrated, embarrassed and completely surprised. But neither is he the common and regular dupe of circumstance, compelled (like a tourist with a pocket dictionary) to consult conscience and emotion at each new turn of events.
>
> (Grudin 1982: 51)

To practice community cultural development with honor and integrity means both a commitment to good work and the knowledge, understanding, and skill to accomplish such work. Toward that end, I suggest to my students that they craft an ethical statement to post and share publically. While many teaching artists create and share teaching manifestos, and many theatre artists create aesthetic statements, I believe we should craft ethical statements as well. I include my own ethical statement below as an example.

> As a professional, my core values revolve around my passion as an artist, a teacher, a scholar, and a citizen. My work moves fluidly between and among these related areas in vital ways creating opportunities for community connectedness, diverse artistic practices and democratic dialogue. I regard my scholarship and my artistic practice as equally important systems exploring fundamental questions about childhood, culture, and civic engagement. I believe my work does not and cannot exist in a vacuum but must come from and go back into community.

In all aspects of my work I believe:

- in mutual respect among persons
- in deliberative democracy
- in the human right to participate in culture
- in the power of the arts to function as sites of civic engagement creating civic publics

Even the practice of crafting such a statement can help integrate theoretical knowledge with practical (procedural) knowledge. Finally, however, as we live our ethics, we negotiate the complex relationships between cultural and personal values, theories on how the world operates, our desires, and the multiple social forces that limit and shape possibilities. Know that this is a lifelong journey.

> **KEY IDEAS**
>
> - Our task is to devise breathtaking theatre that speaks to and enriches both the community itself as well as larger US American culture.
> - TFY CCD depends on craft competency as well as grounded philosophical understandings of the ways in which material culture functions.
> - TFY CCD artists must commit to practices of personal integrity.

## 2.7 AUTHENTIC LEADERSHIP

When I first started teaching community-based processes, I floundered trying to label and differentiate. I used "teaching artist" and "facilitator" contextually based on the primary domains I believed those roles engaged. After working in this manner for several years and refining my own thinking, however, I believe *leadership* is the most appropriate term for how we engage children and youth in community cultural development. First, I need to distinguish between a leader and a boss. A boss has power over individuals structurally. A leader motivates people to follow and work together. When young people tell one another, "you are not the boss of me" they speak to power relationships *and* intrinsic desire—"I do not follow you and you have no power over me." If you think about your own experiences with directors, teachers, or coaches, I feel certain you can distinguish between teachers or coaches who were bosses and those who were leaders. While leadership research in the early- to mid-twentieth century focused on the innate skills and internal psychological characteristics of leaders (leaders are born), more recent literature examines the practices of effective leaders (leaders are made). Most contemporary research agrees leadership:

- Is a collection of skills built over time
- Happens in the moment
- Engages both intellect and emotion
- Sets organizational/ensemble culture.

I particularly draw on leadership research focusing on *authentic leadership*. Bruce Avolio, William Gardner, and Fred Walumbwa write,

> Authentic leaders are leaders who: (a) know who they are and what they believe in; (b) display transparency and consistency between their values, ethical reasoning and actions; (c) focus on developing positive psychological states such as confidence, optimism, hope, and resilience within themselves and their associates; (d) are widely known and respected for their integrity.
> (Avolio, Gardner, and Walumbwa 2005: xxii–xxiii)

Authentic leadership functions in the same manner as individual authenticity. Authenticity touches on the external reflection of internal realities or genuineness. Additionally, authentic people do not depend on others to continually validate their existences or their choices. As Todd Pittinsky and Christopher Tyson note, authenticity not only reflects one's individual psychology, but also social relationships and identity/ies structures (2005: 257). To return for a moment to the diversity wheel explored in Section 2.3, authentic leadership builds on reflective practices. Authentic leaders understand themselves and live their values; they commit to nurturing positive relationships and healthy intrapersonal skills. Authentic leaders do not invest in being right or proving others wrong. Adrian Chan, Sean Hannah, and William Gardner write, "Authentic leadership is a lifelong developmental phenomenon that involves acquiring greater self-awareness along with an unwavering commitment to and regulation of the self" (2005: 35). Additionally, Larry Hughes offers,

> Authentic leaders act according to their values, build relationships that enable followers to offer diverse viewpoints, and build social networks with followers. Authentic leaders also recognize followers' talents and see their job as one in which they nurture followers' talents into strengths [...].
> (2005: 86)

Pittinsky and Tyson break down authentic leadership further: "Individual authenticity [...] includes self-awareness, self-acceptance, and authentic actions. Authentic leader-follower relationships are characterized by (a) transparency, openness, and trust; (b) guidance toward an objective; and (c) an emphasis on follower development [...]" (2005: 256). Within community cultural development, authentic leadership demands honesty, transparency, clear articulation of the focus and structure of the processes, lateral management structures, and reciprocal relationships. Authentic leaders *show* and *tell*.

## 2.7.1 Openness and Emotional Honesty

Larry Hughes offers a notable mnemonic labeling of the key components of what he calls "relational transparency." He writes, "self-disclosure is comprised of the expression of four aspects of self-disclosure: goals/motives, identity, values, and emotions (GIVE)" (2005: 87). Building reciprocity among partners and ensemble members depends on a culture of openness and emotional honesty. Sharing your goals and motivations while honestly disclosing your identity/ies, values, and emotions might alarm you especially in new partnerships or if you have been trained in hierarchical pedagogical structures. Unlike traditional school structures, however, in community-based theatre, most young people connect because they wish to engage, not because adults compel them. Participation choice creates space for more evenly balanced relationships between adults and young people. A skilled community-based artist creates safe environments and builds trust-fostering opportunities for authentic communication. Theatre artists working within this paradigm need to understand how to perform deep listening and to provide appropriate feedback, paying attention to opportunities to raise young people's awareness of creative and dialogic structures. Authentic leadership rests too on skillfully and ethically building relationships with and among partners and ensemble members. Authentic leadership means paying close attention to group and individual processes not just the content and substance of the lesson, workshop, or program. Like all relationships, TFY third space relationships depend on honesty and mutual respect—relational transparency. Relational transparency, however, does not equate to ensemble cultures anchored in leader "specialness." I warn against group culture in which the leader remains at the center of the ensemble and followers build relationships not with one another but with the leader. Such structures rarely foster equal interactions. Relational transparency does not mean making everything about the leader and/or the leader's specialness. Authentic leadership depends equally on self-awareness and self-regulation. Learning how to share enough to create a culture of openness while not hijacking the emotional resonances in a room demands skill.

## 2.7.2 Lateral Management Structures

Hierarchical control structures promote obedience not participation. In addition, creativity research shows that creativity encourages critical and destructive attitudes together with constructive problem solving. Meaning hierarchical control structures short circuit creative processes and are a key target for artistic children and youth who feel them to be oppressive. Hierarchy interferes with TFY third space. Nevertheless, TFY CCD artists must be able to read an environment and to practice effective management, streamlining administrative tasks to maximize time spent immersed in the aesthetic processes. In effect, we need to off-load control by creating an environment of mutual respect and lateral management. Barb McKean suggests that explicitly negotiating the "kind of space and the conditions necessary for everyone to engage actively and productively in the work at hand" (2006: 18). Creating an environment in which all participants feel safe taking risks depends on openly discussing necessary ensemble expectations. I find creativity research particularly useful here as a kind of informational front-loading, allowing participants to explicitly discuss conditions necessary to create and improvise. In addition, I discuss power and hierarchy openly to foster considered discussion of ensemble relationships. Children and youth tend to default to the hierarchical structure with which they have the most familiarity—age. In a culture understanding adulthood as the finished product, age reflects status. Older youth will have more power than younger youth.

Keith Sawyer points out, "Effective teams require participants who can coordinate, communicate, resolve conflicts, solve problems, make decisions, and negotiate […]" (2003: 185). We have to spend time at the beginning of our residency co-constructing an ensemble contract outlining expectations for collaborative and creative work in order to approach effectiveness. Creativity demands both divergent and convergent thinking patterns, unfettered, imaginative play filtered through critical feedback and thoughtful analysis. Different creative phases can demand different rules of engagement. Nevertheless, spreading responsibility through the ensemble rather than centralizing decisions activates group members. Drawbacks of lateral management can include time (decisions need discussion) as well as skillful balancing of chaos and order. Facilitators need to find the sweet spot between the chaos and order and continually work to keep the ensemble balanced.

### 2.7.3 Reciprocity

A central idea within community-based arts, I define reciprocity as mutual benefit. Generally, reciprocity does not describe the general social contract between adults and children and youth in the United States. Instead, "service," "gratitude," or perhaps "duty" would be more appropriate definitions for noncustodial relationships. Nevertheless, TFY third space relationships depend on mutual interchange and transparent communication. Dani Snyder-Young (2013) points out in fact, "[…] identifying 'what's in it for me'—is a crucial first step, if not the entire solution, to the paradox of practitioner privilege" (Synder-Young 2013: 27). Understanding what adult facilitating artists gain is important to this progression. Each residency will provide slightly different advantages.

In some cases, novel relationships will be primary, other residencies might allow facilitating artists to focus on particular cultures or artistic styles. In all cases, however, I have found ensemble relationships grow my artistry in fascinating (and sometimes painful) ways. Creativity research has focused on the ideal composition for group innovation. In an intriguing discussion of this research to date, Mark Runco points out two pertinent facts:

> individuals who have made large investments in their own field of expertise have large knowledge bases, which they can bring to the group in a very useful fashion, but they also have a tendency toward inflexibility.
> (Runco 2007: 166)

> [novices] are most likely to be open-minded and flexible since they have little to lose. A new idea may attract or intrigue them.
> (Runco 2007: 166)

While I do not like to think of myself as inflexible, my years of experience do suggest to me easy solutions or actions or activities. I prefer to understand this aptitude as efficient problem solving rather than inflexibility, but "efficiency" has a downside. And to be honest, I like to be right, which can lead to personal stubbornness (or, ahem, inflexibility). But, I have had innumerable experiences in which my understandings of the aesthetic process or a symbol were humbled by a fresh solution or suggestion from a novice. Even as a parent, I can tell you of experiences in which an off-hand comment from one of my daughters redefined an entire physical space or experience for me in extraordinary ways. Meeting the challenge of ensemble creativity within TFY third space has never gotten old for me. I have to think differently, to expand my understandings of how humans know and perform, to grow artistically and to innovate. The adventure of work within TFY third space always excites and I gain as much as I give. Individual artists will need to come to their own understanding of their gains as human and creative artists. I caution, however, against a "service" mentality that can short circuit creative processes and lead to imaginative and artistic stagnation.

### KEY IDEAS

- Leaders are made not born.
- Leaders motivate people to work together for a common purpose.
- Authentic leadership builds on reflective practices.
- Key characteristics of an authentic leader include: openness and emotional honesty, reciprocity and lateral management structures.

## 2.8 HEALTHY ENSEMBLES

Psychologist Mihalyi Csikszentmihalyi developed a key idea of creativity and happiness research—flow. As he explained in his 1990 text, *Flow: The Psychology of Optimal Experience*, flow is the enjoyable sweet spot where the challenge and our skills perfectly balance—too hard or too easy and we slide into anxiety or boredom. Sawyer builds off Csikszentmihalyi's work to explore ensemble flow. He writes,

> When a group is performing at its peak, I refer to the group as being in group flow, in the same way that an individual performing at his or her peak often experiences a subjective feeling of flow. The concept of group flow is related to Csikszentmihalyi's flow, but with a critical difference. Csikszentmihalyi intended flow to represent a state of consciousness within the individual performer, whereas group flow is a property of the entire group as a collective unit.
>
> (Sawyer 2003: 43)

Building healthy ensembles helps scaffold opportunities for group flow—peak experience. In order to do this, facilitators build complex understandings of individuals within the ensemble as well as mental maps of the group processes themselves. In other words, TFY CCD leaders must understand individuals and ensembles both psychologically and structurally. I use warm-ups and games as opportunities to assess both individuals and group processes. Watching game/warm-up structures as well as the skills practiced tells me quite a bit: Who leads? Who follows? Who is comfortable in their body and who feels exposed? Who takes control? How is control practiced? Who can be silly? Who likes to win? Leaders learn how to see the structures of group process as well as assess individual's emotional states and skills.

The eight components of the outer ring of the diversity wheel in Section 2.3 can be a helpful assessment structure to plot individuals' relationships, psychological habits, and skill sets. Questions to ask include:

- *Method of belonging*: How do individuals relate to the community? How do they understand their community and their position within the structures? How does power flow?
- *Problem solving*: How does the individual solve problems? Does the individual solve problems? What seems to be a primary interest for each individual? What are the stakes for each?

- *Emotional connections*: What relationships already exist? How would you characterize them? What undercurrents are involved subtextually for the children and youth? How are emotional connections reinforced and practiced in the environment?
- *Seniority*: How is seniority defined? Who has internal information the group will find useful? How did they build this information?
- *Aesthetic and symbolic languages*: What are the primary aesthetic and/or symbolic language structures of individuals? How easily do individuals move from system to system? What symbol systems seem to be used the most and how?
- *Network complexity*: How connected is each individual? Internally to the ensemble? Externally to the larger community?
- *Leadership*: Who are the leaders? How do they lead? Who follows? Why? Are there factions? How can you tell?
- *Thinking style*: How would you define the thinking styles in play? Why? Who are the rule breakers and the rule followers? Who needs extra nurturing to take risks and who will need guidance on appropriate risks?

Additionally, never underestimate the power of asking people to tell you about themselves. How do you work best in a group? What kinds of opportunities excite you? What would you say challenges you? Will Weigler suggests using an "Inventory of Skills" when building an ensemble (2001: 20–21), I suggest we expand such thinking to include creativity and collaboration. Edward De Bono (1992) uses the metaphor of "six thinking hats" as a way of fostering lateral thinking skills in his book, *Serious Creativity*. Different colored hats represent different modes of thinking.

- White hat = research and data collection
- Red hat = emotional and intuitive thinking
- Black hat = judgment and criticism
- Yellow hat = optimism and hopeful analysis, focus on best possible outcomes
- Green hat = generating further ideas through deviation amplification or riffing on a theme
- Blue hat = facilitating the processes, meta-thinking and time keeping

Even young children understand this metaphor and can tell you which hat they find most comfortable and which hat challenges them the most. De Bono's hat metaphor also usefully promotes switching modes or roles during ideation/generation activities. Additional questions helpful to understanding the unique aspects of different ensembles include defining risk, defining success, and building trust.

What counts as a risk will be slightly different for different groups. For some, performing live will be their biggest challenge. For others, engaging emotionally or being wrong outlines their fear. Almost everyone, however, irrespective of age, is afraid of humiliation. Facilitation goals depend on fostering a healthy ensemble that can communicate, make decisions, negotiate, and resolve conflict—skills dependent on trust. Creating an environment in which individuals feel comfortable with the possibility of being ridiculous goes a long way toward building ensemble safety and trust. I have long-used games, humor, silliness, and my own comfort with being ridiculous as a way of diffusing ensemble fear. Purposely creating moments in which the ensemble can feel superior to me also allows me to flip traditional hierarchical power structures. Research in effective leadership shows this technique a useful one. Hughes summarizes,

> Vinton (1989) found that humor alleviated status differentials and workplace tension between organization members. […] Furthermore, Vinton (1989) suggested that self-directed ridicule is well used by leaders who wish to communicate to followers that he or she has a sense of humor and can laugh at him or herself. Self-directed humor makes a powerful statement to followers, and thus enables followers to see leaders as accessible rather than remote, capable of adopting detached perspectives on themselves, and worthy of emulation (Kahn, 1989).
>
> (Hughes 2005: 94–95)

I do not mean to suggest that I clown or perform for ensembles, but rather I try to foster a playful environment. Game structures usefully allow me literally to play with ensembles. In fact, play defines my primary facilitation approach.

Play is recreational, enjoyable, autotelic (people play because they wish to play), imaginative, often physical, and with risk/consequences contained in the world of the game or the improvisation. Play is fun. Additionally, David Cohen (2006) points out that play has specific benefits including fostering flexibility and openness:

> […] enrichment through play enhances behavioural flexibility, including the ability to solve novel problems and to respond effectively to novel environments. In this light, play experiences facilitate generalized learning

and problem-solving skills, such as seeking multiple solutions to problems, adjusting problem-solving strategies to the task, and adapting to changing environmental or problem conditions.

(Cohen 2006: 58)

We have a tendency in US America to understand game play within a winner/loser paradigm. Healthy ensembles fundamentally need to understand the difference between competition and collaboration. One of the ways I point this out is through three separate rounds of musical chairs. (If I am working with young people with mobility issues, I replace the chairs with paper or masking tape squares on the floor.) On the first round, we play the game in the traditional manner—removing a chair per round, with individuals progressively "out" when they cannot find a chair (paper square). The second sequence we play teams (boy–girl, or some other easily identifiable characteristic) with the goal a team win rather than individuals. Finally, we play a third round in which everyone wins. The facilitator continues to remove chairs (up to the end when no chairs remain), yet everyone must find space to help one another progressively occupy a smaller and smaller space. (If playing with individuals with mobility impairment, players must find ways to physically link to the player in the last square.) Processing the different rounds, allows participants to discuss their emotional engagement with the different structures; how team play differs from individual play; examine the differences between collaborative play and competitive play. This allows me to point out examples of creative problem solving. I suggest readers find their own playful ways to experientially seed frank conversations on risk, play, and fear. The amazing community-based artist Elizabeth Johnson—long-time associate artistic director for Liz Lerman's Dance Exchange—begins each of her residencies with three instructions learned from Lerman:

1. Turn discomfort into inquiry. If an activity makes you uncomfortable, process why.
2. Keep a smile on your face when you chose not to participate so others do not feel self-conscious.
3. Breathe. Pay attention to the amazing dance inside your own body and know that where you are at this moment is perfect.

My game and Johnson's instructions serve the same function—to lighten stress and name fear while allowing for the growth of trust. When using games, care must be taken, however, to foster collaboration skills rather than competitive ones. While competition is not in and of itself negative, community cultural development and principles of deliberative democracy need gray space beyond black/white, win/lose scenarios. Roger Von Oech's classic text on fostering creativity (2008) explores what he calls the ten blocks to creativity that I believe relate to cultures of fear:

1. Wanting a right answer
2. An exclusive focus on logic
3. Blindly following rules
4. Focus on practicality to the exclusion of flights of fancy
5. Fear of ambiguity
6. Fear of mistakes
7. Avoiding play
8. Tunnel vision
9. Fear of appearing foolish and silly
10. Thinking of oneself or an ensemble as not creative, self-defeating attitude

Fear itself carries great emotional weight. So much so, acting teacher Stephen Wangh notes,

> Most [participants] will have invented clever disguises for their fear, so that they need not acknowledge it, even to themselves. It may look at first like aggression, or sleepiness, or distraction. But it will often 'speak' in clear, non-verbal ways. For instance, fear will show itself in where a student chooses to work in the room, or whether or not he makes eye contact.
> (2013: 65)

Another way of parsing Von Oech's blocks to creativity would be to focus on positive cultures/attitudes rather than negative ones. Runco's creativity text cited a study on organizational climates fostering creative teams and creative work places:

(1) Support for ideas
(2) Challenge
(3) Time for ideas
(4) Freedom
(5) Trust and openness
(6) Dynamism/liveliness
(7) Risk taking
(8) Playfulness and humor
(9) Debates
(10) Conflicts and impediments

(Runco 2007: 164)

While I suppose one could argue that healthy ensembles do not necessarily have to be creative ensembles; for my purposes, they are one and the same. I do want to quibble a bit, however, with Runco's number nine, no matter how useful I find his list. Debate does not equal dialogue. For the purposes of community-based theatre with children and youth, dialogue functions to build intellectual engagement and emotional stakes as well as social capital and relational reciprocity. Debate is competitive. Dialogue is collaborative. Nevertheless, creative capacity needs disagreements and conflicts propelling collaborative choice-making forward. In my experience, a studio process without conflict means participants do not care or are not paying attention.

## 2.8.1 Dialogue and Positive Communication

Healthy ensembles communicate effectively and appropriately. Part of my facilitation strategy rests in collectively creating rules of engagement—lateral management. Rather than avoiding conflict or pretending creative tensions will not occur, we plan for how the ensemble will collectively use tension to propel itself forward. Conflict is not in and of itself negative, but the dominant way we understand disagreement tends to be in competitive terms—judge, insist, diagnose, criticize, attack, debate, win/lose—or what Deborah Tannen (1998) calls the "argument culture." US Americans have a tendency to communicate in terms of what others have "done" to us. For example the phrase, "You are making me angry." As a parent, I can tell you "you are making me angry" does not serve as effective and creative problem solving. Although to be excruciatingly honest, I have said the phrase more than once. Rather than being focused on perspective taking or information sharing, "you are making me angry" functions as a threat. Marshall Rosenberg (2003) developed a communication strategy he calls nonviolent communication. At heart, Rosenberg's tactic depends on practicing exactness in communication. In order to facilitate communication precision and short circuit argument culture, Rosenberg divides communication into Observation, Feelings, Needs, and Requests segments.

- Observations are separate from judgments. We label what we experience without criticizing. Observations use "I" statements and sense data: "When I (see, hear) …"
- Feelings are separated from thoughts, rather than focusing on interpreting or diagnosing, this segment labels feelings, sometimes more difficult than one would imagine. "I feel…"

- Needs or values are expressed not in terms of specific requests rather needs ground requests. "I need…"
- Requests are concrete actions

(Rosenberg 2003)

The four segments combine generally in three to four statements or sentences. "When x, I feel y. I need x. Concrete action suggestion." For example, when I come home to a messy kitchen I could yell at my children, "Gah! I have asked you at least a thousand times to clean up the kitchen when you are done with your snacks!" Using nonviolent communication strategies, I would say, "When I come home to a messy kitchen, I feel overwhelmed. I need a serene space in order to decompress enough to start making dinner. Clean up after yourself." Which is not to say that nonviolent communication strategies are easy. In fact, I have discovered on the whole, most people (including me) have difficulty divorcing observations from judgments. Rosenberger offers several examples distinguishing observation from evaluation.

Rosenberg also cautions against combining feeling segments with personal judgments or self-criticism as well as how we *think* others are behaving or understanding. For example, the phrase, "I feel misunderstood" posits a state of understanding for another person. Likewise, saying "I feel inadequate as an actor" describes how we understand ourselves rather than resting on feeling alone. While this type of linguistic exactness can appear nitpicking, such precision creates communication environments for solving problems and working together. For example, "I feel misunderstood" structures further

| Example of Observation with Evaluation Mixed in | Example of Observation Separate from Evaluation |
| --- | --- |
| You are too generous. | When I see you give all your lunch money to others I think you are being too generous. |
| Doug procrastinates. | Doug only studies for exams the night before. |
| She won't get her work in. | I don't think she'll get her work in. Or she said, "I won't get my work in." |
| If you don't eat balanced meals your health will be impaired. | If you don't eat balanced meals, I fear that your health may be impaired. |
| Hank Smith is a poor soccer player. | Hank Smith has not scored a goal in twenty games. |
| Jim is ugly. | Jim's looks don't appeal to me. |
| You seldom do what I want. | The last three times I initiated an activity you said you didn't want to do it. |
| He frequently comes over. | He comes over at least three times a week. |

(Rosenberg 2003: 30–31)

conversation in such a way that the process can come to a standstill while individuals "prove" understanding or misunderstanding. Alternatively, "I" statements structured as observation/feeling/needs/requests can usefully model effective communication strategies. "I feel misunderstood" transforms to "When we jump from story to story I feel frustrated. I need to know the group heard my concerns. Can we have each speaker summarize previous ideas? Or can we have a recorder write them all down?"

Communication, however, contains both expression and listening. Active listening strategies are necessary factors in effective communication. Active listening has several components.

- *Encouragers*: Encourage the speaker with short verbal or nonverbal cues expressing your interest and attention.
- *Check for understanding by paraphrasing*: "What I hear you saying is…" or asking questions to clarify, "What did you mean by…" or "Could you tell me more?"
- *Emotional labeling*. Emotional labeling describes without evaluating the emotions of the speaker. "I can see you are really upset" or "You sound pretty worried." The phrase, "I understand how you are feeling" does not emotionally label. Instead, emotional labeling shows understanding through verbal acknowledgment.
- *Defer judgment*. I personally have a tendency to think through solutions to other people's problems or to rehearse what I will say in response to a speaker rather than deferring judgment. When I interrupt, however, I waste the group's time and frustrate the speaker. Moreover, thinking about what I want to say limits my understanding of the speaker's message. A strategy I use to short circuit my own bad habit is mirroring or reflecting back to the speaker what he or she just said as a quick encourager. Mirroring forces me to pay close attention when I feel myself wanting to solve the problem.
- *Reflect meaning*. Reflecting meaning checks for understanding and restates the issue. After someone explains a problem, leaders reflect their meaning back to them. Here, Rosenberg's nonviolent communication strategy can be particularly helpful. Reflections should be in four parts: observations, feelings, needs, and requests. Sometimes with young ensembles, leaders need to facilitate the discussion so that individuals arrive at needs and requests—modeling conflict as opportunities for problem solving and visioning.

In his book on empowering students in the performing arts, acting teacher Wangh (2013) devotes an entire chapter on different types of listening needed in studio spaces. He parses his chapter by addressing listening as concentrated focus on the experiences and states of the participants in the moment. Wangh points out that empathy is a kind of listening practice. Empathy here means leveraging our skills as performers, storytellers, and performance decoders to hear our ensembles deeply, fully, and passionately. What people say and do not say; how voices rise and fall; the way individuals occupy space; how comfortable different individuals feel in their bodies, moving their bodies, performing with their bodies, and playing our games. Wangh writes, "all performance disciplines are deeply dependent upon listening. Musicians of all kinds, dancers, and actors must all learn to "listen" aurally, visually, or kinesthetically, to many signals, often to several signals at once" (Wangh 2013: 27). Beyond plotting ensembles' relationships, psychological habits, and skill sets, facilitating a healthy ensemble also means practicing deep, empathetic listening.

In his study on group flow and collaboration, Sawyer points out the necessity for strong communication skills among a creative collaboration. In his research on jazz ensembles, Sawyer suggests for flow to happen, performers must be open and "each performer fully attends to what the others are doing" (2003: 44). Further, Sawyer points to what communication researchers label "interactional synchrony" or the ways communicators visually mirror one another's physical movements, rhythms, and coordinate turn-taking. Sawyer suggests that strong creative ensembles develop highly complex group level interactional synchrony (2003: 37–39). He uses the concept of "entrainment" and "groove" to explain these phenomena: "In entrainment, one person's rhythms become attuned to another, almost like a tuning fork" (Sawyer 2003: 38). Many researchers believe interactional synchrony has a biological basis and "infants show evidence of interactional synchrony with their parents as early as twenty minutes after birth…" (Sawyer 2003: 38). Interactional synchrony physically facilitates communication. I structure exercises in nonverbal communication then along with teaching "I" statements and active listening strategies. Exercises or activities focusing on physical communication and communal reflection—Anne Bogart and Tina Landau's Viewpoints warm-ups, for example, or contact improvisation—work extremely well. Even a simple activity like fill the space (participants walk the space keeping equidistant from one another and attempting to leave no open areas) can encourage ensemble groove.

Of course, these strategies will not solve all problems but can go a long way in building space for trusting, generous, and productive collaborations. No matter how careful we are though, sometimes people get hurt, feel diminished, or share a story so personal that others will not know how to respond. This is normal. Pat Griffin (1997) uses the term "trigger" to refer to an issue, policy, story, or term laden with emotional baggage for listeners (78). Knowing general responses to triggers can help facilitators process difficult moments collectively and/or intellectually. TFY third space depends on dialogue in all phases of the work so understanding triggers also can help ensembles process conversations with audiences and adult partners. Trigger responses can include internal and external manifestations:

Internal:
- *Avoidance*. Avoiding future encounters and withdrawing emotionally from people or situations that trigger us
- *Internalizing*. Believing the trigger to be true and/or appropriate, for example, youth are risks, incarcerated youth are throwaways not worthy of love
- *Misinterpreting*. Feeling on guard and expecting to be triggered, we misinterpret something said and are triggered by our misinterpretation, not the words
- *Silence*. Not responding to the situation although it is upsetting, not saying or doing anything

External:
- *Attacking*. Responding with the intent to lash back or hurt whoever has triggered us
- *Laughing*. Being overcome by awkwardness or tension and laughing
- *Launching asides or side conversations*. Being unable to suppress commentary

(Griffin 1997: 78–79)

Paying attention, listening with your entire artistic self can help facilitators identify moments of productive tension as well as moments in which we need to stop and process or back away. Margaret Wheatley (2002) suggests that we foster relational structures that at once assume good intent as well as rely on human goodness. By this, Wheatley suggests frames for engagement focused not on what people have "done" to us or on mapping all instances of power discrepancy and aggravation, but on possibilities and movement forward. Assume good intentions and individual goodness. Nevertheless, triggers in particular can be moments of profound ensemble difficulty. I suggest that naming and bracketing the trigger can work to diffuse tension. CCD residencies cannot do all and be all, but healthy ensembles depend on building space for honest and perhaps painful conversations. Ultimately, however, getting to know one another's quirks, learning to hear the unspoken stories, and developing trust will depend on adequate time together. A nine-month residency program will be able to accomplish much deeper work than a week-long residency.

> **KEY IDEAS**
>
> - Building healthy ensembles helps scaffold opportunities for group flow—peak experiences.
> - Facilitators build complex understandings of individuals within the ensemble as well as mental maps of the group processes themselves to foster collaboration, playfulness, and creative openness.
> - Fear is the enemy of creativity.
> - Healthy ensembles communicate effectively and appropriately.
> - Argument culture does not provide appropriate communication skills for healthy ensembles.
> - Nonviolent communication demands exactness. Rosenberg divides communication into observation, feelings, needs and requests segments.

## 2.9 FOSTERING CREATIVITY

A key component of community-based residencies depends on leveraging and building creative capacity within participants and partnerships. Creativity research has grown exponentially in recent years and provides an evidence-based platform for structuring community-based processes. Creativity functions like a muscle training can enhance, rather than a romantic, innate characteristic of individuals. Creativity and collaboration researcher, Sawyer points out, "[m]ost psychologists today believe that innate creative talent is overrated," adding "[r]esearchers have discovered that creativity is largely the result of hard work. There is no magic, no secret" (2006: 53). For the purposes of this book, I use Mark Runco's psychologically based definition of creativity developed in his comprehensive 2007 text, *Creativity Theories and Themes: Research, Development, and Practice*. There, Runco advances a multifaceted explanation of creativity pointing out:

- "Creativity is a complex or syndrome" (Runco 2007: 322)
- "Creativity is a reflection of cognition, metacognition", which Runco defines as "self awareness and self control" (Runco 2007: 322)
- Creativity is "attitude, motivation, affect, disposition, and temperament" (Runco 2007: 320)

Within psychology creativity then becomes a set of phenomena occurring together. The clinical definition of "syndrome" builds from sets of symptoms or behaviors appearing together, examples include Stockholm syndrome or post-traumatic stress disorder. While most of us associate "symptom" and "syndrome" with illness, Runco's model allows for the specificity needed to ground experimental research protocols investigating creativity. Central to Runco's definition, creativity is not a "thing" but a process, a habit of thought and emotional investment—a pattern.

Additionally, however, I use the systems model of creativity developed by Mihalyi Csikszentmihalyi. Csikszentmihalyi claims that creativity can only be found in the dynamic relationship of three interrelated components: (1) the person, (2) the domain, and (3) the field: "a culture that contains symbolic rules, a person who brings novelty into the domain, and a field of experts who recognize and validate the innovation" (Csikszentmihalyi 1997: 6). In other words, domains (e.g., visual art, theatre, or classical music) nest inside of cultures with both the domain and the culture composed of specific rules, behaviors, performances, languages, and symbol systems. Individuals use these domain-specific conventions and established norms as primary source material to create something. The field, however, must recognize the product or process as "creative" or "innovative." The field includes the established gatekeepers, for example, university scholars, archivists, national organizations, and recognized critics. For the visual art world, the field would include universities, museums, granting organizations, the National Endowment for the Arts, curators, et cetera. Sawyer points out,

> Domain includes the 'raw materials' available to the creative individual, and the rules and procedures which can be used to combine them. Individual acts that do not satisfy the constraints of the domain are rarely viewed as 'creative' by the field, the social group that defines a type of creative activity.
>
> (Sawyer 2003: 52)

Creativity can be understood to happen within communities and systems while also employing specific conventions and symbolic languages. Both Runco's definition of creativity and Csikszentmihalyi's occur with feedback loops and complex interactions among skills, systems, symbols, and established conventions. Creativity involves habits, processes, affective states, and knowledge—creativity can be taught and improved. The implications of these two definitions of creativity for third space facilitation include four specific effects that, although deeply related, I excerpt individually for ease in discussion: (1) domain, field, and the structure of feeling, (2) individual creativity, (3) raw materials, and (4) creative processes.

## 2.9.1 Domains, Fields and Circulating Symbolic Meanings

Creativity and innovation occur in complex systems and require feedback mechanisms in order to be understood fundamentally as creative. Residencies then need to cultivate both community "gatekeepers" as well as "gatekeepers" within theatre and performance—to "speak to" the partnering community and to be considered an artistic product in the larger ecology of theatre and performance. In other words, for a process and product to foster creative capacity and be understood as artistic, we need to build feedback structures into the process as well as the product or performance. In TFY, we tend to speak dismissively of "gatekeepers" yet, according to a systems model of creativity, the creative products, performances, and acts must be viewed by "outsiders" as creative. For example, projects can invite local artists to visit a studio showing and provide feedback. Or, projects can take in-progress work to friendly open-mike nights. In TFY third space, the circulation of creative potential and the recognition of that potential reinforce the creative capacity of youthful participants while also contributing to the symbolic ecology of the communal "place" while building status and power for the ensemble's work. Placemaking hangs on this circulation. Additionally, ensembles need to build the skills necessary to manage feedback loops for their own creative growth not to mention building craft—understanding that the creative process of art-making is part of the engagement process. As Sawyer points out, "creativity is fundamentally social and collaborative" (Sawyer 2006: 257). Part of third space facilitation includes making this social and collaborative system explicit to partners and to participants. This approach directly collides with the dominant US American myth of creativity as a solo flight of genius delivered in a lightning burst from the heavens. Additionally, this approach fights against "self-esteem" structures that foster attitudes understanding criticism and feedback as negative or destructive. Adults can be reluctant to provide feedback to children, but the creative process demands genuine response from the "field" engaged. TFY third space has to replace the artist-genius myth with experientially based understandings of creativity as a process. In my experience, foregrounding the hard work of development (through open studios or structured showings, for example) increases not only craft skills, but also adult partners' understandings of the real capacity of children and youth to thoughtfully add value to their communities. Thus, we circulate value and leverage different kinds of capital into power.

Necessary to understanding how creative symbolic actions circulate in communities is a concept Raymond Williams calls "structures of feeling." A structure of feeling concerns "meanings and values as they are actively lived and felt, and the relations between these and formal or systematic beliefs" (Williams 1977: 132). Structures of feelings revolve around our daily, lived experience as our life paths intersect and collide with others' and with the formal beliefs systems and hegemonies of our material existence. Community-based theatre projects with children and youth, by their nature, deeply engage a community's structure of feeling. Negotiating the "structure of feeling" can be fraught, and in my experience, the ethical ramifications of the systems of values in play depend on insider knowledge to understand fully. Bruce McConachie writes,

> because audiences have as much control as theatre workers over the mutual images constructed and experienced, the local context always inflects the specific structure of feeling that emerges in performance. Like any group of spectators, local folks bring a wide variety of desires, anxieties, and agendas with them to the theatre; there is never a single context shaping the response of local citizens to a community-based production.
> (McConachie 1998: 41)

As an ideological transaction, theatre and performance depend on shared systems. Feedback loops then become a necessary component both creatively and ethically. I have had multiple experiences in which an audience member's reaction to the youth's art surprised me. For example, in a nine-month digital storytelling residency conducted with high-school indigenous youth on the Gila River Indian Community, the youth chose to explore the meaning of "happiness." Over the course of the school year, the youth spent extended time devising material and probing how "happiness" was understood on the Rez. They created a frank section on drug use, compared and contrasted the diversity of elders' understandings with their own, and honestly probed their own familial and romantic relationships. Toward the end of the experience, we had several structured feedback sections inviting teachers, coaches, parents, and all the elders interviewed in the course of the project. The youth requested feedback in both open talk-back sessions and through the use of a written instrument. As a team, we had been most concerned with the drug-use section of the piece as that had been an issue in a prior digital storytelling residency. Somewhat surprisingly, the community members were most touched by the honest exploration of drug use and most offended by what I considered a chaste kiss. The feedback sessions allowed the youth to ask questions about their work, to engage their own critical eye, and to make choices concerning the material generated. The ensemble discussion over whether to include the kiss in their final edit engaged principles of deliberative democracy and ultimately the team was able to effectively articulate, to any questioning community member, why they made specific creative choices. The adults and civic leaders also communicated frankly with the youth, explaining their reasoning and requests for revisions in ways honoring the youths' interpretations. The reality of community-based theatre with children and youth entails creating a mechanism to circulate both aesthetic and ideological choice-consequence constructions: structural flow if you will.

## 2.9.2 Individual Creativity

In any residency, TFY CCD artists will need to explicitly model individual creative capacity while fostering an environment nurturing those same behaviors and attitudes. While creativity is both a process/syndrome and dispersed in systems, there are certain attitudes and characteristics associated with creativity. Sawyer notes, "Creative achievement requires a complex combination of both divergent and convergent thinking, and creative people are good at switching back and forth at different points in the creative process" (Sawyer 2006: 45). Arthur Cropley and David Cropley (2009) suggest, "Some personality traits make it easier to become creative. These traits include autonomy, flexibility, preference for complexity, self-confidence, and ego-strength. Taken together, such characteristics define a special pattern of personality we call openness" (104). In order to train and strengthen creative capacity, facilitators should foster independence, flexibility, preference for complexity, self-confidence, emotional stability, and resiliency within our ensembles and ourselves. From the ways in which we design engagements to the activities we use, to how we question and interact with our partnering young artists, we can build opportunities to strengthen creative openness. For example, switching from writing to creative movement to scene work can foster flexibility. An artist's willingness to jettison a workshop plan in order to meet the needs and desires of the ensemble increases leadership flexibility.

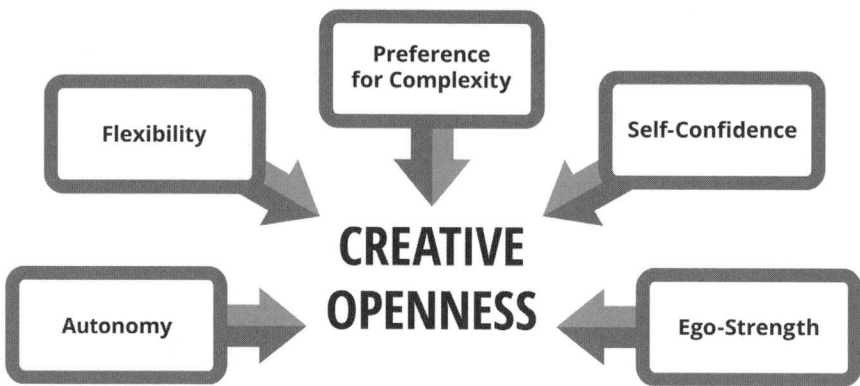

**Figure 2.3:** Fostering creative openness.

How we ask questions can build independence and help develop comfort with complexity. An understanding of how openness can build creative capacity also allows TFY CCD artists to assess groups and individuals from the beginning of a residency to build stronger collaborative processes. The graphic below parses this information visually. Part of TFY community cultural development involves structuring workshops and entire residencies to foster creative openness in order to strengthen creative capacity within both individuals and the community.

Theatre and performance artists develop deep relationships to their own creative processes as well as clear understandings of the risks and rewards involved in working with others' creative processes. US America sustains the myth that artists are erratic, weird, or neurotic. In reality, creative people are not more flighty or difficult than other humans. Instead, experimental evidence demonstrates creative personalities "are characterized by seven polarities:

1. openness combined with drive to close incomplete gestalts,
2. acceptance of fantasy combined with maintenance of a strong sense of reality,
3. critical and destructive attitudes together with constructive problem solving,
4. cool neutrality combined with passionate engagement,
5. self-centeredness coexisting with altruism,
6. self-criticism and self-doubt together with self-confidence, and
7. tension and concentration side by side with relaxedness.

(Cropley and Cropley 2009: 116–117)

If you are like me, reading this list probably caused you to smile and nod to yourself in recognition. What does this list of seven polarities mean for community-engaged artists? First, if third space facilitators perform their tasks well then they can expect to nurture moments appearing exuberantly out-of-control to outsiders. Embrace the knowledge and expect the chaos. Which is not to say that creativity demands the absence of self-control or ensemble discipline. In fact, creativity depends on self-awareness and self-control. Second, TFY CCD artists need to build space to nurture individual awareness of the mental and affective states of individual creativity in addition to building awareness of group processes (discussed further below). Understanding the making process through creativity structures, labels and provides space for artistic moments and experiences while also grounding ensemble experiences in language easily understood by adult partners.

### 2.9.3 Raw Materials and Group Creativity

In any residency, TFY CCD artists must chart and understand their raw materials: the dominant languages, aesthetics, narratives, and symbol systems of the community with whom they work, as well as traditional theatrical conventions, narrative constructs, and symbol systems. This means employing both anthropological skills and dramaturgical skills. Mapping how a specific community understands space, time, color, rhythm, humor, beauty, story, performance of self, and other, can, of course, take a lifetime—as can keen attention to one's own theatrical craft and performance technique. Unless TFY CCD artists work within their own micro-communities, however, they will never be cultural insiders. Our task will then be to build enough common language to explore the raw material of the residency with the expert guidance of the ensemble and community partners. Sawyer points out, "Group creativity involves distributed cognition—when each member of the team contributes an essential piece of the solution, and these individual components are all integrated together to form the collective product" (Sawyer 2006: 121). This, in fact, is a deep part of the asset-mapping necessary to a successful residency. McConachie points out, "Simply put, *how* the show communicates and *what* is communicated must draw on conventions that are locally familiar. In this way, residents can be induced to put their imaginations to work in the symbolic building of community during the show" (1998: 39, original emphasis). Part of fostering creativity within the artistic team will be measured by how competent the participants feel. "Creativity requires a person to become an extremely knowledgeable expert in his or her domain of activity" (Sawyer 2006: 300). Mapping the expert status of your youthful participants, as well as your adult community partners, generally involves bringing taken for granted knowledge into conscious control. All people develop contextual knowledge through the course of their everyday existence. Before their first birthday, babies learn how to make the dominant sounds of their native tongue and develop mind maps of the physics and culture of their world—gravity, fluid dynamics, rules of environmental, and social interaction. Your youthful participants will have remarkable skills and knowledge within specific areas as will your adult community partners. Take nothing for granted. For one, your partners will be cultural insiders with instinctual knowledge of how power is performed, what counts as beauty, and important stories/locations. However, they could also be expert joke tellers or have 100 years of baseball statistics at their fingertips. One person might be able to create and sing rap improvisationally while another can spin a basketball on her head. I once had an ensemble participant who could fart on demand; she called herself, "the master gasser."

*What you and your ensemble do with this raw material, however, defines whether your performance qualifies as innovative or creative.* Farting, for example, is not inherently a creative act although in the right context farts can serve as humorous performance punctuation. Sawyer holds that while there is a strong bias to understand creativity and innovation as a "product," the *process* of creativity—particularly in improvisational performance—patterns creativity in slightly different ways. The "process is the product," he claims (Sawyer 2003: 98). Creativity will not only be found in ensembles, however, facilitating in TFY third space demands high levels of improvisational creativity.

Additionally, Sawyer's work on ensemble creativity adds to my assertion that process and the product need equal attention in TFY third space. Creativity depends on oscillating patterns of divergent thinking and convergent thinking. Sawyer points out,

> A tradition in creativity research [...] holds that creativity occurs in (at least) two stages. [...C]reativity researchers have usually placed the source of novelty in divergent thinking, an 'ideation stage' that often occurs below the level of consciousness. In this formulation, the conscious mind then filters or evaluates these many ideas, using convergent or critical thought processes.
>
> (2003: 173)

Cropley and Cropley list some of the characteristics of convergent and divergent thinking that I find useful (see page 137).

|  | **Convergent** | **Divergent** |
|---|---|---|
| **Typical Processes** | Being logical | Being unconventional |
|  | Recognizing the familiar | Seeing the known in a new light |
|  | Combining what "belongs together" | Combining the disparate |
|  | Homing in on the single best answer | Producing multiple answers |
|  | Reapplying set techniques | Shifting perspectives |
|  | Preserving the already known | Transforming the known |
|  | Being accurate and correct | Seeing new possibilities |
| **Typical Results** | Greater familiarity with what already exists | Alternative or multiple solutions |
|  | Better grasp of the facts | Deviation from the usual |
|  | A quick "correct" answer | Surprising answer |
|  | Improvement of existing skills | New lines of attack or ways of doing things |
|  | Closure on an issue | Opening up of exciting or risky possibilities |

(Cropley and Cropley 2009: 48)

Evidentially, grounded suggestions for increasing imaginative manipulation of a domain and a community's raw materials serve well here too. Mark Runco has a list of suggestions to foster divergent or ideation stage creativity:

- Shift perspectives: literally or figuratively
- Flip the idea/situation
- Find or apply analogy or metaphor
- Borrow, adapt, or steal from other domains
- Environmental suggestions, look to the natural world or take a walk
- Simplify
- Experiment and play
- Deviation amplifications—variations on a theme
- Persistence—creativity takes time and hard work
- Question assumptions, list assumptions, make assumptions
- Redefine problems
- Change representations—move genre, or representational form
- Zoom in/Zoom out: play with scale

(Runco 2007: 324–373)

Many of these techniques should be quite familiar to theatre artists. We shift perspectives, think metaphorically, adapt, and experiment de facto in our studio practice; other suggestions dovetail nicely with performance devising practices. Labeling our studio processes, however, especially through the use of creativity terminology foregrounds the intellectual and emotional labor of the imaginative fields while nurturing creative capital. Again, a long-term goal in TFY CCD practices includes consciously building the social, political, economic, and/or cultural power of the community. Demystifying the creative process, teaching artistic habits of mind, and foregrounding studio structures form the backbone of this strategy.

## 2.9.4 Creative Processes

Some creativity researchers (Runco and Chand 1995; Amabile 1999) particularly focus on the stages of creativity noting creative development occurs in both linear and circular patterns. What can research tell us, however, about the steps of creativity? Sawyer explains,

> Psychologists have been studying the creative process for decades. They have several different theories about how it works, but most of them agree that the creative process has four basic stages: preparation, incubation, insight, and verification.
>
> - Preparation is the initial phase of preliminary work: collecting data and information, searching for related ideas, listening to suggestions.
> - Incubation is the delay between preparation and the moment of insight; during this time, the prepared material is internally elaborated and organized.
> - Insight is the subjective experience of having the idea—the 'aha' or 'eureka' moment.
> - Verification includes two substages: the evaluation of the worth of the insight, and elaboration into its complete form.
>
> (Sawyer 2006: 58–59)

Not satisfied with the generalized stages defined by many psychologists, Cropley and Cropley are interested in illuminating unconscious components as well as how various stages of creativity create subproducts understandable as creative in and of themselves. Their work focuses on understanding creativity for the purposes of teaching creativity and so they developed an extended model of the four stage creative process (see page 140).

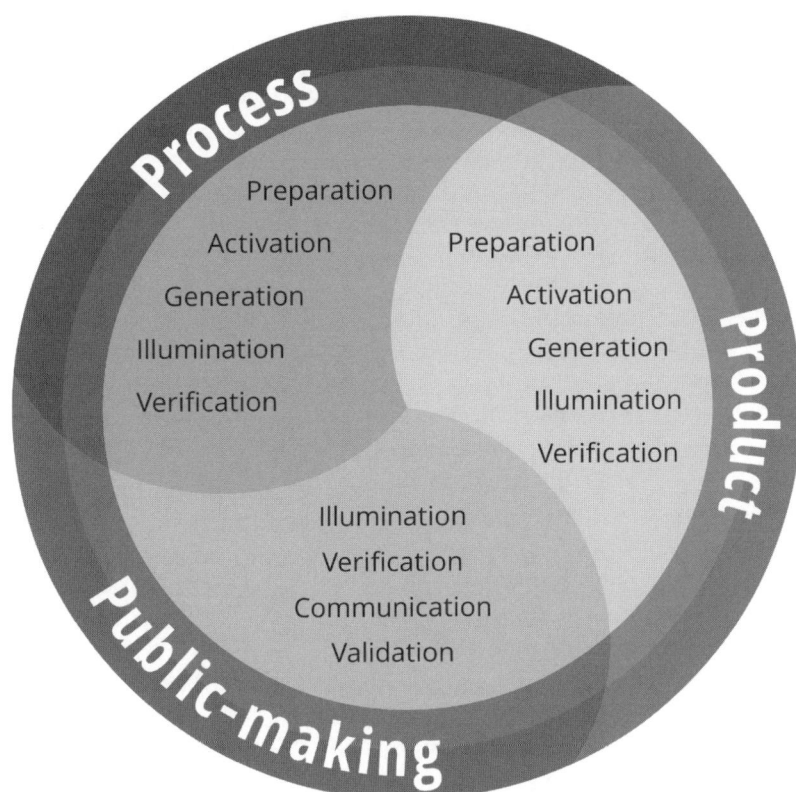

**Figure 2.4** TFY CCD creative processes.

Cropley and Cropley's model exhibits a preference for product-oriented creativity although they recognize that the arts pose unique examples of products including objects, "interesting, exciting, or provocative ideas" and performances (Cropley and Cropley 2009: 29). Understanding the Cropleys' model as an iterative one helps remind us of the circular nature of community-based engagements as a whole. In fact as an artist, I find the four-stage creative process most helpful for facilitation purposes—preparation, incubation, insight, and verification (extended version preparation, activation, generation, illumination, verification)—but believe Cropley and Cropley's extended model works well for the TFY CCD process as a whole. In fact, we can map the extended creative process onto the graphic from Section 1.9 (see Figure 2.4).

| Phase | Process | Subproduct |
|---|---|---|
| **Preparation** | • "uncensored" intake of information<br>• Acquisition of broad general knowledge<br>• Acquisition of specific knowledge | • Identification of problem<br>• Establishment of goals |
| **Activation** | • Problem recognition<br>• Problem construction | • Understanding of the dimensions of the problem<br>• Establishment of broad solution criteria |
| **Generation** | • Boundary breaking<br>• Making remote associations<br>• Restructuring ideas<br>• Producing configurations | • Many candidate solutions |
| **Illumination** | • Recognizing appropriate configurations<br>• Building new categories | • Apparently appropriate configurations |
| **Verification** | • Exploration of own ideas<br>• Elaborating and extending ideas<br>• Recognition of a solution | • Privately explored novelty<br>• A single optimal solution |
| **Communication** | • Making the novelty available to other people | • A working prototype |
| **Validation** | • External exploration of ideas<br>• Seeing wider implications | • Publicly explored novelty: a "truly creative product" |

(Cropley and Cropley 2009: 62–63)

While real life never approaches the simplicity of a graphic; nevertheless, the stages of creativity easily align with the general structure of community-based projects. Of course, we would expect this to be so, because theatre and performance inherently engages creativity. Recognizing the recursive nature of these stages, via the process-product-placemaking visual, can bring creative work into clear focus while promoting further conscious control of the process. Although, I want to point out that Cropley and Cropley's extended model functions linearly while civic practice with children and youth functions recursively—although bound in time. Nevertheless, labeling the types of creative phases can help with planning, assessment, and evaluation. I return to these ideas later in this text.

**KEY IDEAS**

- Creativity then can be understood to happen within communities and systems while also employing specific conventions and symbolic languages.
- Creativity involves habits, processes, affective states, and knowledge—creativity can be taught and improved.
- TFY third space needs feedback loops in the process and the product that advance public-making.
- Feedback should come from the community itself.
- Feedback should also come from the domain of theatre and performance. For example, projects can invite local theatre artists to visit a studio showing and provide feedback.
- Fostering ensemble and individual independence, flexibility, preference for complexity, self-confidence, emotional stability, and resiliency helps grow creative openness and creative risk-taking.
- Fostering self-discipline and self-awareness can also help grow creative capacity.
- For each residency, TFY CCD artists map their raw materials: the dominant languages, aesthetics, narratives, and symbol systems of the community with whom they work, as well as theatrical conventions, narrative constructs, and symbol systems.
- Cultivating ensemble creativity requires enabling alternating patterns of convergent and divergent thinking/processes.
- Creative development occurs in both linear and recursive ways.
- Creative processes move through at least four stages: preparation, incubation, insight, and verification.
- Cropley and Cropley extend those four stages into seven: preparation, activation, generation, illumination, verification, communication, and validation.

## 2.10 THEATRE AND PERFORMANCE SKILLS

I want to highlight the importance of knowing the conventions and rules of a creative domain. Rather than limiting, conventions liberate. Like understanding the alphabet prior to learning to read, collaborating artists need to know the basic building blocks of theatrical performance in order to manipulate them into new constructions. Sawyer points out, "In both the arts and the sciences, creative individuals must become familiar with what has come before, and only then can they begin to generate truly original products" (Sawyer 2003: 52). Writing about jazz ensembles, Sawyer says, "Musicians practice and perform the same songs repeatedly, and can often express themselves more effectively when they have a predeveloped set of musical ideas available" (2003: 58). A tricky balancing act, third space facilitators need to structure residencies to provide both generative studio time and in-depth study of theatrical/performance conventions and rules. A wrench in the creative motor, however, comes from research done with very young children. In an article published in *Scientific America*, Alison Gropnik writes,

> My group found that young children who think they are being instructed […] may become less creative as a result. The experiment showed four-year-olds a toy that would play music if you performed the right sequence of actions on it […]. For some children, the experimenter said: 'I don't know how this toy works—let's figure it out.' She proceeded to try out various longer action sequences for the children, some that ended with the short sequence and made music and some that did not. When she asked the children to make the toy work, many of them tried the correct short sequence, astutely omitting actions that were probably superfluous based on the statistics of what they had seen. With the other children, the experimenter said that she would teach them how the toy worked by showing them sequences that did and did not produce music, and then she acted on the toy in exactly the same way. When asked to make the toy work, these children never tried a shortcut. Instead they mimicked the entire sequence of actions.
> (Gropnik 2010: 80–81)

In other words, when we frame our actions with young children as teacher/learner children mimic, while the exact same sequence framed through experimentation and play fosters youth ownership and engagement. Relational categories matter. For some circumstances, mimicry and modeling will be absolutely appropriate; and in other cases, mimicry and modeling will be absolutely inappropriate. Allowing ensemble participants to be masters of their own experiences, while also teaching them the fundamentals of theatre and performance, tests community cultural development artists' craft. Third space residencies need pedagogical skills, but mechanical teaching runs the risk of short circuiting the creative process if used inappropriately.

Teaching theatrical craft depends upon a knowledge or skill specialist—an expert. If we are not carefully monitoring ensemble temperament, however, the expert-novice structure can suggest right/wrong binaries. The adults' knowledge is complete, finished, and whole. The youths' knowledge is incomplete, surface, and in process. Such constructs short circuit creativity by squashing innovative and fluid understandings developed by more novice participants and reinforcing expert rigidity. Nevertheless, trust also builds from understanding facilitators' abilities and knowing these skills are in service to ensemble creativity and innovation. Poor performance skills can tank an otherwise solid project and make everyone uncomfortable.

Facilitators need competency for teaching artistic and aesthetic techniques. Mastery of a field or domain of knowledge does not necessarily mean an automatic and equal skill in teaching others to master that domain. In order to instruct, TFY CCD artists need to understand the innate organization of their field(s) and be able to build programs addressing that organization. For example, curricula often develop structurally with simple information becoming more complex over time. An art class one of my daughters took, for example, began by teaching the children about primary colors, then how to navigate the color wheel to produce secondary colors. When I first began learning how to play the bodhrán (a traditional Irish drum), I spent an exhaustive several weeks simply learning how to hold the drum and manipulate the tipper (double-headed beater). TFY CCD artists divide field information in such a way that participants can progress from basic understandings to more complex skills. Parsing information also means being able to predict how long ensembles will need to linger at any one level. In other words, what are the fundamental tenets of a field and what are secondary facts or skills? Finally, domains have two distinct segments demanding different learning goals—knowing and doing. All domains contain certain given facts, histories, and philosophical belief systems, but they also contain skill sets; for example, in theatrical performance, an acting student needs to know how to score a script, create a character history, physically embody a character, vocally project, and enunciate—performance skills. That student also must be aware of the historical differences in performance techniques (like, for example, the differences between the techniques of Meyerhold and Brecht), be able to chart the development of realism and naturalistic acting methodologies (like Chekhov and Arthur Miller), and have basic literacy with regard to poetic verse (e.g., Shakespeare)—performance history and theory. Educators often refer to this distinction as the difference between domain facts and domain skills. There are no hard and fast rules about maintaining balance between facts and skills; each residency and each ensemble will demand different outcomes. The question I always ask myself is what do I need to teach in order to accomplish our project and residency goals? That being said, I believe there are essential skills needed in all performance residencies:

- Embodied storytelling
- Character development
- Narrative pacing and tension.

I do not have easy answers but fall back on Cropley and Cropley's suggestion to teach specific understandings of creativity along with domain knowledge. Meaning, I highlight what I am doing and why all along the process. Additionally, planning through the creative process can help facilitating artists negotiate *when* to focus on domain knowledge and skill building. I tend to locate knowledge and skill building during the preparation and verification (elaboration) stages. In addition, asset mapping among ensembles should address skill deficits head on. While all my residencies revolve around storytelling and representation, we have created digital stories, podcasts, installations, illustrated books, websites as well as traditional theatrical performances of devised or scripted work. The CCD artists' difficult task is balancing what the ensemble wants to say with how they need to say it in order to be heard and understood aesthetically. What can one accomplish given the diverse parameters and limits of each residency? The key to the planning process rests in remembering that community cultural development's ability to foster change and build capital depends on being understood as *art*: not education, nor self-esteem structures.

Children and youth walk into studio spaces with hours of television and movie viewing under their belts—they have advanced televisual skills. Sometimes, merely helping them articulate those skills adds greatly to their sophisticated use of narrative and character. Young performers too often need additional physical training in order to control their bodies. TFY CCD artists will never have enough process time, however, so I default to using the essential elements of theatrical performance to help plan what skills my residencies must tackle versus what skills can be handled lightly:

- Duration
- Embodiment
- Ensemble
- Gesture

- Reenactment of an original
- Imaginative location
- Sound/music
- Spectacle
- Text.

Residency time is the most precious resource—we never have enough time. As Cohen-Cruz reminds us, "Artists who aspire to make a difference in a social situation must assess the relationship between their goals and the scale on which they are able to work" (2010: 196). Learning how to parse information and skill effectively is a necessary skill for CCD facilitators.

Knowing how to balance time spent learning the conventions and rules of the creative domain versus time spent refining the CCD product comes from building familiarity with the artistic choices appropriate in contextual environments—what is possible? Probable? Necessary? Part of this familiarity comes from experience, and part results from planning. Working in TFY third space often means your success and failure will be judged by outsiders from the performance event. However, the performance equals only a third of your responsibility to your residency project. TFY third space artists need the ability to explain and to warrant what creative and communicative practices, as well as theatrical skills, participants employed, and how those skills contribute to expanding cultural, human capital, and participant power. The creativity myth in the United States grows from a belief in genius and unconscious manipulation of symbol systems. Research (and practical experience) proves creativity and innovation grow from hard work and conscious manipulation of symbol systems. The TFY CCD artist's ultimate goal here will be to hand the creativity engine keys to the ensemble and partnering organization.

### KEY IDEAS

- A tricky balancing act, third space facilitators need to structure the residency to provide both generative studio time and in-depth study of theatrical/performance conventions and rules.
- Facilitators need competency in teaching techniques as well as deep understanding of when *not* to teach.
- Key performance skills for TFY CCD ensembles include embodied storytelling, character development, and narrative pacing and tension.

## 2.11 FACILITATING CREATIVE PROCESSES AND PRODUCTS

Making art with community can be frustrating, overwhelming, and glorious. This section explores collaboratively creating performance and creative products. Of course, shelves of books explore this same subject with more detail and clarity than I can provide here. So really, this is a section about my idiosyncratic processes. Rather than create lists of my favorite games or activities, I focus this section on the kinds of aesthetic structures and frames I use and why. Studio practices and environments are unique to the facilitator, participants, and communities, demanding immense processual creativity from facilitating artists. Sawyer points out, the "process is the product" (2003: 98). In general, I devise original material with children and youth. Less often, I adapt published stories, poems, plays, or books. Starting from a question or theme decided upon by the group, I ground my planning in the placemaking approach we have chosen. Devising material allows me to start with the passion of the participants while also building "a language of performance that uniquely suits the actors' particular identities, strengths and abilities" (Govan, Nicholson, and Normington 2007: 6). Starting in the real allows the ensemble to build interactional synchrony or groove while also supporting space for creative playing as we specifically address placemaking. Emma Govan, Helen Nicholson, and Katie Normington point out, "Devising performance is socially imaginative as well as culturally responsive, and articulates between the local and the global, the fictional and the real, the community and the individual, the social and the psychological" (2007:194). In this way then, devising allows me to tailor my structures to placemaking, community cultural development, and the specificity of the ensemble's identities, strengths, and aesthetic/symbolic abilities.

### 2.11.1 Studio as a Space of Games and Play

I use games and play as both frame and structuring device in workshops and session designs. First, of course, to play and a play relate deeply. As Johan Huizinga reminds us, "Play is older than culture, for culture, however inadequately defined, always presupposes human society, and animals have not waited for man to teach them their playing" (1950: 1). A case can be made for theatre as the aesthetic formalization of play, especially pretend play. While we can generally recognize play when we see playing, play itself is pretty complex. Anthony Pellegrini (2010) points out,

After reviewing the vast human and nonhuman animal play literature, it seems clear that play is a multidimensional construct and should be considered from a structural, functional, and causal criteria, simultaneously. With this said, probably the most basic and necessary aspects of play relate to the means over ends and nonfunctional dimensions.

(20)

In other words, play focuses on processes not products and while play uses behaviors from the real world, it does so with non-real consequences. For example, we can pretend to cook while using actual pots and pans but all recognize we are not really cooking. Our play cooking is nonfunctional or as behaviorists would say, noninstrumental. Play then can be characterized by a set of conditions or components:

- Play is intrinsically motivated
- Play involves pleasurable emotional states
- Play relates to instrumental behaviors but is free from instrumental consequences
- Play pays attention to the means not the end.

Many species play and some have theorized that there are unique adaptive mechanisms associated with this behavior. However, for our purposes, using play as a structuring device sparks distinctive understandings of artistic studio processes and devising structures. Artists play. Deliberatively using play also allows me to talk about creativity and helps set the stage for an ensemble space free of fear. Play does not have real-world consequences, although play does involve risk. Play is, above all other things, fun. We play because we enjoy playing. In his qualitative research dissertation on youth participation in theatre productions, Craig Kosnik (2014) emphasizes how important fun was for his youth informants. "This idea of fun cannot be a throwaway concept in youth theatre," he writes (Kosnik 2014: 50). Engaging in TFY third space should be enjoyable, which is not to say we do not make serious work too. Cohen (2006) points out that we have

> […] strong evidence for the claim that enrichment through play enhances behavioural flexibility, including the ability to solve novel problems and to respond effectively to novel environments. In this light, play experiences facilitate generalized learning and problem-solving skills, such as seeking multiple solutions to problems, adjusting problem-solving strategies to the task, and adapting to changing environmental or problem conditions.

(58)

|  | **Divergent** |
| --- | --- |
| **Typical Processes** | Being unconventional |
|  | Seeing the known in a new light |
|  | Combining the disparate |
|  | Producing multiple answers |
|  | Shifting perspectives |
|  | Transforming the known |
|  | Seeing new possibilities |
| **Typical Results** | Alternative or multiple solutions |
|  | Deviation from the usual |
|  | Surprising answer |
|  | New lines of attack or ways of doing things |
|  | Opening up of exciting or risky possibilities |

(Cropley and Cropley 2009: 48)

We learn and experience through playing, particularly adaptive and creative processes. Play enhances divergent thinking patterns. In Section 2.9.3, I quoted Cropley and Cropley's (2009) examples of convergent and divergent thinking. I highlight their divergent thinking examples above for your reference.

Playing engages patterns of divergent thinking. In my work over the years, only rarely will my adult community collaborators answer "yes" when I ask them if they understand themselves as artists. Almost all children and many teens will answer "yes" without hesitation however. Creativity and playing connect profoundly. However, how do we structure spaces of play?

As theatre artists, we pretend play all the time although we do not, of course, call it that. In addition, we all have multiple experiences of play. I am interested in building structural connections, however, between play and creativity, and so I again return to Section 2.9.3 and highlight selected suggestions from Runco (2007: 324–373) for stage creativity (see Figure 2.5).

Again, how do I use these to structure playful devising? Well, the possibilities seem endless and relate to how individual resident artists understand devising. Here, I offer my particular riff. Start, for example, with a mission of expanding mainstream understandings of youth homelessness. We want to build knowledge around the issues with an assumption that most people do not understand why and how youth become homeless, nor what life is like for youth without a residence. Our placemaking strategy is building effective connections and shared values and we want to leverage the unique problem-solving abilities homeless youth possess. We could devise scenes in which kids get kicked out of their residences for various reasons. We

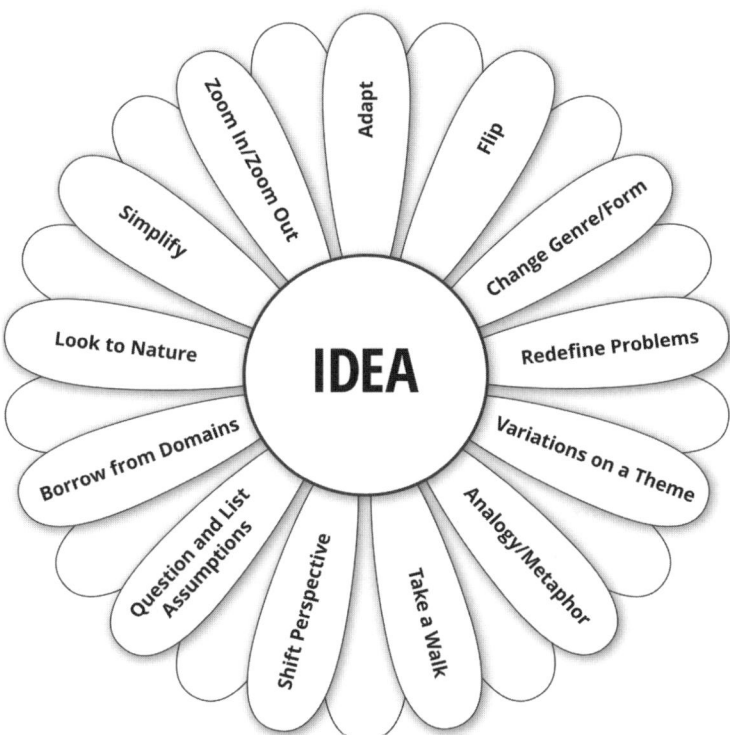

**Figure 2.5:** Devising Daisy.

could shift time and imagine a world in which there is no teen homelessness and create a documentary on how the city solved the issues. We could find poems, stories, and songs about the issue. We could interview city council people, police, and social workers to hear their understandings. We could adapt classical plays or mythology á la *Polaroid Stories*. We could map key locations for homeless youth in the city and create a travelogue or tour or a geo-tagged map in Google Maps with an accompanying photo essay. We can also take one of these ideas and move it through playful iterations. For example, if we were going to start with scenes of youth getting kicked out of their residences:

- We could shift perspectives away from the youth and to the individual kicking the young person out, or we could shift to a news anchor reporting on the story.
- We could explore what a "home" means, or what we need to take from a home to survive using trash bags and gestural representation.

- Like Brecht we can find a metaphorical way to address the issue, through history or mythology.
- Taking a literal or figurative walk with the subject, we could generate word poems about moving away or moving toward.

Again, possibilities are endless but the studio negotiations of this devising need to address the key components of the play state: intrinsic motivation, pleasure, means not an end, and be free of instrumental consequences.

Games are a particular form of playing and I use game structure to facilitate creative processes and products. In his classic text on games, Roger Caillois (1961) defines games as activities having the following characteristics, many related, of course, to play:

- Separate from real life with a beginning and an end
- Governed by rules different from everyday life
- Free from instrumental consequences
- Fun
- Outcomes are unknown (not all games have winners or losers but we do not know what will happen)
- Pretend

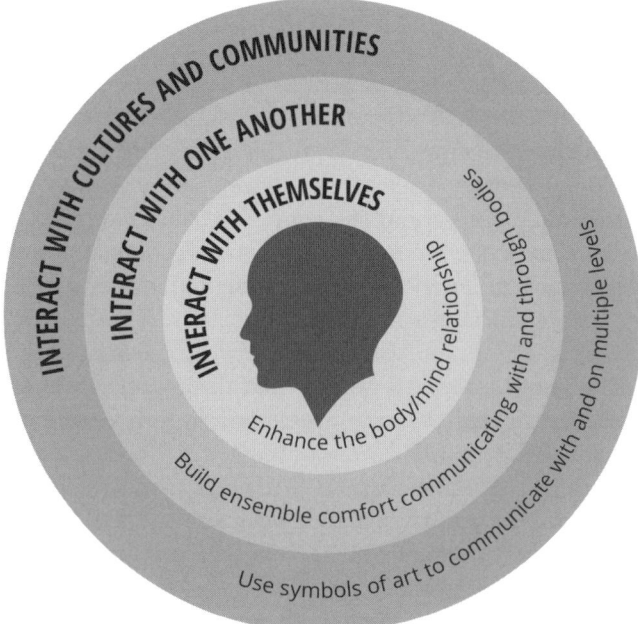

**Figure 2.6:** Boal's internal to external relationships.

While we have a bias toward understanding games as competition in US America, I try to avoid creating win/lose scenarios. For my purposes, game structure allows me to do several things simultaneously. First, theatre has a vast archive and tradition of games and these games easily lend themselves toward devising. Second, games help structure studio space as play space quickly while adding to the fun quotient and helping short circuit fear. We tend to forget as theatre artists how frightened most individuals feel when speaking or performing in front of a group. Game structure shunts individuals' attention away from performance anxiety and toward their task or game goal. Third, game building with set rules, timed beginning and end, and pretend play structure allows me to optimize the ensemble's skills with the requirements of the activities in order to facilitate flow. Fourth, Boal argues in *Theatre of the Oppressed* for a four-part structure transforming passive spectators into actors: physical exercises to relearn/reawaken the body; exercises to enhance bodily expression; exercises to learn theatrical forms while practicing theatre as a language; and, finally, theatre as discourse or conversation. I use Boal's organization loosely as indicated in Figure 2.6. I understand these structures to be interconnected rather than sequential.

Let me provide an example from an activity I typically use in first/second class periods with my graduate students. After playing several theatre warm-up games focused on physicality and communication, I provide my students an "I am" poem template. Ubiquitous in K-12 circles and available on multiple sites online, the "I am" poem asks individuals to self-disclose information in a nonthreatening form. I use the following structure:

FIRST STANZA

I am _____
  (two special characteristics you have)
I wonder _____
  (something you are actually curious about)
I hear _____
  (an imaginary sound)
I see _____
  (an imaginary sight)
I want _____
  (an actual desire)
I am _____
  (the first line of the poem repeated)

## SECOND STANZA

I live _____
    (something about graduate school)
I feel _____
    (a feeling about something imaginary)
I touch _____
    (a sense perception about living in the desert)
I worry _____
    (something that really bothers you)
I cry _____
    (something that makes you feel sorrowful)
I am _____
    (the first line of the poem repeated)

## THIRD STANZA

I understand _____
    (something you know is true)
I say _____
    (something you believe in)
I dream _____
    (something about how you want to impact others with your art)
I try _____
    (something you really make an effort about)
I hope _____
    (something you actually hope for)
I am _____
    (the first line of the poem repeated)

After allowing the group enough time to complete their poem, I use a game structure as a devising protocol. Most video games have one large adventure separated by what is often called mini-games. Using this mini-game structure, I create timed "stations" or "levels" in which the artists, using their poem as primary text, play. For example, mini-games I have used include:

1. Create three movements for your first stanza. One movement must include your entire body, one should involve just your head, and your third movement should take three seconds to complete. When you have finished your movement sequence, put your words and movement together. When do you start? Is there stillness? Why? Do the words and actions happen together? Are there echoes? GO!

2. You are starring in your own cartoon superhero series. Hum your theme song. Use the first phrase of your poem as your tag line. What will your opening credits look like? GO!
3. You are an astronaut on the international space station and your oxygen is slowly leaking out. Your poem contains the instructions for how to stop the leak and save your life. But, remember there is no gravity in space. Lie on your back and learn your life-saving instructions/sequence using all six surfaces of the room. Once you have learned how to stop the leak. Get up and GO!
4. Pretend your poem is a giant cookie. Eat the cookie. What is your secret ingredient? How long does it take you to eat your poem? What is your favorite part? Do you eat it all in two bites? Savor the cookie by slowly letting it crumble in your mouth? Nibble around the edges? Now say your poem as if you are eating it. Play with the sounds in your mouth, let the gooey bits melt and lick them off your fingers. GO!
5. You are a secret agent who can only communicate with your body. Spy on the other stations and copy people's bodies with your own. Learn their secret languages and codes so that you can report back to your handlers. Don't let them catch you! GO!
6. Choose from these ten songs on the karaoke machine (iPad karaoke app) now replace the song's lyrics with your poem. Are you on the R&B charts? A rock star? Beat boxer or K-Pop Band? Sing it to the heavens for your 27,000 fans in this stadium, but use the headphones. GO!

Individuals generally cycle through the levels separately; although with younger groups, I tend to use whole group mini-games with much less involved rules. Game rules can be as simple or as complex as the skills of the group indicate. Mini-game subjects can be as prosaic or as outlandish as needed while focusing on different kinds of aesthetic or symbolic structures. These games swing between the innermost circle (interact with self) and the largest circle (interact with culture/community) while also fostering divergent thinking.

In the next phase of the game play, I would bring the group back together again for collaborative play and the final "boss" level. Collaborative play could include improvisation games or physical warm-ups. For example, the group could pretend to be playing baseball or kickball, but the only words they can say must come from their poems. Or, the group could play the theatre game, bus stop, again incorporating text from their poems. I sometimes overlay physical activities, like "Fill the Space" or the Viewpoints version of "Flocking" with the texts of the poems. Flocking, for example, groups players together in a triangle form—one player at the point and two in the base.

(I use all kinds of shapes not just triangles.) I start with music to influence how the "flock" moves around the room. Again, I default to rules of game play, in this case Atari's pong. When the flock meets an obstacle (any obstacle) they must bounce back and switch directions changing leaders seamlessly. At all times, the flock must maintain consistent alignment and velocity. When I overlay the poem onto the flock structure, I have the flock "leader" say a line from the leader's poem when the leader takes control of the momentum and movement—for example, " I want …." The flock responds together, "You want …." The final level or "boss" level moves back to a more individual focus. I explain that by completing the mini-games, each participant earned "prizes" needed for their final "battle." Individuals would need to decide on their own their mini-game's prize and combine them with their poem. Ultimately, each artist would perform their poem for the group incorporating the "prizes" into their performance. With a group of beginning artists, I would set specific rules for the boss-level integration/performance. For example, one prize needs to be verbal; one prize should be an eight-count physical movement series; one prize involves a secret musical phrase, et cetera. With advanced artists, they make their own choices.

Game structure allows me to manipulate how we interact and decide on potential outcomes while also creating space for playful engagement and enhancing divergent thinking patterns. The group takes pleasure too in discussing how differently they each responded to the mini-games and like trying to identify the "prizes" won in each game. The group unpacks the game play and discusses strategies just as if they were playing a real video or board game. I seek to build spaces for peak creative experiences and believe playful game structure fits my needs. Finally, building spaces of play and "enjoyment" allows for the possibility of a collective experience of *mudita*. A Sanskrit word, *mudita*, means the pleasurable state of enjoying another's joy. The opposite of *schadenfreude*, or pleasure in another's pain, *mudita* experiences are addictive, building off one another and enhancing the ensemble experience and collaborative synergy.

## 2.11.2 Spiral Devising

While I use game organization with session designs, I structure the overall residency using the four stages of creativity—preparation, incubation, insight, and verification—and a process I call spiral devising. Over the years, I have noticed both new artists and young artists tend to rest in the concrete rather than creating abstract material or moving into more structurally sophisticated symbolic manipulation. As I follow a devising process starting in the real, this reliance on the concrete can impede the creative process, as ensembles spin their wheels in the preparation section never moving to insight or verification/elaboration. In popular culture, "realistic" and "good" often become interchangeable concealing the real dramaturgy of filmic or narrative practices. I use spiral devising in order to move ensembles from the concrete while still honoring the real.

Springing from the real stories, feelings and experiences of the ensemble I use the spiral to build toward more abstract expressions. As I spiral down, I recursively have the ensemble work on their expressive forms by building on previous ones. For example, if I were to start with selected lines of an "I am" poem, I could move through the primary components of theatrical expression—duration, embodiment, ensemble, gesture, reenactment of an original, imaginative location, sound/music, spectacle, and text—as well as nontheatrical art forms such as painting, photography, collage, or digital storytelling. As a theatre artist, I believe one of the true strengths of my art form rests in how theatre folds other art forms into itself. So to provide a concrete example of a spiral process and how game structures contribute, I return to my hypothetical project with homeless youth in central Phoenix. Our mission rests on expanding mainstream understandings of youth homelessness with the assumption that if we transform how people understand the issue, we can build toward attitudinal and behavioral change. Our placemaking strategy is building effective connections and sharing values and we want to leverage the unique problem-solving abilities homeless youth possess. For clarity, I abstract the spiral process from inside workshop structures but spiral devising only forms one part of what we would do.

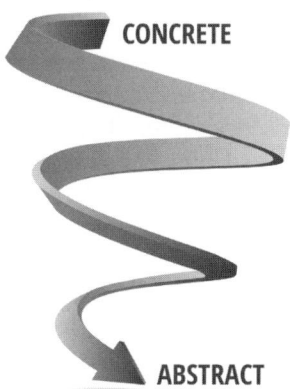

**Figure 2.7:** Spiral devising.

1. Ensemble members create short scenes drawn from their real lives around the moments they were kicked out or aged out. They would share these with a partner for editing and clarifying questions. We then would read them aloud. Authors will revise once again. And again, we would perform the revised scenes as a group.
2. While watching the scenes from One, ensemble members serving as audience will complete different tasks.
    a. One group will cluster around a large sheet of paper and write evocative phrases, moments and words from the scenes.
    b. Another group will use digital cameras to capture haunting and powerful body shapes; alternatively they could create these shapes themselves from the words they hear and document through photography.
    c. The final group will pay attention to characterization. On sheets of paper with a human figure outline, they will pick one character set on which to focus for all the scenes (the youth or the adult). On the inside of the body, they will write internal states of the characters they watch (e.g., fear, anger, despair, and relief) and on the outside they will write descriptive phrases (e.g., mother, pimp, and social worker).
3. After collating the responses from Two (or having the ensemble do so depending on time), the facilitator would return with several different devising tasks ensemble members could choose from.
    a. The images from 2b (printed on several contact sheets and cut up) would become a movement score. Dividing into groups, each group could arrange their score in whatever way feels right, practice and then perform for each other. This activity would be turned into a game with rules dictating duration, repetition, and rhythm.
    b. The words from 2a would be written on post-it notes using different colors to help separate moods. Using sidewalk chalk (or painters tape), the group would create a single-line journey and then place post-it notes along the path in an order that makes the most sense to the individuals involved. Ensemble members would take turns walking the path while performing their collage text.
    c. After collating 2c characters into two separate silhouettes (one for the youth kicked out and one for the adult), ensemble members would choose one body sheet and create an imaginary character. They would create a biography page for this person by using a social media interface (perhaps a work sheet in the style of Facebook or a Twitter account). Thereafter, using the profile, ensemble members

would create five posts or tweets their character would write. Two before, one during, and two after the moment explored in activity one.

As you can glean from these sample activities, we build on the real but move toward the abstract. Activities could go through multiple iterations and move more or less quickly into the abstract. I purposefully steer ensembles away from the creation and direct playing of their own personal narrative. In order to foster play, we need distance from real life. Remember the components of play include:

- Intrinsic motivation
- Pleasurable emotional state
- Freedom from instrumental consequences
- Attention to the means not the end.

In order to use personal narratives, facilitators have to build psychological and emotional distancing into the representational structures in order not to harm or infect (reinfect) ensembles with anger or anguish. Rage, fear, and instrumental consequences negate spaces of play. Further, manipulating ensembles to stage personal narratives of trauma or pathos can victimize collaborators (Cohen-Cruz 2010: 122; Thompson 2005: 25). TFY CCD practices rest in building ensemble/community power, capacity, and cultural capital.

## 2.11.3 Compositional Practices and Aesthetic Considerations

Of course, once we devise work, we need to put that work together into a cohesive frame—a production or art action. Again, I present to you my own particular practices without suggesting my choices will serve everyone. All products, of course, will be unique to the facilitator, participants, and community. Additionally, products should be grounded in aesthetic frames and symbolic languages, recognizing the community's structures of feeling as well as serving the overall theory of change and placemaking strategy. That said, I tend to default to compositional practices to structure products rather than narrative- or plot-driven Freytag-style dramas. I do this for several reasons. The players' direct relationship to the subject matter of the production remains a hallmark of community-based theatre. As Cohen-Cruz notes, "Community-based performance relies on artists guiding the creation of original work or material adapted to and with, people with a primary relationship to the content, not necessarily to the craft" (2005: 2–3). As performers, the ensemble will be doubly coded, perceived through both the frame of the performance (as performers) and their identity status as community insiders. Multiple understandings of realness then circulate around the product no matter what the production's aesthetic frame is. Audiences will be inclined to understand the performance as *descriptive* rather than symbolic. Understanding aesthetic distance to be the separation between the real and the not-real, I default to compositional practices in order to balance aesthetic distancing between the real and not-real components of the production or art action. Additionally, compositional practices help me to balance the diversity of performers' skills while promoting multiple connection points to the product beyond that of "performer" or "actor." Finally, as Manon van de Water (2012) points out,

> a work of art neither stands by itself nor is it an expression of a social group but it is in the complex social, historical, and cultural interactions that it is produced as, and believed to be, a work of art and thus acquires its symbolic value.
>
> (43)

In order for the community cultural engagement to be seen as art, it must be named "art" and produced in a structure validating the "artness" of the product as well as the process. Compositional practices help me highlight the "artness" of the product, hopefully allowing for the transfer of capital from one system to another. I believe the power and status gained by young people as "artists" outweigh that gained through structures building self-esteem.

Matthias Rebstock and David Roesner (2012) define compositional theatre as theatre constructed and understood through musical composition practices applied to "extra-musical materials as movement, speech, actions, lighting or whatever" (21). Additionally, composed theatre/performance

> consists in the aesthetic conviction of the independence and absence of hierarchy among elements of theatre, or, to put it another way, in the conviction that in principle no element should so dominate that the others would be reduced to illustrating, underpinning or reinforcing the first.
>
> (Rebstock and Roesner 2012: 20)

While US American theatre for young audiences, including educational theatre practices, tends to default to a theatrical practice valuing narrative and character above all other theatre elements, I prefer compositional and Viewpoints strategies (Bogart 1995) over Aristotelian or well-made play structures for the reasons elaborated above. In practice, this means I tend to think in "scores" rather than "scripts." I understand the primary elements of music as:

- Rhythm—pattern, duration
- Dynamic—volume, duration
- Melody—progression (tends to hold listener's attention), duration, (story)
- Harmony—chords played together
- Timbre—tone and color
- Texture—relationships and layers
- Form—genre and construction

Mapping these onto the compositional elements of theatre, I get:

1. Duration—time, rhythm, dynamics, tempo, kinesthetic response, repetition
2. Embodiment—real bodies and characters, spatial relationships, kinesthetic response, timbre
3. Ensemble—collaborative group, spatial relationships, flow
4. Gesture—expressive and behavioral
5. Reenactment of an original (story/memory) and melody
6. Imaginative location—architecture (e.g., solid mass, texture, light, and color), topography, setting
7. Sound/music—rhythm, dynamic, melody, harmony
8. Spectacle—shape, gesture, architecture, topography
9. Text—texture, timbre, melody, rhythm
10. Form—genre and shape and bracketed experience

As I work with groups, I use the above list to plan activities, structures, and games that take advantage of the imaginative possibilities created through compositional practices. Additionally, I use these ten compositional elements to build performance scores in which we work to build art actions, communicating experience in nonliteral and nonlinear frameworks. As I build performance scores, I keep several questions in mind to guide my steps:

- Do I privilege continuity or discontinuity?
- Is there a balance between form and content?
- What holds the elements of the performance together?
- Is the mise-en-scène coherent?
- What is the relationship between the audience and the playing space? How does this relationship support the community cultural development goals?
- What do we show and what do we conceal? What are the primary signs and evocative imaginaries of the performance?

- What is the function of noise and silence in the overall performance? What is the rhythm of the overall performance?
- What overall story are we telling? How is the plot constructed by the ten compositional elements? Are we as concise as possible? What fluff can be eliminated?
- How do we manipulate the spectator's attention? Emotion? Comprehension?
- Is there space for the actors to be successful? What is the relationship between actor/character? What is the relationship between text and the body? What is our kinesthetic approach?

Of course, these are only my idiosyncratic practices, and in each residency I work to incorporate the primary aesthetic languages of the ensemble and the community. All art actions then will look vastly different.

> **KEY IDEAS**
>
> - I use games and play as both frame and structuring device in workshops and session designs.
> - Game structure facilitates creativity processes.
> - I use spiral devising to move ensembles from the concrete into the abstract while honoring ensemble stories and memories.
> - I default to compositional practices in order to balance aesthetic distancing between the real and not-real components of the production or art action.

## Section 3

Partnering, Project Management, Planning, and Evaluating

*To achieve great things, two things are needed: a plan and not quite enough time.*

– Leonard Bernstein

This section explores working in communities moving from the philosophical to the practical. This section gives readers practical advice on how to plan residencies, approach institutional partners, create trajectories toward true collaboration, and build budgets. Building an action-oriented/process definition of *community*, Sections 3.1 through 3.2 focus on institutional relationships and the diverse ways in which partnerships can be structured. In Sections 3.4 through 3.6, I focus on how to build projects moving from the conceptual to the specific. In Section 3.7, I explore *change* and how to plan for change. Section 3.8 provides detailed information on how to design project proposals and ongoing project management. Finally, Section 3.9 discusses the need for ongoing and practical assessment strategies. Here, I explore processes of *collaborative assessment* in which institutional and community partners collectively define *success* as well as what evidence will be needed to "prove" success or failure. Finally, I discuss writing project reports for institutional partners and funders, and exit strategies to end residencies/projects. Here is a quick note on the two key terms I use frequently in this section: *partners* and *projects*. For the purposes of this section, "partners" generally refers to institutional and/or community organizations run by adults. Only rarely are children and youth imbedded in leadership roles within institutional or community organizations. Ideally, organizations will have a youth advisory board that helps to plan and evaluate residency programs and projects. Pragmatically, I have found such youth boards to be rare. When I use "projects" here, I particularly mean time-bound activities. "Partnerships" can last years with multiple "projects" happening across those years.

## THINKING THROUGH *COMMUNITY*

I once had a student tell me, "Two things I hate about group work, my group and the work." While more than a little silly, such comments acknowledge how easily collaboration can lead to aggravation. Of course, theatre inherently engages group, as does Community Cultural Development (CCD). Nevertheless, both collaboration and community can be hard. However, as Suzanne Morse reminds us, "The best answers to our most wrenching issues or glorious opportunities come when there is collective deliberation, judgment, and ideas" (2004: 49). Or as my father pointed out—about a hundred times a week when I was a teenager, "If it's not hard, it's not worth doing." This section explores the pragmatics of working in community and builds from previous definitions and understandings of community, touches on cooperating/collaborating with community organizations, basic project management, and project evaluation as well as leveraging resources and capabilities development in both the planning and the evaluation processes.

First, however, I need to return to the key points on *community* advanced in Section 1.8:

- Community defines and distinguishes.
- We all belong to multiple communities.
- Community is the social and symbolic space of humanness.
- People construct community symbolically attaching diverse meanings to those symbols.
- However, community is not generalized abstraction.
- Fluid and partial, community appears only in social action.
- We internally and externally regulate community.
- Communities depend on mutuality and interdependent recognition.
- Theatre/performance expresses the web of relations.

Humans create community moment-to-moment through symbolic and social interaction. When humans come together and are present with one another, we create what Hannah Arendt (1958) calls the "space of appearance." We "appear" to one another not as objects but as actors, as agents. We manifest the complex and unpredictable web of human relationships through and in our interaction. Like Harry Boyte's "publics," Arendt's "space of appearance" is a creative moment of possibility structured through human relationships and deliberation. In fact, Arendt claims social action as true moments of humanness (remember in Arendt's conception of human we are primarily social beings). In fact, we *become* human through and in the web of relationships crafted in the spaces of appearance. What do the above interpretations of community and humanness mean for participatory art-making in and with communities? First, community can only be expressed and understood partially; therefore, CCD artists should not be afraid of complexity—either in the process or in the product. In fact, we should depend on complexity as indicator of creative possibilities. In addition, CCD artists develop understandings of particular communities in the social space of interaction—the web of relations—therefore spending time "hanging out" becomes important to solid aesthetic choices and to uncovering the particularized symbols and narratives already in use. Morse (2004) points out "community evolves around three nexuses: the community of relationships, the community of interests, and the community of place" (Morse 2004: 2). Complex and layered, these social spaces of interaction structure both overt and covert behaviors. CCD artists understand that their partners are community experts and work to uncover the layered interpretations possible. CCD artists also pay attention to the symbolic membranes containing community as well as to the internal performances of belonging. An understanding of how the community defines its boundaries symbolically, and literally, can build deeper interpretations of a community's spaces of appearance. Additionally, community appears only in specific, particularized actions—so CCD artists should actively avoid essentializing or stereotyping. Performatively generalizing community not only raises ethical and cultural concerns, but also aesthetic ones. CCD artists and ensembles create and perform a web of relations not only literally in their own studio practices, but also through representing community itself. Although I note the difference between generalizing and abstracting, stereotyping can only result in bad art as stereotypes misrepresent the specificity of the web of relations.

CCD artists need to mark the limits of community. All communities enforce and regulate membership. Communities who understand themselves as "in crisis" or oppositionally can invest heavily in policing community members' behaviors and demanding uniformity. James DeFilippis, Robert Fisher, and Eric Shragge (2010) argue against the prevailing notion interpreting "community" as always and everywhere positive or a force for good. They write, "Communities can not only function to reproduce a structurally unjust status quo but they also have connotations of homogeneity. People in communities are often assumed to be almost uniform in their interests, lifestyles, perspectives, and so forth" (DeFilippis, Fisher, and Shragge 2010: 24). Mark Valdez once spoke to my students about an experience he had working on the 2003 *You Can't Take it With You, An American Muslim Remix* for Cornerstone Theatre Company's Faith-Based Cycle. Valdez told us of a conflict between members of the community/performance over representation of gay and lesbian Muslims. One LGBTQ participant wanted to recreate the characters of Rheba and Donald (the household staff) as a gay couple. Other members of the community vehemently objected. The collaborators held an open meeting and consulted an Imam. Ultimately, the majority of the community participants and community leaders felt the inclusion of a gay couple too incendiary, particularly two years after 9/11. The

LGBTQ participant felt marginalized and discounted by his community and betrayed by Cornerstone. He abandoned the production entirely. I share this story not to call out this particular community or even to pass judgment on the decision. Sometimes there are no good answers. After all, by its nature CCD places the values and needs of a majority over the individual. Moreover, "communities are, to no small degree, products of their larger social contexts" (DeFilippis, Fisher, and Shragge 2010: 24). Here, I warn against romanticizing community. Community can hurt; communities can enforce narrow definitions of "human" and they can rigidly control who belongs. White supremacists count as a community, but I would not consider them a force for good.

> **KEY IDEAS**
>
> - We become truly human in the web of relations—humans are social beings.
> - Collaboration takes care.
> - CCD practices express the web of relations—symbolically complex, messy, and aesthetically rich with possibility.
> - Do not romanticize community.

## 3.1 PARTNERING TO FOSTER CHANGE AND SOCIAL TRANSFORMATION

In her over twenty years of leadership in the civic and community change arena—first at the Kettering Foundation and then at Pew Partnerships for Civic Change—Suzanne Morse developed solid strategies for working in and with communities to accomplish change. She identifies seven "high leverage points" common to all successful "smart communities." Morse writes,

Communities that were having success were doing the following:

- Investing right the first time
- Working together
- Building on community strengths
- Practicing democracy
- Preserving the past
- Growing leaders
- Inventing a brighter future

(Morse 2004: ix)

Partnering, Project Management, Planning, and Evaluating

In her book, Morse devotes a chapter to each of these seven leverage points along with case studies illustrating each. Many of these seven bullet points align with the principles of CCD with children and youth already discussed—working together, building on community strengths, inventing a brighter future, practicing democracy, and growing leaders. Her understandings of these terms and processes, however, usefully serve as a starting point to think about partnerships and collaborations, programs, and project planning. Morse points out,

> Americans choose to work together in different ways and for different reasons. Sometimes it is sporadic and necessary because of an incident or circumstance. However, it is clear that sustained efforts—those developed for a purpose and that work over time—must have a structure for working together that has broad implications for building social capital, creating unusual partnerships, and taking action on systemic issues.
> (2004: 47)

The communities with whom Morse typically works lean heavily toward civic institutions and governmental entities. TFY CCD specialists, however, also work with nonprofits, education institutions (both formal and informal), religious institutions, cultural institutions, and sometimes recreational programs. Over the years, for example, I have partnered with museums, libraries, schools, school districts, churches and parishes, mental health facilities, government agencies, nonprofit social-service providers, arts centers, and tribal organizations. In all cases, partners have to create a "structure for working together." Morse categorizes "working together" in a continuum noting that each category needs diverse commitments of (1) time, (2) trust, and (3) access: coalition building; networking; coordination; cooperation; collaboration (Morse 2004: 51–53). Morse particularly explores the inter-workings of organizations, but her continuum works with some adaptation for TFY third space artists. Figure 3.1 reflects this, again, with diverse commitments of time, trust, and access. Coordination takes the least amount of time, trust and access, while integration requires the most time, trust, and access.

For any successful partnership, partners need to create clearly defined relationships as well as specific goals/outcomes for the partnership as well as

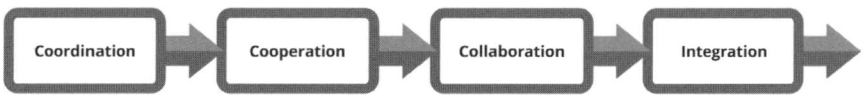

**Figure 3.1:** Etheridge Woodson adaptation of Morse continuum.

167

any projects. Morse goes on to describe the attributes of "working together" in a chart she developed from Himmelman's 1994 article, "Communities working collaboratively for change." I adapt her chart extensively to focus on TFY CCD and to reflect my own working experiences. I have two givens that readers should keep in mind as they examine the chart. First, I assume that the TFY CCD artist functions as a project director. A project director's time commitments do not necessarily lessen across the continuum in the same way as a partnering institution's would. Time commitments in project direction depend on the skill sets of the involved artists, the complexity of the partnerships, and the scale of the program/projects. Second, project complexity and duration do not depend on the complexity of the "working together" structure. In other words, *how* partners work together does not necessarily correlate to the *kinds of projects possible*. I use this chart (see page 169) with my project partners both to plan residencies and to assess how our partnerships are working. In this way, the chart serves to open discussions focused on *how* we will work together before we get into the specifics of the individual projects we will accomplish.

*Coordination*: In a coordinated partnership, partners create their own visions and understandings of a project while agreeing on a placemaking approach and the impacts sought. Partners meet infrequently and work in parallel toward project goals. Project partners spend minimal amounts of time developing partnering relationships and solve structural problems as necessary. Impact strategies focus on leveraging extant resources primarily to grow individual capacities. Short term and individual changes generally are targets. Evaluations are conducted separately with the project director often authoring a final report.

*Cooperation*: In a cooperative partnership, partners work toward a common goal and have set reporting mechanisms. Partners trust one another within the boundaries of their established roles and address structural conflicts proactively. While partners agree on overarching goals (e.g., placemaking approach, assets, and capabilities targeted), they likely have separate institutional objectives as well and conduct evaluation separately to meet their diverse needs. The project director often authors the major components of the final assessment report and multiple drafts can circulate between partners cooperatively. Short term and individual change is possible as well as limited potential for organizational impacts.

*Collaboration*: In a collaborative partnership, partners meet regularly and engage in collaborative strategic planning. Here, partners pool resources, share authority and risk-taking. Generally, organizational and structural conflict will be addressed proactively. Planning and evaluation happen collaboratively and comprehensively. Short- to mid-range impact is possible

| | Coordination | Cooperation | Collaboration | Integration |
|---|---|---|---|---|
| **Communication** | Partners exchange information and meet when necessary | Partners exchange information fluidly and regularly | Regular and established strategic planning meetings | Ongoing comprehensive strategic planning and communication; partners frequently share space |
| **Roles** | Individuals maintain authority over their own vision | Partners establish project roles and reporting mechanisms | Partners share authority and responsibility | Fluid roles with shared responsibilities shaped to the moment |
| **Partnering Organization Time Commitment** | Low | Low/medium | Medium/high | High |
| **Relationship** | Low-risk, conflict generally ignored or worked around | Low-risk, structural conflict addressed in context of project roles | Medium-risk, structural and interpersonal conflict addressed, partners influence each other's mission | High-risk, inter- and intrapersonal conflict addressed, partners create new collaborative mission |
| **Planning and Evaluation** | Participants set and evaluate individual and internal goals, while agreeing on project goals, evaluation conducted separately or only by project director | Participants agree on goals, generally conduct evaluation separately or only the project director | Participants set goals and conduct evaluation together | Ongoing adaptation and assessment of collaborative goals |

Adapted from Morse (2004: 55).

in this structure with potential for institutional and organizational impacts too. Community-level impact is possible depending on the project's goals and focus. Final project/program reports tend to be written in a collaborative format, generally with the project director or an assigned project evaluator taking leadership responsibility. Again, multiple drafts will circulate.

*Integration*: In integrative partnerships, project partners create new organizational structures. Partners cease to represent different organizations and instead become constituent members of a new organization. Fluid roles reflect shared responsibility. Resources are pooled and new missions are created in order to achieve maximum and sustained targeted impacts. New structures and roles will be created to support the nascent organization. In the for-profit world, these "spin off" companies often focus on a particular product or process.

*Working together versus work for hire*: A frequent "working" structure common to teaching artists is pay-for-hire or contract work. In my considered opinion, however, pay-for-hire or contractor status does not structurally support development processes oriented toward change. In the teaching-artist economy, schools and other organizations contract with a teaching artist to provide certain services (much like other contractors or vendors). Contract work rarely functions as "working together." And perhaps more importantly, the boundaries of these structured understandings or contracts preclude the significant planning necessary to implementing collaborative public-making strategies. A central function of CCD revolves around change making through asset and capabilities development. In this, I do not discount teaching artistry's ability to add value; however, only rarely do partnering organizations interpret "teaching" beyond individual or classroom knowledge/skill acquisition. Dorothy Gamble and Marie Weil (2010) point out,

> The terms used in community work to describe these mutual relationships are participants, partners, group members, and community members. We work with people not in dependency relationships but in mutual relationships in their roles as citizens, immigrants, refugees—as members of groups and communities, and member carries a very different connotation than the dependency relationship implied with client [...].
> 
> (Gamble and Weil 2010: 97)

I understand CCD with children and youth as categorically different from teaching-artistry, although they build on many of the same skills and creative protocols. Nevertheless, many organizations who work frequently with contractors or vendors will understand CCD through work-for-hire or service-provider models first. Practitioners have to help partnering organizations understand the differences between service/product delivery and CCD practices.

Bringle, Clayton, and Price (2009) write,

> One of the defining characteristics of contemporary models of civic engagement is mutually-beneficial collaboration, in which all persons contribute knowledge, skills, and experience in determining the issues to be addressed, the questions to be asked, the problems to be resolved, the strategies to be used, the outcomes that are considered desirable, and the indicators of success.
>
> (1)

The vast number of my partnerships have been either cooperative partnerships or collaborative partnerships although I have coordinated partnerships too. In my lengthiest partnerships, we move up and down the continuum depending on the personnel involved, scope of our projects, and funding cycles. Collaboration and integration—and theatre with children and youth tends to use these terms more than we should—depend on nonhierarchical relationships with mutual trust and willingness to jointly participate in ongoing structured planning, program delivery, and assessment. Collaboration and integration also depend on mutual risk taking. Integration creates new organizations or imbeds artists inside organizations that change and adapt to take advantage of the unique skills artists bring to the table. In my experience, true collaboration is almost structurally impossible for solo TFY CCD artists unless the partner imbeds the artist into their organization. In other words, to truly function collaboratively, solo TFY CCD specialists must be interdependent with the organization. For example, from 2005 to 2008, the Seattle Office of Arts and Culture partnered with the Seattle Department of Transportation to integrate a resident artist into the planning phases of public transit. Rather than leaving space for artists at the end of the process, Seattle wished to explore how integrating artists in planning processes could add value to all phases of their public works. In this case, the artist functioned as an employee of the Department of Transportation—albeit one whose salary was paid by an external organization.

I want to introduce a final framework for planning and evaluating healthy collaborations. Robert Bringle, Patti Clayton, and Mary Price (2009) created what they refer to as the "E-T-T model of relationship outcomes," which addresses "the degree to which [relationships] are exploitive, or are transactional, or are transformational (E-T-T)" (Bringle, Clayton, and Price 2009: 7). Exploitive relationships depend on hierarchical/specialist status relationships and sap capacity among participants rather than build capital.

"Exploitive relationships lack closeness, equity, and integrity because they possess unrewarding or harmful outcomes and are not satisfying to one or both persons, even if they are maintained" (Bringle, Clayton, and Price 2009: 7). Transactional relationships generally can be understood as relationships built to complete a task. Transformational relationships literally transform individuals; they are characterized by growth and development on both sides. While TFY CCD is characterized by reciprocity (everyone gains something), understanding the diversity of collaboration schema and relational outcomes helps to bring reciprocal structures into sharp focus. In fact, the building of those reciprocal structures and partnering relationships needs just as much attention from TFY CCD artists as program planning or facilitation does. While I find the E-T-T structure especially useful for evaluation, I also believe that listing intended outcomes in preliminary partnership meetings can help potential partners and TFY CCD artists express their systems of values to one another. Additionally, a focus on intended partnership outcomes allows partners to identify and evaluate indicators.

At Arizona State University (ASU), I maintain two long-term partnerships: one with a homeless youth services organization in central Phoenix and another at a children's hospital in the hematology and oncology unit. Our partnership with the youth services organization is collaborative. Trained like any other employee, the resident artist functions as a staff member. The artist keeps regular hours, meets weekly with her supervisor at the center, and goes on street outreach. All planning, assessment, and youth case management happens in teams. I am not sure, however, that I would label this relationship as transformational. Although, the graduate student resident artists do change and grow. Our residency at the hospital functions quite differently. There, I would categorize the partnership as coordinated or cooperative. While the resident artist attends volunteer training and becomes certified as "safe" to work with medically fragile humans, the artist does not function as a staff member but as a "volunteer." I regularly assess the program and report to the hospital once a semester, but we undertake little comprehensive planning or collaborative assessment. At the hospital, our mission literally includes noninterference in hospital operations. This only makes sense. Hospitals work to save lives, cure disease, and promote healthy living. Our work as resident artists there revolves around a shared understanding of positive youth development as a function of health—understood broadly. However, many of the young people admitted to the hospital have acute medical crises and we cannot interfere in the real work of saving their lives. Nor does the hospital have the resources, or desire, to commit to a different structure. Here too, I would understand our partnership primarily as transactional. Different partnerships demand different structures of working together.

How do you know which working together structure will function best? Each step up the continuum demands more trust, time, and access, and often partnership parameters will be more limited than infinite. Nevertheless, all working relationships, David Chrislip (2002) articulates, build:

> A series of progressively deeper and more comprehensive agreements among stakeholders. The evolution of these agreements follows a general pattern and [shape] the phases of a collaborative process.
>
> 1. Agreement that shared concerns exist that should be addressed
> 2. Agreement to work together to address the concerns
> 3. Agreement on how to work together
> 4. Agreement on a shared understanding of the relevant information
> 5. Agreement on the definition of the problem or the vision
> 6. Agreement on the solutions to the problem or the strategies to achieve the vision
> 7. Agreement on the action steps or implementation plans for implementing the solutions or stategies
>
> (Chrislip 2002: 54)

Being able to engage in structured partnerships depends on time, trust, and access as well as the collaborating artist's commitment to engaging and understanding the context of the collaborative environment. Additionally, understanding the implicit and explicit agreements needed, help in crafting thoughtful participatory structures that ultimately promote successful partnerships.

> **KEY IDEAS**
>
> - In order for partnerships to function productively, we have to create an agreement on *how* to work together.
> - There are multiple ways to partner, each with different time, trust, and access commitments.
> - Project complexity does not necessarily depend on the complexity of partners' working relationships.

## 3.2 BARRIERS TO WORKING TOGETHER

To go back to a statement from the beginning of this section, working together can be hard. At any point in a partnership process roadblocks can occur. Often when I plan for a long-term or potentially complex collaboration, I first determine the feasibility of a partnership by using what I call a *proof-of-concept* or a *road-test*. I plan a small, short-term residency using minimal resources and truncated planning processes. Such projects allow me and my potential allies to develop common language, introduce my potential allies to the creative potential of theatrical engagement, allow me to get to know some of the youth in a community, and assess the working parameters of an organization. In my experience, many prospective partners do not understand the creative potential of theatre art actions and CCD with children and youth. Giving them a taste of what we can accomplish, builds awareness, knowledge, common vocabulary, and greater understandings. Proof-of-concept projects create the opportunities, trust, and capacity for in-depth working together. Additionally, a proof-of-concept does not take huge amounts of resources, so if we discover barriers to a collaborative process that either cannot, or should not, be surmounted, we minimize our risks.

What barriers might you face? Well, roadblocks can happen at multiple levels and for multiple reasons. To go back to Chrislip's seven phases of collaboration, difficulties can arise at all seven stages as well as around the edges of the project. Morse points out that turf wars and ethnic or cultural issues can divide groups and organizations, preventing trust from forming (2004: 56). Russell Linden (2002) in his book, *Working Across Boundaries*, divides barriers to collaboration into communication issues, interpersonal differences, organizational hurdles, and project problems such as "fragmentation of responsibility" (35). Specific roadblocks he mentions include:

Interpersonal

- What's in it for me
- Self-serving bias (my work is good, but not so sure about yours)
- Fear of losing control
- Fear of loss of autonomy
- Worries about quality
- Worry over resources
- Turf concerns
- Trust issues

Organizational

- Immediate costs, remote benefits
- Differing goals and measures
- Low credit or reward systems
- Individually oriented appraisal systems
- Line item budget systems

(Linden 2002: 38–49)

I believe the interpersonal roadblocks self-explanatory but want to unpack a few of the organizational difficulties that Linden outlines. Many institutions need their employees/members to collaborate or to at least coordinate tasks. At ASU, for example, official language promotes breaking down the silos between different fields and knowledge systems. In fact, "fuse intellectual disciplines" is a core value of what our president, Michael Crow, calls the New American University. However, organizational structures still impede internal and external collaboration at ASU. To speak of the internal difficulties, the university evaluates professors and clinical faculty based on criteria promoting only individual excellence, not collaborative performance. Teaching distributions of effort do not allow for collaborative, shared, or co-teaching practices. Tenure and promotion rest on narratives explaining how faculty members perform differently—competitively—than anyone else in their field. Internal grant cycles do not recognize remote benefits or stepped progress. When professors wish to include external community partners, the academic year calendar makes planning projects with communities on fiscal or calendar years difficult. Collaborating well takes immense effort and planning but faculty's labor-making success can only be addressed through "service" metaphors, which in effect often erases the actual work being accomplished. In other words, the structures of academia have not caught up to the realities of collaborative living and working in the twenty-first century.

TFY CCD artists need to pay particular attention to structures and strategies in order to address or plan around inherent organizational barriers. The Chinese strategist and military philosopher, Sun Tzu wrote 2500 years ago, "victorious warriors win first and then go to war, while defeated warriors go to war first and then seek to win." Poor planning, in other words, capsizes more projects than almost anything else. We cannot solve all the problems all at once, of course, but knowing what questions to ask, what issues might lurk around blind corners, and what elements are essential for a successful project become necessary to strategic planning. Additionally, William Cleveland's grounded research in community-based arts programming (2012), culled from interviews and evaluations of multiple projects, summarizes strategies and barriers to keep in mind when building CCD relationships:

- Power imbalances between large and small organizations are particularly difficult to overcome and destabilize long-term planning and successes. Particularly when the larger organization is an arts organization based outside of the geographical area involved.
- Local ownership is key: Our research also shows that the success of community-based work is often tied to the role the community has in identifying its own needs, formulating possible solutions, doing the work, and owning the result.

- Outreach both in concept and in process is NOT successful nor reciprocal.
- Partnerships are important. Successful practitioners say over and over that their most important resources are relationships.
- Clear intentions produce better outcomes.
- Community art making is slow and specific. Our research tells us that assumptions and expectation as accrued from other sites can inform our programs but should not drive them. This is not because those experiences are not potentially valuable and informative but because the time spent learning about a community's culture is an indispensable part of building community trust.

(305–307)

Know the context for working together. Understand the politics involved and the structures of your partners' organizations. Hear potential partners' fears, and build credibility and collaborative capacity through proof-of-concept projects. Determine whether you can work together. Finally, knowing your own and/or your organization's tolerance for risk and uncertainty can help you map the parameters of possibilities. Sun Tzu also pointed out that:

> It is said that if you know your enemies and know yourself, you will not be imperiled in a hundred battles; if you do not know your enemies but do know yourself, you will win one and lose one; if you do not know your enemies nor yourself, you will be imperiled in every single battle.

While TFY CCD can in no way be considered a battle, Sun Tzu's advice rests in the need to understand the complexities of the contexts and communities with whom we engage *and* to know our own tolerances, needs, and preferred working-together strategies. Reciprocity functions as a critical value in TFY third space, crafting the space to build reciprocal participatory structures demands unique skills in engagement, relational management, and strategy.

### KEY IDEAS

- Poor planning destroys projects.
- A proof-of-concept or road-test project can help map potential partnership difficulties while also building common vocabulary and realistic expectations.
- Successful project strategizing and managing depend on TFY CCD artists' knowledge of themselves and of the particular community contexts.

## 3.3 QUALITIES HELPFUL TO OVERCOMING BARRIERS

Messy, provisional, chaotic—working in CCD with children and youth demands advanced capacities in multitasking. In my experience, four traits go a long way toward cultivating positivity and joy in the experience. I do not speaking here of aesthetic or facilitation skills, which are discussed in Section 2, but rather attitudes and modes of thought.

First, *flexibility*: I guarantee that no matter how specific and thoughtful your project proposal or how detailed your memorandum of understanding with your project partners is, things will change. Personnel will change, space will change, the church choir will need the rehearsal space, and you will have to relocate to a conference room totally unsuited to physical movement. Someone will steal your musical equipment or lose the wall charger for your amplifier. So-and-so will need the van to pick up youth who missed the bus and you will miss a crucial site visit. A camera will break; a child will accidently delete all 162 documentary photos off your hard drive. One project partner will consistently answer e-mails but provide incorrect information and another will never respond unless you call on the phone, between 7 and 8:05 in the morning. I cannot emphasize enough how important nurturing flexibility will be to your practice. Being adaptable in changing circumstances is both a matter of personality but also of cultivated attitudes and skills. In my experience, the less trust individuals have in their own capacity to creatively problem solve, the less adaptable they are. In other words, flexibility depends on building confidence in your problem-solving skills, your creative adaptation, and your ability to think quickly. Flexibility also depends on developing tolerance for change and the wrenches daily living will throw in your works. I was not born tolerant of change: like a toddler, I crave routine and stability. I do not even care to make transitions ... inertia rules. Clear knowledge of my own creative processes combined with strategic attention to the necessary steps needed to move toward project success have helped me develop a tolerance for change. I guarantee change will happen. Positive adaptability also depends on cultivating a sense of humor. Enjoying the absurdity allows CCD artists to use problem solving and creative adaptation to propel the work forward rather than holding it back. Finally, we have to allow our project partners and collaborating youth to *see* this work—and solving problems is work. Muse out loud as you labor through possibilities. Creative problem solving then becomes part of the creative aptitudes you bring to the community table. Additionally, allowing the process to be visible reinforces deliberative principles and creates what education experts call "teachable moments." Remember community becomes visible—becomes real—in the web of relations. Allow yourself to participate in community in those moments.

*Ability to tolerate ambiguity*: CCD with children and youth inherently functions as a gray space without clearly delineated lines. In fact, the real work of the project depends on who enters the room and what they seek to give and gain. We can plan for days and pages, but the truth of the matter can be found in uncertainty and unknowing. I never know who will walk through the door and what they will want to do. The great Dorothy Heathcote practiced theatre in this manner. She asked youth what they wanted to explore and created elaborate and compelling narrative engagements on demand. Like flexibility, the ability to tolerate ambiguity grows from self-confidence and experience. In a similar manner, cultivating positivity and an attitude of abundance rather than fear can color ambiguity in delight. Meaning, what amazing skills will your unknown collaborators bring to the studio? What knowledge or stories will they share with you? What will you learn that you never before knew? How will they show you their capacities and abilities—with their eyes? With their words? Using their bodies? No matter how much experience I accrue, I start new projects with a belly full of anticipation and anxiety. I enjoy the feeling of risk and surprise, and my butterflies help me remember my new partners will likely be feeling exactly the same way.

*Proactive versus reactive stance*: At first, I was going to call this quality "proactive vs. reactive problem solving," but frankly taking initiative frames more than problem solving. Part of both successful collaborative aesthetic work and successful project management depends on proactive thinking that builds forward momentum. Like the epigram opening this section, CCD with children and youth depends on a plan without enough time. If you wait for problems to come to you, conflict to dissipate, or ambiguity to solidify, forward momentum could come to a screeching halt. Time will always be your most precious resource—how can you use the minutes you have to create the strongest creative act of public making? Being aware of small problems before they grow, not shying away from difficult conversations, and paying close attention allows CCD specialists to strategically handle decision making. Additionally, help your collaborators understand how their tasks are necessary to moving forward. Set deadlines, hold partners accountable, and reliably accomplish your own tasks: these are components of a proactive stance. In Section 2, I offer suggestions for negotiating conflict, but understand conflict will occur. Do not fear conflict; instead, catch it small before the conflict can spread to new spaces and people.

*Improvisation* skills grow in fertile, prepared minds that have clear and specific knowledge of their domains, methods of working, and artistic craft. Knowing the project thoroughly while paying attention to specific assets and the diverse capital you can leverage, promotes skills to change tracks, riff on new subjects, and work toward social change productively. Related to flexibility, improvisation depends on three things: being present; building common language and understandings; and a grasp of the project's flow. Scholar Keith Sawyer studies collaborative creativity. He writes,

> There's a growing body of research into the creativity of performance [...] these studies tell us:
> - Everyday creativity is collaborative;
> - Everyday creativity is improvised;
> - Everyday creativity can't be planned in advance, or carefully revised before execution;
> - Everyday creativity emerges unpredictably from a group of people;
> - Everyday creativity depends on shared cultural knowledge;
> - In everyday creativity, the process is the product.
>
> (Sawyer 2006: 296)

Sawyer's research points out the conditional knowledge as well as shared frames built by skilled improvisers. In performance improvisation, actors or musicians pull from a well of stories or themes shared among the group. Being present and actively listening to the group allows improvisers to work inside of the narrative or musical landscape already present while adding innovation, addressing change, and working collaboratively. Skills needed by improvisers include keen focus, adjusting to and accommodating others, and being present—actively engaged in the moment. Third-space CCD specialists function like able theatrical improvisers.

Reading all four of these traits together highlights the provisional nature of working in community, for community, and with community. Morse reminds us:

> Community development is about people, place, process, and outcomes. The needle cannot be moved permanently until attention is paid to building the capacity of the community to work together (people and process) to create results where people live (places and outcomes).
>
> (Morse 2004: 85)

CCD, too, is about people, place, process, and outcome. Complex and messy, specific and particular, working in third-space CCD demands presence, planning, and flexibility. I have found no other application of my art form that demands more creativity from me than this.

> **KEY IDEA**
>
> - Flexibility, comfort with ambiguity, skills in improvisation and a proactive stance go a long way toward cultivating positivity and joy and overcoming barriers in TFY CCD partnerships.

## 3.4 CONCEPTUALIZING PROJECTS

TFY CCD builds projects and partnership focused on capabilities development rather than need statements. In other words, TFY CCD strategic planning uses asset development models, not deficit structures. Moving from deficit models to asset models can be more difficult than it first appears. John McKnight and Peter Block (2010) use the metaphor of "abundance" to discuss thriving communities. They compare and contrast social identities available through a consumer economy versus those drawn from an abundant community. In many ways, their metaphor tracks with the way I conceptualize TFY third space and is useful for thinking though project conceptualization. They note the principles of an abundant community as:

- What we have is enough. […] We do not need to operate on the half-full glass of scarcity to give value to things or qualities.
- We have the capacity to provide what we need in the face of the human condition. […] We can imagine creating together a future beyond this moment. We can learn how to make visible and harvest what up to now has been invisible and treated as though it were scarce.
- We organize our world in a context of cooperation and satisfaction. We do not need competition to motivate our children or ourselves.
- We are responsible for each other.
- We live with the reality of the human condition. We understand what we can and cannot do. Sorrow, aging, illness, celebration, fallibility, failure, misfortunate, and joy are natural and inevitable. Life is not a problem to be solved or services to be obtained.

(McKnight and Block 2010: 66)

Human flourishing does not function as a zero sum game or a set of inputs for defined outputs. Instead, a focus on flourishing grows from understanding abundance and plenty, not lack or risk or problems. In this manner, TFY CCD artists become partners or even catalysts in the conceptualization of community as a space of power and wealth.

Communities *require* aesthetic/symbolic exploration and collaborative meaning-making experiences. Both Nussbaum (2011) and Alkire (2005) include aesthetics, sensual, and imaginative engagements of meaning as core human capabilities—the absence of which marks life as not worth living. While I in no way suggest theatre and performance are the only way to experience aesthetic meaning making, ensemble theatre and performance uniquely engage the web of relations and therefore the space of being human. Art is necessary, not frivolous. Art inherently can perform functions other actions cannot. TFY CCD artists frame moments in which participants share in social expression, public-making, and agentic equality.

Roy Baumeister, in a book-length cross-disciplinary study on the meaning of life (1991), postulates that there are four human requirements for meaning: purpose, value, efficacy, and self-worth. He points out—like Arendt—we acquire meaning socially, in the web of relations and through the space of appearance. "Meaning is shared mental representations of possible relationships [...]. Thus, meaning connects things" (Baumeister 1991: 15). I bring up Baumeister's work here because I believe his construction of the human drive toward meaning has application to generalized project conceptualization as well as how we create project frames to share with potential community partners. I outline Baumeister's theory in the table below. Keeping these four components in mind helps conceptualize projects with particular intentionality aligning with both the capabilities approach and positive youth development models.

### Components of Human Need for Meaning

| | |
|---|---|
| **Purpose** | People want their lives to have purpose. |
| | Purpose can be broken down into extrinsic goals (the desire to get a college degree or earn enough money to travel) and intrinsic goals that Baumeister calls "fulfillment," and I suggest we could also call "self-integration" and "practical reason." |
| | Meaning enables the person to organize current behaviors around the goal state. As a need for meaning, purpose involves at least three things. First, the goal or state is imagined and conceptualized. Second, current behavior options are analyzed and evaluated according to whether they will help bring about this desired goal state. Third, the person makes choices to achieve the goal. |
| **Value** | As a need for meaning, this need for value refers to people's motivation to feel that their actions are right, good, and justifiable. |
| | The belief that a particular action is right and good is one reason that people will do it, just as the belief that an action is wrong will help prevent people from doing it. Value is thus a form of motivation. |
| **Efficacy** | People need to believe they have some control over events. |
| | Simply put, efficacy means feeling capable and strong. Having a meaningful life is more than having goals and values; you must also feel |

| | |
|---|---|
| | that you have some capability to achieve these goals and realize these values. In the language of capabilities, efficacy could also be understood as "agency." |
| **Self-Worth** | People need to make sense of their lives in a way that enables them to feel they have positive value. |
| | More precisely, the need is to find some basis for positive self-worth. People seek some criteria according to which they can regard themselves and convince others to regard them positively. It is a need to have some claim on respect—both self-respect and the respect of others. |
| | Self-worth can have either an individual or a collective basis. People's identities are substantially based on belonging to certain groups or categories. |

(Baumeister 1991: 32–36)

I in no way mean to suggest that TFY CCD practices *provide* meaning. We do not make meaning for someone else; people craft meanings contextually and socially. Baumeister's work here functions to organize development principles and project frames of reference. As a TFY CCD artist, I use these four components as a check on my own work. Beyond the twenty key ideas developed in Section 1, Baumeister's theory combined with the framework of abundance helps articulate why TFY third space *matters*. Additionally, Baumeister's components help serve as a check and balance on program conceptualization as a whole. Am I articulating a community's values clearly? Have I created space and processes for the community to communally develop goals and articulate behaviors and steps necessary to move planning forward? Do I address freedom? Do we have formative assessments to keep the project aligned with community understandings of the good, or their values? Do I ensure participants engage their own values in the context of community motivations? Do I promote participants' and partners' real control and agency within the TFY CCD processes? Do I partner with children and youth participants in such a ways as to ensure adult partners can respect the youths' social practices? Does the project adds value, increase community power, and claim publics such that participants feel worthwhile and respected? Do participants function in the economy of art? Principles of abundance and meaning frame TFY CCD intentionality.

In order to discuss the *pragmatics* of conceptualizing projects with children and youth aimed toward human flourishing I return to material presented in Section 1, in particular Figure 3.2. First, what do I mean specifically when I say, "project?" A "project" is a series of activities supported by resources intended to achieve specific outcomes.

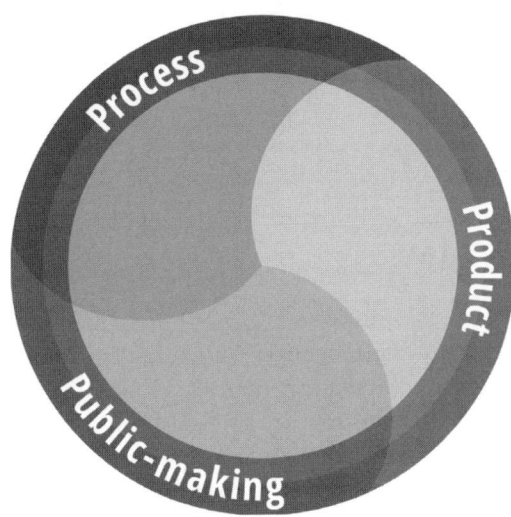

**Figure 3.2:** TFY third space.

TFY CCD uses participatory art making and sharing to thoughtfully claim publics with children and youth while building capacity and community capital. In a CCD process, particularly one focused on human capabilities and flourishing, the community must be involved in conceptualizing projects. Artists can seek out partnerships and approach communities, *but they cannot plan projects on their own.* In order to craft art actions, claim publics, and increase capabilities significant to the community, artists must collaborate across the entire spectrum of decision making from start to finish. Remember the foundation of the capabilities approach roots in freedom, freedom to live lives, and make "choices [communities] have reason to value" (Sen 1999: 293). Who decides and what decisions are made become key questions for a planning process. "Participatory approaches see well-being and participation as inherently connected" (Alkire 2005: 127). Alkire goes on to define "participation" as "discussion, information gathering, conflict, and eventual decision-making, implementation, and evaluation by the group(s) directly affected by an activity" (2005: 129). Sections 1.11, 1.12, and 1.13 articulate what kinds of decision making and planning I specifically mean here. Participation in decision making not only functions to highlight deliberative democratic skills and techniques, but participation and agency have normative value in and of themselves. If TFY CCD artists cannot plan projects alone then how do we ever get new projects off the ground? I approach communities or organizations with project ideas or frames, first, rather than fully fleshed out programs.

> **KEY IDEA**
>
> - Project concepts spring from a space of abundance and productively use the human desire for meaning (purpose, value, efficacy, and self-worth) to frame asset development.

## 3.5 PROJECT FRAMES

What are the components of a project frame? I understand the components to be an impulse, information gathering including informal meetings, and then a written paragraph or two articulating ideas as well as potential next steps. First, an impulse or a desire: this can come from the artist or from a potential partner. In many cases, the impulse arises because of previous relationships. Recently, a teacher whose daughter is friends with one of my kids requested I work on a project with his classroom. The impetus for my work with Child Protective Services (CPS) was my mother, a Texas social worker. She wanted to know why I was not working already with CPS, and because I am still trained to obey my mother, I approached them. (As an icebreaker, explaining how I am still slightly intimidated by my mother during cold calls worked really well, too.) I once met the Executive Director of nonprofit organization focused on homeless youth, in that meeting, during a break, he said I should talk to one of his project directors. That brief conversation led to a solid eight-year relationship. Impulses can also come from admiration or curiosity about a potential partner. Sometimes, I simply want to get to know an organization better.

The second component of a project frame includes research about potential partners and/or organizations. Where are they located? What are their facilities? What do they say about themselves online? What do others say about them? What is their mission? This research allows me to build a hazy snapshot in my head of the scope and sequence of a potential project. Then I request an informal meeting to discuss the possibilities of a project together. Knowing what questions to ask and how to frame the benefits of what you offer is particularly important in this first informational meeting. Discovering what is important to an organization and their vision for the future provides useful information helping connect an organization's literal activities with their stated mission, vision, and values. I generally walk away from these meetings with several potential ideas for partnerships that I write up as a paragraph or two and send back to my contact. I often include previous project proposals and final reports from past partnerships so that potential partners understand the scope and sequence of TFY third space. Additionally, I include my curriculum vita and ethical statement. Finally, I include a list of action items if we decide to move forward. Looking back at Chrislip's (2002) key steps of building a partnership you can see how each step becomes an action item:

1. An agreement to work together.
2. An agreement on *how* to work together.
   a. Crafting structures for planning
   b. Crafting structures to include young people's input and concerns
   c. Pragmatic planning including memos of understanding with primary contacts, process assessments of the relationship, and key responsibilities
3. An agreement on the placemaking approach/goal. Will we:
   a. Build effective connections and shared values?
   b. Intensify civic participation and engagement?
   c. Solve a particular problem?
   d. Find problems or articulate gaps in community understandings?
   e. Vision for the future?
4. Build shared and agreed upon understandings of CCD objectives.
   a. What developmental assets will we leverage and strengthen?
   b. What capabilities are important?
   c. What capital assets will we leverage and build?
   d. What are the structures for growing youth and community power?
   e. How will we claim publics? (What public? How will we define public?)
5. An agreement on the project vision and planning.
   a. Collaboratively crafting a detailed project proposal
   b. Thinking through project inputs and outputs as well as outcomes
   c. Building shared understandings of success
6. An agreement on the project assessment and evaluation.
   a. How will we know if our partnership is a success?
   b. How will we know if our project is a success?
   c. What data matter?
   d. Who will collect and analyze the data?

Remember, Bill Cleveland's point that relationships are the most important resource in community-based arts. Resource development takes time, energy, and involves real risk. In addition, being able to articulate what resources a partnership will demand from a partner helps organizations decide if my proposal is worth their investment. Once you and a partner have agreed to begin a project together, you can begin to plan and strategize the actual project. Additionally, you can respond to requests for proposals (RFPs) from target organizations in order to build a track record and personal relationship with them.

> **KEY IDEAS**
>
> - The components of a project frame include: impulse, information gathering, and a written paragraph or two articulating ideas as well as potential next steps.
> - The key steps to building a partnership include:
>   1. An agreement to work together
>   2. An agreement on *how* to work together
>   3. An agreement on the placemaking approach/goal
>   4. Building shared and agreed upon understandings of CCD objectives
>   5. An agreement on the project vision and planning
>   6. An agreement on the project assessment and evaluation

## 3.6 ARTICULATING A THEORY OF SOCIAL CHANGE

Figure 1.8 and 3.2 highlight the need to articulate a theory of change and how change is understood. Working toward change means creating structured action plans built from a solid concept of *change* itself. Projects should articulate specific methods—the why of the project or what a colleague calls the "so what." Theories of change address ideas and concepts relationally. Designing effective residency projects, programs, and partnerships depend on using contextually appropriate theories and strategies. Social science and allied health science "theories of change" begin primarily with a problem. However, a "theory of change" in and of itself does not have to be problem-based. A theory of change articulates *how* you expect to move from one condition to another and *why*. If you are trained in pedagogy, theories of change should not pose any difficulty for you. Basically, a theory of change articulates pathways to outcomes. Different fields refer to theories of change with diverse terminology: rubric, roadmap to success, logic model, and logical framework analysis. What all theories of change have in common, however, is a list or map of prospective results and brief narrative or list of assumptions: "document the assumptions that underlie your initiative, including philosophies, principles or values; ways to work together; community context and other assumptions on which you have based your change effort" (Reisman and Gienapp 2004: 2).

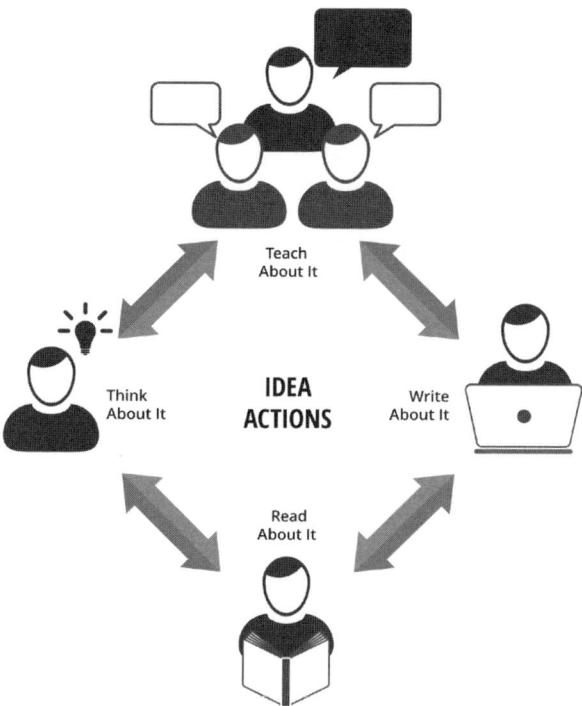

**Figure 3.3:** Theory of change for TFY third space.

Theories of change use graphic mapping to organize complex relationships between short- and long-term goals, common outcomes, and indicators. In other words, *we represent our theory of change visually, not in narrative.* My theory of change is represented in Figure 3.3.

In Figure 3.3 I define *impact* as the circulation and growth of ideas and actions. My *strategy* includes writing a theoretically sound but practically oriented book. I leverage personal assets here, including many years of personal artistic practice, many years of teaching graduate students the practice and methods, and skill in research and philosophy (along with mental processes that focus on systems). *Methods* include research, writing, revision, peer-review, graphic information, student-review, and personal storytelling. My key *assumptions* particularly revolve around the way universities and academics circulate and grow ideas and actions through training programs, research, and writing. This theory of change is *emergent*. Meaning, I understand change to happen in a chaotic system. The path toward adopting Theatre for Youth (TFY) for CCD will be slow and uneven. Individuals will make choices and mark the path toward change through personal and lived experiences.

The book here serves as my "art action" but I will also need to work toward bringing the ideas of the text into publics. I will need to speak about and give master classes on the ideas here, as well as giving conference presentations, and serving as a resource for both community organizations and TFY CCD artists to bring about the social change I desire.

Doug Reeler, of the Community Development Resource Association, usefully articulates three different conceptual categories of change: *emergent*, *transformative*, and *projectable*. Reeler points out that most western funders assume linear models of cause and effect that pull primarily from manufacturing and business models. However, change in social systems is infinitely more complex. Reeler does not understand these categories to be mutual exclusive. Nor can they be considered sequential. Rather, he describes different types of change that can and do exist simultaneously in complex systems. An organization may be particularly stable and using projectable change for projects with adult constituencies within the organization, but have an emergent relationship to their young people. In his essay (2007) published by the Center for Developmental Practice, Reeler says, "Understanding deeply and respecting what change processes already exist can help us to respond to and work within a deeper sense of reality, rather than its shallowly perceived set of problems and needs" (7). Different change conditions will produce different scales of results and impacts, but in all cases "understanding deeply and respecting" the change processes extant allows TFY CCD artists to leverage resources and build assets valued by the community. In all cases, CCD artists need to learn what kind of social change orientation organizations and partners use. Theories of change cannot be imposed externally but rather bubble up from the inside systems. In some cases, CCD processes can work toward articulating understandings of change rather than attempting change itself. To move the needle, first we must understand the gage.

## 3.6.1 Reeler's "Emergent Change"

While we can be either aware or unaware of emergent change in systems, change is always happening. In many ways, life itself can be understood as an emergent system. People learn developmentally and our life paths become clear only as we move forward. The word *emerge* points toward connotations of development, appearings or happenings, and becoming known. Reeler points out,

> This is likely the most prevalent and enduring form of change existing in any living system. Whole books, under various notions of complex systems, chaos theory and emergence, have been written about this kind of change,

describing how small accumulative changes at the margins can affect each other in barely noticeable ways and add up to significant systemic patterns and changes over time; how apparently chaotic systems are governed by deeper, complex social principles that defy easy understanding or manipulation, that confound the best-laid plans, where paths of cause and effect are elusive, caught in eddies of vicious and virtuous circles. Emergent change is paradoxical, where perceptions, feelings and intentions are as powerful as the facts they engage with.

(2007: 10)

Reeler divides emergent change into unconscious and conscious patterns. In each, movement toward change happens erratically lead by personality, emotion, and developmental processes of growth and decay. Reeler graphically represents these ideas in Figure 3.4 & Figure 3.5.

**Figure 3.4:** Reeler's Unconscious Emergent Change Theory (Reeler 2007: 10).

**Figure 3.5:** Reeler's Conscious Emergent Theory of Change (Reeler 2007: 10).

As you can see from these figures, unconscious emergent change environments might be difficult to plan for and to anticipate. Change emerges and then flattens organically. More conscious emergent change environments may be characterized by stable relationships and structures, but not always. In my experience, classrooms, in general, are places of emergent change depending on teacher leadership, time of year, and how the kids are feeling in any given moment. Emergent change happens slowly, developmentally, and gradually. As TFY CCD artists in emergent systems, our largest focus will need to be on reflexive learning and ongoing assessments. Like creative drama lesson plans, we cycle through plan-play-revise-plan-play-revise iterations. TFY third space projects can accomplish disparate goals that include (but are not limited to):

- Art actions can feed change emergence by reflecting back extant relationships, power structures, identities, et cetera. In this way, TFY manifests the change environment itself.
- Art actions can focus on processes and relationships.
- Art action can be a form of action research.
- Art actions can focus on the life of the people while mapping resources and building networks of abundance.

My experience in emergent environments also leads me to point out several inherent risks. Art actions tend to be much more successful at modest levels. Clearly articulating outcomes can also be difficult and frequent monitoring and revision of expected outcomes and indicators can be helpful. Finally, in chaotic systems, the system itself can coalesce around CCD artists fostering a climate of "expertness" rather than investments in the system itself. In other words, rather than promoting abundance, relationships with third-space artists can highlight the "specialness" of the project or program (or the artist), placing it outside of the normal systems as something "other." Public-making will need to be highly choreographed in order to avoid these outcomes.

### 3.6.2 Reeler's "Transformative Change"

Reeler characterizes emergent change as systems of learning and transformative change as systems of *unlearning*. His introduction to transformative change is "through crisis and unlearning" (2007: 11). Based on the U-model of change developed first by Friedrich Glasl and Dirk Lemson in the 1970s (Glasl and Kopp 1999), Reeler describes transformative change as change environments arising from conflict, crisis, or "stuckness." This form of change environment can happen at any level from the small (one human or perhaps a pair relationship) to the epic (the Arab Spring and World War II). Graphically, Reeler represents transformative change in Figure 3.6.

In this Figure you can see how the environment (or the organization, or community, et cetera) moves from a recognition of the crisis, to an investigation of the causes and patterns undergirding the crisis, through a conscious turning point and adoption of new ideas and values. Not all people

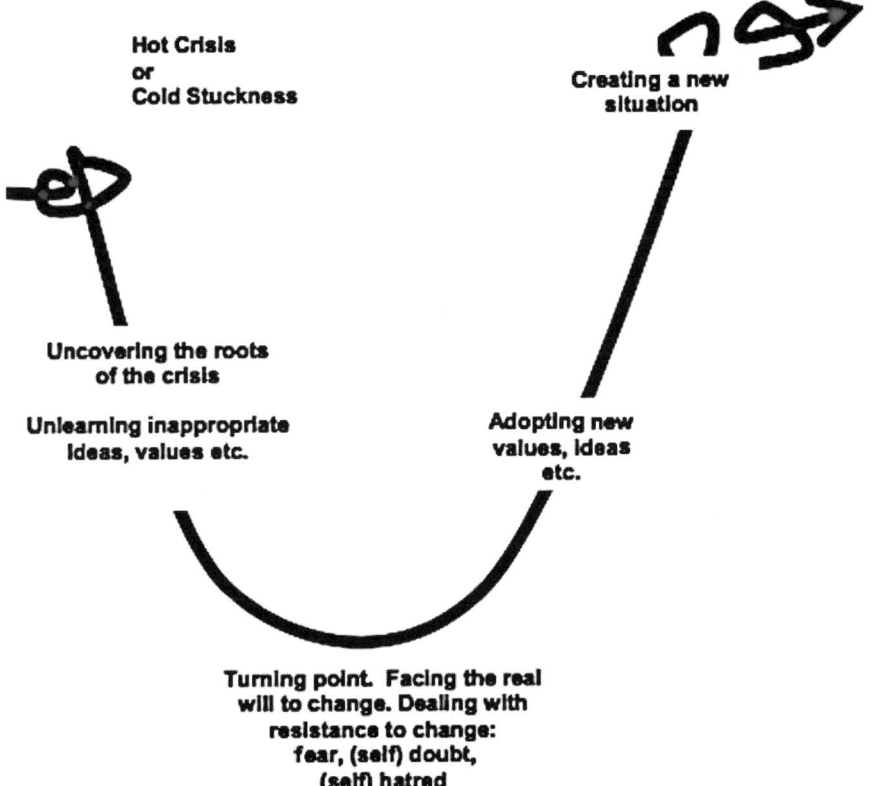

**Figure 3.6:** Reeler's Transformative Change Theory (Reeler 2007: 12).

move through transformative change at the same pace, nor will everyone agree on the underlying causes of the crisis. As the 2014 protests and news coverage in Ferguson, Missouri, make clear, not all people will even agree that there *is* a crisis or stuckness. Reeler points out, "For practitioners, understanding existing transformative change processes or change conditions demands a surfacing of relationships and dynamics that are by their nature contested, denied or hidden and resistant to easy reading" (Reeler 2007: 12). Working in this environment means addressing both advocates for transformation and resistance to transformation. In each case, CCD artists can focus on exposing a community's or organization's values, visions, and beliefs while building space for public discussion and deliberation. Reeler notes,

> Often this means working with resistance to change, most commonly rooted in fear of what might be lost, of doubt or self-doubt as to whether

there is any real alternative that can be embraced, or of hatred, resentment or self-hatred, the residues of the crisis that needs to be dealt with. A period or process of grieving what has to be let go of by those whose identities have been vested in the past may be required. Resistance to change stemming from these things needs to be surfaced and dealt with before any real or lasting change can ensue.

In other words, TFY CCD can expose and embrace transformative change environments, but it cannot create transformation or the will to solve underlying issues. In my work, for example, on the Tohono O'odham reservation mentioned in the preface to this book, the youth surfaced real and painful difficulties with the state of education in their village. We were able to help youth and their elders articulate their values and beliefs and build space for conversation. However, we did not solve the issue nor were we able to create an environment for "unlearning." Each group of stakeholders did agree after our project, however, that a cold stuckness existed. So what can art actions accomplish in transformative environments?

- Art actions in crises can helpfully articulate problems and solutions. Or TFY CCD projects can avoid this binary by focusing on future visioning for the community or organization.
- Projects can uncover the roots of the crisis or stuckness.
- Projects can bring focus to the diversity of community values and identity structures.
- TFY CCD projects and programs can work toward creating momentum toward change by negotiating fear, doubt, and resistance and focusing on abundance and communal meanings.
- After crisis turning points, art actions can promote ideas and new values, and vision toward the future.

These suggestions are not all such projects can accomplish of course, but they are a helpful starting point. An example of an extensive project in this vein is the Sojourn Theatre's Witness Our Schools. Sojourn built a documentary theatre performance around 500 plus interviews conducted in the state of Oregon. The central question of the project was, "What is the mission of public education in our communities today?" Linda Frye Burnham notes,

> The company's goals [...] were to present a performance piece about education that would describe what's happening inside Oregon schools, personify the issues, personalize the voices, clarify existing values and

validate and reveal the wide diversity of community opinions in an atmosphere of mutual respect.

(September 2005: n.p.)

The art action occurred once a week for 36 weeks and was free to the public. After each performance, the company facilitated a town-hall-style dialogue in each location (including the state capital with legislators). The project spanned two years and a key component of the process included interviewing and representing a large diversity of opinions and values. Here, we see an example of a large and intricate CCD work focused on uncovering the roots of the educational crisis in Oregon. Finally, I want to note some of the risks inherent in transformative environments. Any crisis will surface deep and passionate viewpoints that are generally in conflict. Conflict then will be pervasive. Learning how to negotiate conflict while using it to propel creative openness demands deft facilitation and deep listening. People can be afraid and aggressive in their fear and that attitude can sometimes spill over onto the TFY CCD artist. In some cases, CCD artists can be approached by communities or organizations in crisis to alleviate stress in order to foster the status quo. Such projects spark moral concerns about TFY CCD being used as "bread and circuses." Finally, not all communities come out of the conflict turning-point better or more just. Working toward social change demands understanding and clear attention to detail, and is never a forgone conclusion.

### 3.6.3 Reeler's "Projectable Change"

Projectable change may be most familiar to those with experience in business, marketing, manufacturing, public health, and some granting and social service organizations. Projectable change occurs in stable environments with integrated social structures and predictable outcomes. Vaccinations, for example, were a large-scale, projectable change project. When the vaccine for polio was first discovered to be effective in public trials, US federal and state governments, along with community and professional organizations, crafted a detailed and multiyear plan to eradicate the disease further prompted by several severe outbreaks. In the 1980s, the US government and their allies extended disease eradication plans throughout the American Hemisphere. In countries with less stable environments, these efforts were much less successful. In other words, projectable social change needs a constellation of givens in order to function effectively. Reeler notes, "Where the internal and external environments, especially

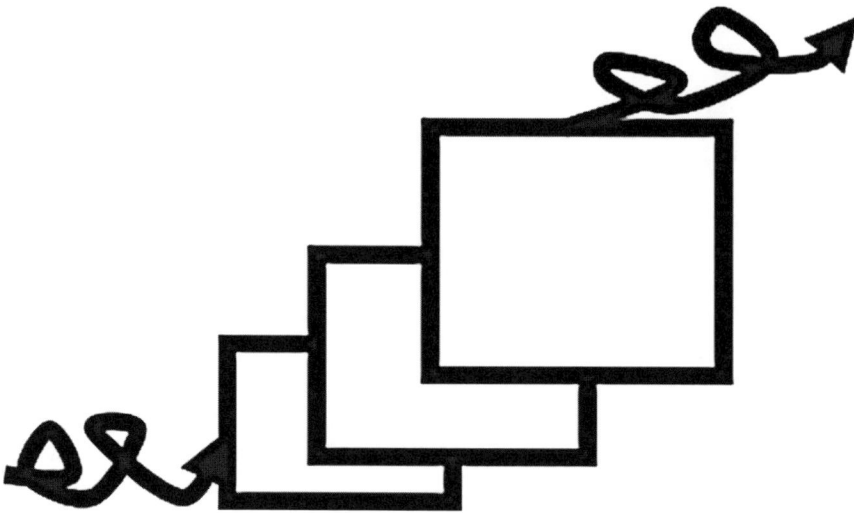

**Figure 3.7:** Reeler's Projectable Change Theory (Reeler 2007: 13).

the relationships, of a system are coherent, stable and predictable enough, and where unpredictable outcomes do not threaten desired results, then the conditions for projectable change arise" (2007: 13). In practice, communities and practitioners often assume a projectable change environment and understand social change through systematic causal patterns. In my experience, however, chaotic systems are much more common than stable ones and social change only rarely occurs in projectable formats. Reeler graphically represents projectable change in Figure 3.7. Projectable social change engagements start by visioning a future time (solving a problem, imagining a future, et cetera) and then work backwards using an "if then" logic model. Art actions and TFY CCD projects function effectively in stable environments.

Jane Reisman and Anne Gienapp (2004) suggest using a "so that" structure to devise projectable theories of change and highlight their causal nature: we do X *so that* Y happens. Generally projectable change environments can be found in highly organized systems in which partners have clear visions of their needs, desired outcomes, and causal pathways to success. Projectable change theories can be quite helpful in organizing large projects over multiple years and provide clear roadmaps for organizing, planning, and assessing projects. Projectable change theories depend on articulating clear and coherent causality. Key here is working in organized systems and with community partners who understand exactly what they want to accomplish and the necessary conditions for success. Generally, I have been contracted by communities or organizations to accomplish extremely specific objectives in support of their overall change plans. Such work can:

- Articulate multiple possible solutions to a problem
- Conceptualize potential outcomes of potential solutions
- Vision toward the future
- Manifest indigenous knowledge and solutions
- Build dialogue in diverse constituencies
- Build community buy-in or investment in the change orientation.

In many ways, the work of a TFY CCD artist in projectable change environments will be to support the community's or organization's planning and practices. Like all change environments, however, working in this way has risk. For one, problem-solving projects imposed from outside communities will only rarely engage the full participation and buy-in of the community. I believe TFY CCD projects should live in the context of the community rather than be dictated. In the case of work with children and marginalized communities, projectable change initiatives can project "needs" onto youth and communities of color. These well-meaning but ethically bankrupt environments default to stereotype and universalist belief structures. In addition, causality can be quite difficult to prove and humans tend to project backwards from effects to draw conclusions not based in authentic knowledge or complex understandings of social structures. For example, US poverty is understood by some to be a function of "laziness" rather than systemic structures prohibiting some from learning or even accessing the tools to survive and flourish.

In order to create work oriented toward social change, we need to clearly articulate, for ourselves and our partners, our theory of change itself. Articulating the change possible in any given environment is an entirely different step to planning the project itself, by the way. Care in thinking through what change can occur promotes TFY CCD practices and the claiming of publics. The different conceptual categories—emergent, transformative, and projectable—contain radically different possibilities. Despite a perhaps inherent desire to affect enormous and lasting social justice change, not all change is possible. An organization or classroom characterized by emergent change cannot craft a project to propel large-scale city-wide change, for example. If an organization is in transformative change cycles, we cannot depend on the status quo remaining stable enough for multiyear, large, complex, projectable change projects. Changes in personnel, for example, can precipitate transformation or be an indicator of transformation already in process. Theories of change can be frustratingly complex and demand both progressive thinking and regressive thinking—meaning hypothesizing forwards and backwards in time.

Malcolm Gladwell (2000) and Alex Begg (2000) separately argue that change in social systems should be understood not like a decision or a revolution—a moment in time or a particular event—but through epidemiological terms—like an infection.

> Instead of social psychology, I would suggest that the epidemiology of ideas is the appropriate discipline for research into social change. In the language of epidemiology, the agent of infection spreads through 'vectors', endlessly reproducing and reinfecting. I would suggest that ideas, practices, modes of behavior, model relationships and dynamics of power are the infective agents, capable of growing, reproducing and transmitting themselves through the vectors. An epidemic is said to occur at surprisingly low levels of infection—as few as 400 per 100,000 new cases a day for an infection lasting only a few days.
>
> (Begg 2000: 255–256)

While the "infection" metaphor took me aback when I first read it, ideas spread from person to person. Anyone active on Facebook or Twitter will have noticed how particular news stories or memes cycle through their feeds in waves and eddies. In addition, change happens incrementally and through every-day acts, be they large or small, as well as in brilliant bursts of transformative learning and experience. Theatre and performance can play a role in both every-day acts and brilliant bursts of transformative experience. I argue in fact that the unique nature of the embodied and communal experience of theatrical performance creates space for radical understandings (Arendt's space of appearances). However, change is not, of course, inherently good. Reeler points out, "All faculties and great sensitivity must be brought to bear in attempting to read the changing processes of people" (Reeler 2007: 19). Understanding these change processes, however, allows us to craft programs, projects, and partnerships paying attention to what Krishna Kumar (2013) calls the five criteria in democratic interventions: effectiveness, efficiency, impact, sustainability, and relevance (12–13).

**KEY IDEAS**

- Working toward change means creating structured action plans built from a solid concept of *change* itself.
- A theory of change articulates *how* you expect to move from one condition to another and *why*.

- Theories of change use graphic mapping to organize complex relationships between short- and long-term goals, common outcomes, and indicators.
- Change environments can be characterized into three overlapping and fluid typographies: emergent, transformative, and projectable.
- Different change conditions produce different scales of possible results and impacts.
- The limits of change depend on what building blocks exist in the community environment and how the attempt at change leverages both existing resources (assets and capital structures) while creating further opportunities.
- Developing a theory of change is a creative visualization activity allowing project/program allies to work together to build outcome specific language while fostering flexible thinking.
- Projectable change environments use causal logic or "so that" statements.
- Emergent and transformative change environments need metaphorical, lateral, and fluid conceptualizations.

## 3.7 PROJECT PLANNING, PROPOSALS, AND MANAGEMENT

### 3.7.1 Project Planning

All projects basically move through the same generic steps:

1. Conceptualizing the project
2. Planning the project/program with your partners (including the placemaking goal, CCD objectives, project inputs, project activities, project outputs, and project outcomes)
3. Collaboratively establishing indicators of success and what evidence will be needed in order to evaluate or assess goals and objectives
4. Doing the project/program
5. Checking that you performed the project/program and created what you said you would create to the level of success promised—evaluation, documentation, and a final report
6. Finally, closing the project down.

In theatre terms, we would talk about planning, producing, rehearsing, performing, and striking, although of course, art actions do not compose the entirety of projects. No project can succeed unless you first begin with the needed components to accomplish the project: what James Lewis (2007) refers to as the "definition of requirements" or the without-which-nots. These requirements could be particular stakeholders, specific knowledge, space, participants, buy-in, funding, transportation, et cetera. To parse a project's requirements, we need to think through project scope, quality, time, cost, and risk. Scope refers to the dimensions of the project. Quality here means how we define success and how we will know success when we see it. Time literally refers to the project's time line or life cycle. Cost itemizes necessary resources including money, of course, but also people, equipment, material, and space—project inputs. Risk means understanding what could go wrong and what could cause the project to fail.

When I went to school I learned the theories, philosophies, and practices of the theatre and theatre with youth but never learned the pragmatics of producing or project management. I learned through trial and error—painful error—that ignoring logistics causes trauma at best and failure at worst. Sun Tzu notes, "The line between disorder and order lies in logistics." Of course, the larger the project the more necessary proper attention to logistical concerns becomes. I now create detailed project proposals to ground community relationships, planning, and evaluation. I am, in fact, a mad fiend for planning. And while I will admit that the hours of planning necessary to produce high-quality projects and partnerships can be frustrating, I hate to fail. Even worse, knowing I failed through lack of planning and due diligence. Cleveland notes, "clear intentions produce better outcomes" (2012: 306). Figure 3.8 graphically represents the logic model I use when planning a TFY CCD project and crafting a formal proposal. What will we do in order to produce the desired outcome?

The processes of TFY third space follow a particular iterative cycle that I explain using Figure 3.9. In Section 1, I explained this graphic by pointing out that each box represents crucial decision locations and I offered several taxonomies or frames of reference useful for the planning and strategic development of both the placemaking approach and the CCD objectives. Figure 3.8 articulates how TFY CCD works.

It is important to consider these figures together because you will note that project outcomes hinge on how change itself is understood and articulated.

A few questions help navigate the planning process. I advocate the following:

1. Who is your community?
2. What is your placemaking goal?
3. What assets and capabilities will your program/project/partnership grow?
4. What resources are needed to make the program possible? What capital systems, behaviors, structures, assets or capacities will you leverage? How

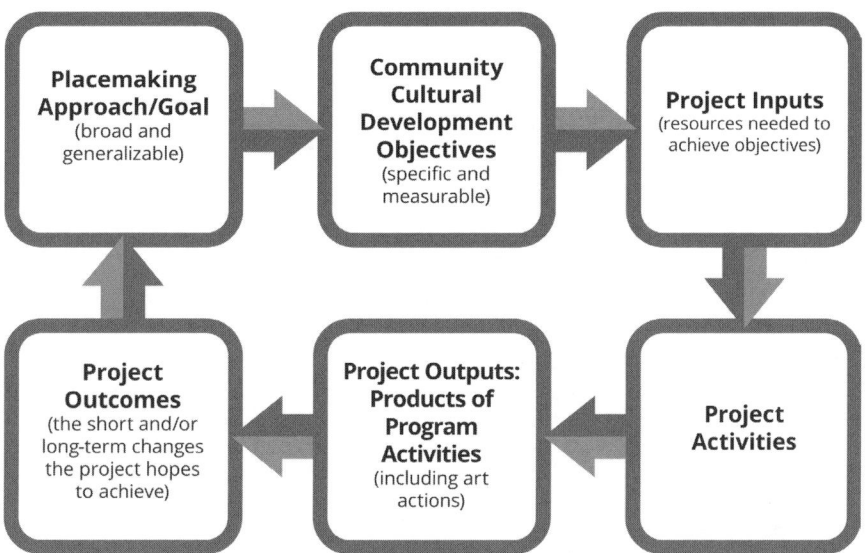

**Figure 3.8:** Project planning logic model.

will you negotiate building capabilities? What are the project/project's objectives?
5. What change are you hoping to achieve?
6. What is the change environment?
7. What does your program/project plan do to create the desired change?
8. What products will result from program activities?
9. What defines success? What level or amount of change needs to occur for you and your allies to feel successful? Short-term outcomes? Long-term outcomes?
10. If you achieve these outcomes, will the conditions in #2 and #3 be addressed?
11. Is it logical to believe that the products of your program activities (#8) have the potential to produce your desired outcomes and results (#5)?
12. What indicators will you use to evaluate your project's effectiveness, efficiency, impact, sustainability and relevance?

An example will be helpful here. Every year I teach a project-based, graduate-level course in community-based theatre with children and youth. There, I plan a community-based project in which class members function as an artistic team while also learning the knowledge, skills, processes, and ethics of CCD. In the fall of 2013, a local fifth-grade teacher contacted me to ask whether I would partner with his English Language Learners class. His curriculum covers US government and history and he wondered whether

**Figure 3.9:** TFY CCD process.

we could help him teach the continental congress in an engaging form. I first explained we were not teaching artists but CCD specialists, and helped him understand the difference. He became excited about the possibilities. We decided on *civic participation and engagement* as our placemaking approach. I write this from the point of view of my preliminary planning so you can look over my shoulder. So, let us walk through some of these questions.

1. *Who is your community?* An elementary school with before and after school care, the school serves kindergarten through fifth grade. In my preliminary research, I learn that the school is a Title I school, which means over half of the youth there are considered low income by the federal government. Title I funding also means that the school has a Site Council: a group of parents, teachers, and community members who help provide governance and do a certain amount of resource allocation. Looking online, I discover the students at the school perform adequately on the math portion of our state's standardized test but rather poorly on

writing and reading. Mapping the census data onto the school's location, I discover a high majority of homes in which English is not the first language. Reading the school's website, I learn the school also has a parent–teacher organization and focuses on technology. The school provides each student a laptop. To learn more about this particular community, however, I will need to go and meet with all these groups, and spend time at the site: learning, observing, and hanging out. I discover the principal is quite new, in his first year of service, and the Arizona Department of Education school report and the school's current website do not quite match. For example, the new principal seems to have changed the school's mission statement to focus on achievement. Given new leadership, I believe the school will be either in emergent or transformative change; however, without more time in situ, I cannot make that determination.

2. *What is your placemaking goal?* The teacher and I decide on increasing civic participation and engagement as our approach.
3. *What assets and capabilities will your program/project/partnership grow?* We plan to divide the youth and my students into small teams allowing each to address their own desired capability and asset. We plan to start conversations with these teams using Nussbaum's "senses, imagination, and thought" and/or "affiliation" capabilities and/or Alkire's "friendship" or "self-integration" capabilities. I know from conversations with the teacher that bullying has been an issue under negotiation in the classroom for several months so we may want to focus on interpersonal and intrapersonal growth. However, without discussion with the youth themselves, we do not yet know what assets the youth wish to address.
4. *What kind of change are you hoping to achieve?* We will not know this until we have a conversation with the fifth-grade teams. Knowing what questions to ask them will be important.
5. *What is the change environment?* Again, like the previous questions, we do not have enough information yet to make this determination. However, based on my conversations with the teacher and my read of the school's website and department of education "report card," I expect we will discover an emergent or transformative space of change.
6. *What does your program/project plan do to create the desired change?* Once we know what the small teams wish to address, we can productively strategize on what kinds of creative art actions and public-makings will be most useful and efficient in achieving the students' goals and objectives.
7. *What resources are needed to make the program possible? What capital systems, behaviors, structures, assets or capacities will you leverage? How will you negotiate building capabilities? What are the program/project's objectives?* Currently, I do not have enough information to know

these things; however, I do know that we will have multiple objectives including learning objectives from the classroom teacher supporting our state's "college and career readiness standards" and learning objectives supporting my graduate course outcomes. Other resources I know we will need include time, access, and permissions from parents/guardians. Additionally, if the primary school can provide my class a room for our course meetings, we will be able to streamline transition time from the ASU to the elementary school. We do not yet know enough to understand what capital systems and personal and cultural assets the youth will be able to leverage toward achieving their objectives.

8. *What products will result from program activities?* Again, this is unknown as of yet; however, we will need to integrate into the learning environment of the school and the classroom. We will therefore need to integrate products displaying pertinent learning goals and educational achievement objectives. We will frame these using the Arizona College and Career Readiness Standards.
9. *What defines success? What level or amount of change needs to occur for you and your allies to feel successful? Short-term outcomes? Long-term outcomes?* Defining success will need to be based on nested sets of outcomes. Given the time frame, only short-term outcomes will be possible. Added to this, projects will need to meet: the youth and partnering graduate students' definitions of success; my definitions as the instructor for the graduate-level class; the partnering teacher's definitions of success; as well as the principal's and district's definitions. If the parent–teacher organization or the site council is involved, their understandings too will need to be taken into account.
10. *If you achieve these outcomes, will the conditions in #2 and #3 be addressed?* This question is an important and vital check on the relationship between the desired change and the program activities. This question asks teams to parse the logic of their plans of action and plan appropriate public-making.
11. *Is it logical to believe the products of your program activities (#7) have the potential to produce your desired outcomes and results (#3 & #4)?* Like question ten, this question asks teams to consider the logic of their activities as well as the relationships of activities to desired outcomes. Carefully, thinking through questions ten and eleven allows CCD artists and their partners and allies to build effective, efficient, and relevant programs aimed at achieving intended outcomes.
12. *What indicators will you use to evaluate your project's effectiveness, efficiency, impact, sustainability, and relevance?* Conceptualizing/planning and evaluation are two sides of the same sheet of paper. We measure what

we care about and the simple fact is that we are more likely to achieve our goals and objectives if we define and measure them carefully. I discuss measurement and evaluation in more detail later in Section 3.9.

In order to move to the next step in my planning, I have to do more research and develop a closer relationship with my partnering teacher. At this point in my discovery process, I do not know if the school itself will also be a partner.

Taking the above real example as a base, I want to create hypothetical social change outcome for this project using an emergent theory of change in order to provide an example of how we create a project or program's change theory. Say one team of fifth graders decides to address "bullying." From previous research and life experiences, I understand bullying as the *purposive and reoccurring victimization of one child or group by another child or group*. Bullying has multiple causes but is characterized both by repetition and by verbal, social, or physical threats. Bullying is about the practice of *power over* another through violence. In my own experiences in classroom environments and as a mother, I also know that young people (and adults) frequently conflate rudeness and meanness with bullying. A focus on building assets and capabilities in friendship, interpersonal, and intrapersonal knowledge can help promote more positive social environments. In Figure 3.10 you can see that conceptualizing a change theory involves articulating desired *impact*, *strategies*, *methods*, and *assumptions*.

What can a particular project accomplish? Animating Democracy, a program of Americans for the Arts has a large section of their website devoted to understanding the impact of the arts. Over the many years they have been working on civically engaged arts practices, they have developed a model articulating the most common impacts of the arts on social living and civic

**Figure 3.10:** TFY CCD Processes Detail.

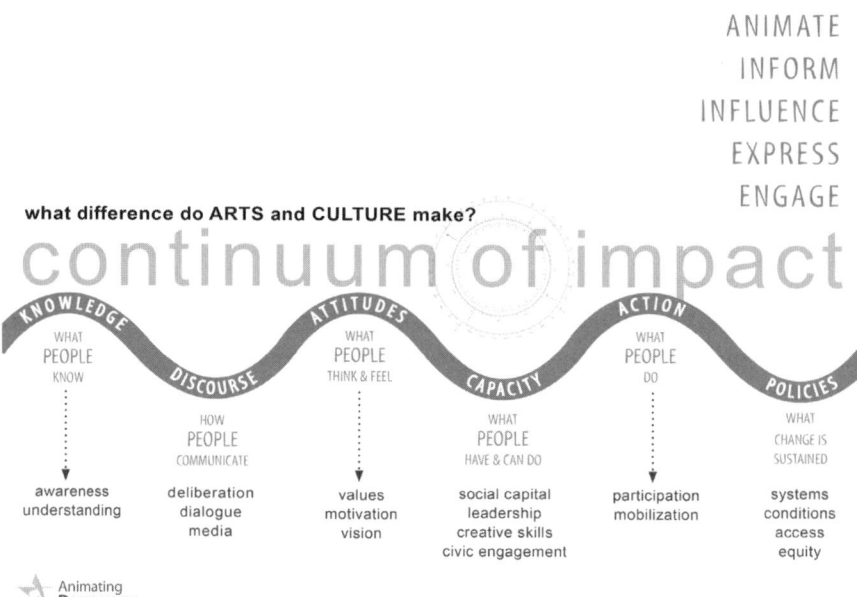

**Figure 3.11:** Animating Democracy 2013: http://animatingdemocracy.org/sites/default/files/sites/default/files/ContinuumOFImpactFINAL.pdf.

practices. Figure 3.11 maps typical influences art actions can have in social change arenas.

This illustration organizes change from the individual to the system but should not be understood as sequential. The "policies" section could literally wrap around to meet "knowledge" like a Mobius strip. Social change, as explored in the previous section, depends on what structures already exist and how attempts at change leverage both existing resources (i.e., assets and capital structures) while creating opportunity for further change. Animating Democracy's continuum can help in another way, too; in planning, deciding what action to take, what process to engage, and which stakeholders are needed in the planning process.

Developing a theory of change should be considered a creative visualization activity allowing project/program allies to work together to build outcome-specific language while also fostering flexible thinking. The different change environments demand different visual logic structures. Only in the projectable change environment can planners use causal logic or "if then" statements. Emergent and transformative change environments need more metaphorical, lateral, and fluid thought. From conversations with the teacher, I understand that the class has spent considerable time discussing bullying, particularly around the emotional responses of the

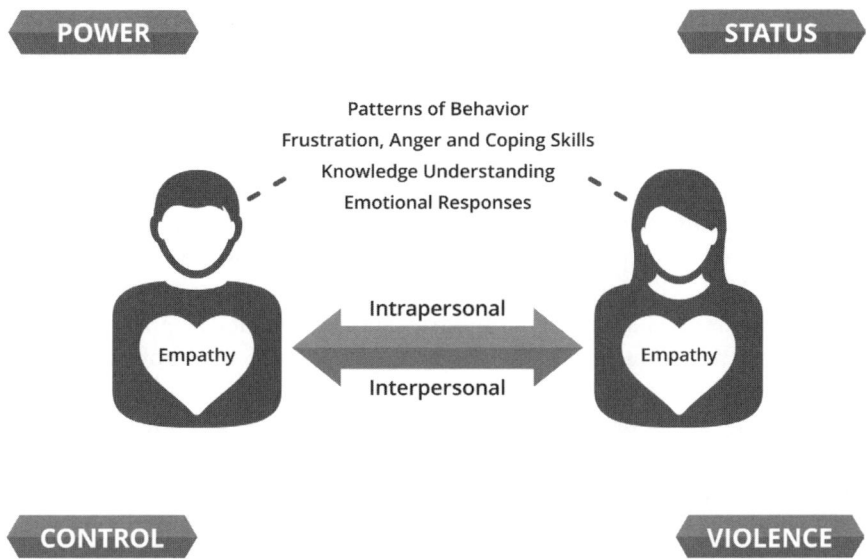

**Figure 3.12:** Anti-bullying Emergent Change Theory.

victims and strategies for negotiating conflict directly. Returning to our questions, the hypothetical condition we wish to address is "bullying." We hope to achieve a decrease in bullying behavior in both the classroom and fifth grade (three classrooms) by building further assets in "friendship" and "self-integration" capabilities. An emergent change environment is characterized by learning in action, by development in fits and starts, and by diversity. Figure 3.12 is my graphic of a preliminary theory of emergent change to decrease bullying in the fifth-grade classroom. I particularly focus on an impact of knowledge, awareness, and understanding with a secondary focus on changing how people communicate with themselves and others.

We define our project's contribution to social change, our *impact*, as a change in how people communicate. I *assume* many individuals will not be aware of their own patterns of behavior, preferred power negotiations or the manner in which they handle frustration and anger. My assumptions also include the vexed association between power, status, control, and violence. Our *strategies* focus on building empathy along with practical skills in self-regulation and nonviolent communication. In a real scenario, this theory of change would, of course, be built with my fifth-grade partners, who likely would have different assumptions. While adult experiences and knowledge systems can help guide collaborative theories of change, youthful partners should have as much say in the process as adults. In a theory of change, strategies lead directly to *methods*; if we assume self-regulation skills and nonviolent communication skills will be useful then we will methodologically teach and evaluate those skills. In an emergent change scenario, learning happens *in action* highlighting the need for formative assessments and iterative planning/playing cycles. In my experience working with youth toward social change, emergent change environments tend to be quite common. Finally, in an emergent system, no plan should be considered a recipe for success; rather plans should be understood as fluid and infinitely malleable to the needs of the emerging environment. Art action designs should be similarly fluid acknowledging the multiple symbolic representations of the theory. Additionally, the above theory of change highlights particularly foci for the making/devising/studio practices of the project and program, including nonviolent communication skills, modeling self-regulation, labeling, and exploring emotional responses to violent stimuli.

A solid and thoughtful change theory forms one of the keystones of the TFY CCD practice. Methodologies used brings us back to a discussion on crafting project proposals.

Richard Newton (2006) advises there are six activities in producing a project plan:

1. Divide the overall project into component tasks, and continue to divide the component tasks into smaller tasks until you have a comprehensive list of things that must be done to complete the project.
2. Estimate the length of time each task will take.
3. Order the tasks into the right sequence.
4. Determine the people, money and other resources you need to meet this plan and determine their associated costs.
5. Check what resources you actually have available and refine your plan to take account of this. Once you have done this you have a complete plan.
6. Review the plan—does it match your needs? Looking at the plan—can you actually do it, and should you do it?

(Newton 2006: 38)

Taking the advice above into account, let me share the specific components of the project proposals I create:

1. Project title
2. Key personnel contact information
3. Executive summary

4. Project placemaking approach/goal
5. CCD objectives
6. Project description
7. Project theory of change
8. Project requirements and budget
9. Project time line
10. Project risks
11. Exit criteria and evaluation protocols
12. Organization/artist information

Let us break down the above sections.

## 3.7.2 Proposal Components

A *project title* should be clear and easy to remember. An advertising friend teases me for including ":" in my project titles, but sometimes subtitles work for me. You will have to make you own decisions with regard to titles. In the best of projects, community members including children and youth name their work. I tend to prefer evocative and poetic titles but my partners frequently prefer descriptive titles. Titles help create anticipation while also becoming a synecdoche for the project as a whole.

Including *key personnel contact information* allows partners to quickly and easily get in touch without having to hunt through old e-mails or cell phone contacts.

An *executive summary* briefly condenses an entire project into one paragraph.

I discuss *project placemaking goals* extensively elsewhere in this text. The five general approaches include: building effective connections and shared values; intensifying civic participation and engagement; solving a particular problem; problem finding; and visioning for the future.

*Project objectives* should be clear and specific. The CCD objectives I use (covered extensively in Section 1) grow from positive youth development protocols, capabilities development, deliberative democracy, the politics of recognition, and an ecological framework of community cultural capital. Project objectives form the cornerstone for both project development and assessment. A key component of TFY CCD practices includes reflective practice. In other words, we are responsible for measuring our accomplishments. Flerx points out,

- Program planning and evaluation should occur simultaneously.

- A clearly articulated program plan is the first step for both program development and evaluation planning.
- The broad goals of the program must be broken down into objectives that are specific, observable and measurable.
- The target population must be well-defined.
- There must be a theoretical link between the goals and objectives, the program activities (strategies/interventions), and the desired outcomes.
- Program evaluation includes an assessment of the program's success in implementation (process evaluation), as well as in achieving the desired outcomes (outcome evaluation).
- A successful program achieves outcomes that match the outcome objectives set during the planning phase.

(Flerx 2007: 159)

Working more succinctly, Lewis notes objectives should be *SMART*, or *s*pecific, *m*easurable, *a*ttainable, *r*ealistic, *t*ime-limited (Lewis 2007: 51). I have a tendency to overload projects with objectives. However, for every objective I add, I am responsible for assessing how well we achieved that objective. Reminding myself to keep objectives SMART helps me to remain practical.

The *project description* performs exactly that task in as few paragraphs as possible. The more succinct and pointed your proposal, the better. Here, you should include the ways in which the project addresses the approach. For example in a project I completed in 2013, we focused on "building effective connections and shared values." The project partnered cultural institutions in Mesa, Arizona (two museums and an arts center) with youth from a local Boys and Girls Club. The topic of the larger project—of which we were one wing—was "At Home in the Desert." Our partnering organizations wanted to focus on bringing more youth, particularly low-income youth, into their organizations. Additionally, the organizations wanted to learn how youth understood them as *places*. We created a digital storytelling residency in which youth composed short video pieces exploring the three sites, explaining through narrative and image the *why* of each place. We used geocaching—a treasuring hunting game using GPS coordinates and smart phones—to cache the stories. By scanning a quick read code, anyone discovering the cache (created by a local visual artist) could enjoy the short digital story. The pieces created shared connections between the youth and the cultural places. In each, youth shared *why* individuals might wish to participate and how they understood each location. By caching the stories, we mapped the young people's values and visions directly onto the sites so the placemaking and public-making could continue as an iterative process.

Again, we have discussed *theories of change*. Theories of change function best as graphic representations or "infographics." What specifically will be the project's targeted impact? What are the strategies to achieve the impact and what assumptions does the project make? What methods will be used?

*Project requirements and budget* detail the resources necessary to successfully complete the project. These can be as simple as rehearsal space and an auditorium or as complex as the needs of a festival with thousands of attendees. Be sure and detail what resources and assets you will leverage as well as ones you need. In the storytelling geocache project, we leveraged proximity—all Mesa project partners were within two miles of one another, of School of Film, Dance & Theatre students and equipment, and of the social capital held by the education director at one of the partnering institutions, and the credibility she had built from having long-term relationships and trust. I divide support into in-kind support and direct support. In-kind support can include space, equipment, personnel time, et cetera. Direct support refers to money and consumable materials. If your project depends on advertising or direct recruitment—for example, to bring a diverse audience to a performance and open forum—do not forget to include that here. Additionally, do not forget to include information and feedback needs in your assessment. Closed lines of communication create untenable conditions and are a risk in and of themselves.

*A project time line* will most likely be in the form of a calendar with project milestones and ongoing assessment times noted.

*Project risks* include anything that logically might cause the project to fail. Although, I note that while an asteroid might hit the earth during your project, statistically it would be illogical to build a contingency plan for such an event.

*Exit criteria and evaluation protocols* relate directly back to the project's objectives and theory of change. How will you collect information along the way and monitor your progress? What will you document and how? Will you create a final project report? Will project partners meet for exit evaluations or focus interviews? Measurement does not of course always mean quantification. I explore evaluation and assessment in detail in the next section, but clear planning creates clear evaluation. We evaluate what we care about, and achieving what we say we will speaks to our integrity. Michael Smith (2010) notes, "very concretely, at least a modest amount, around 15% of a program budget, should be allocated to evaluation of a program" (Smith 2010: 7). Here, you should remember a "budget" includes much more than money, encompassing all project requirements necessary for success, including time. For several years now, I have been working with colleagues across the United States as part of Imagining America's Assessing the Practices of Public Scholarship and Art research group (APPS). While primarily exploring university/community partnerships, APPS focuses on how assessment and evaluation undergirds all aspects of community partnership and collaboration, using the term *integrated assessment*. APPS lists the following core values of integrated assessment on their website, http://imaginingamerica.org/research/assessment:

> *Collaboration*—An integrated approach to assessment engages community- and university-based stakeholders in defining what are meaningful outcomes and indicators of success, long before the assessment itself begins, and often in implementing the evaluation activity itself. It is grounded in a shared understanding of interrelated goals.
>
> *Reciprocity*—An integrated approach to assessment is useful to community- and university-based stakeholders. It goes back to the stakeholders involved; it invites reflection, feedback, and critique.
>
> *Generativity*—An integrated approach to assessment feeds the project, program, or course at hand. At the same time, it looks beyond the semester or project unit and invites stakeholders to evaluate the overall, long-term relationships at the heart of community-based education and public scholarship. It is part of an ongoing and dynamic process of programmatic, institutional, community, and/or regional development.
>
> *Rigor*—An integrated approach to assessment utilizes sound evaluation methodologies and practices.
>
> *Practicability*—An integrated approach to assessment promotes activities that are proportionate to the project and resources available.

Keeping these principles in mind helps craft evaluation protocols. Exit criteria include how you will close a project down. What are the final deliverables? How will you ritually mark project closure while promoting creative sustainability?

*Organization/artist information* includes brief biographies of the artists or company involved. I include an ethical statement and an aesthetic statement, too. If you are proposing a new project to a community with whom you have never worked, you might want to include work samples (e.g., images or brief video clips) of past projects you have successfully completed. If you work outside of an established theatre company, I suggest creating and maintaining a digital portfolio easily accessible to potential allies or partners.

Developing action plans and managing multiple project components can seem overwhelming but theatre artists perform these functions all the time. We plan, produce, rehearse, perform, and strike. We make plans for what could go wrong and how we will solve the problems. Theatre artists' favorite "war stories" revolve around forgotten lines, lost props, botched entrances, or rushing to bail the play's lead out of jail. Well-written project proposals create roadmaps for logistical and strategic success. An example of a project proposal might be helpful here. As we have already extensively discussed my course-based, fifth-grade spring 2014 project, let me share the actual proposal developed with my partnering teacher.

## 3.7.3 Project Proposal Example

Teacher Name
X Elementary School
ELD 5th Grade—ASU THP 514 Projects in Community-based Theatre Partnership Plan

*Never doubt that a small group of thoughtful, committed, citizens can change the world. Indeed, it is the only thing that ever has.*
*– Margaret Mead*

**Project title:** X Scholars Making the World a Better Place.

**Executive summary**
This Spring 2014 partnership between X's 5th Grade class at X Elementary and Stephani Etheridge Woodson's THP 514 class at ASU will focus on inquiry-based performance processes for each group of learners. Divided into five teams and six 5th graders and two/three graduate students), each team will each team will

1. Decide on an issue or problem and the measurements of 'success' they wish to use
2. Conduct background research
3. Devise a creative solution or approach using an art action
4. Present an "informance" to an appropriate and public audience on 23 April
5. Collaboratively evaluate project success (30 April) and pizza party

*(continued)*

Conducted on Wednesdays, from 2–3pm, the project has ten–twelve contact hours and associated individual work.

**Project approach**
Intensify civic participation and engagement through the creation of a civic project positioning youthful participants as experts and creative assets to their classroom, school and surrounding community.

**Project Objectives: 5th Grade Students Learning Objectives**
<u>AZ College and Career Readiness Standards</u>

- Write informative/explanatory texts to examine a topic and convey ideas and information clearly (5.W.2)
- Write narratives to develop real or imagined experiences or events using effective technique, descriptive details, and clear event sequences (5.W.3)
- Conduct short research projects that use several sources to build knowledge through investigation of different aspects of a topic (5.W.7)
- Recall relevant information from experiences or gather relevant information from print and digital sources; summarize or paraphrase information in notes and finished work, and provide a list of sources (5.W.8)
- Adapt speech to a variety of contexts and tasks, using formal English when appropriate to task and situation (see Grade 5 5 Language standards 1 and 3 for specific expectations.) (5.SL.6)

<u>Vocabulary Targets</u>

| | |
|---|---|
| Town meeting | Protest |
| Humane | Boycott |
| Equality | Justice |
| Poverty | Diversity |
| Famine | Culture |
| Legislature | |

**Asset Development**
<u>Creativity Skills</u>

The following graphic illustrates the five key components of "creative openness" the project will focus on building.

*(continued)*

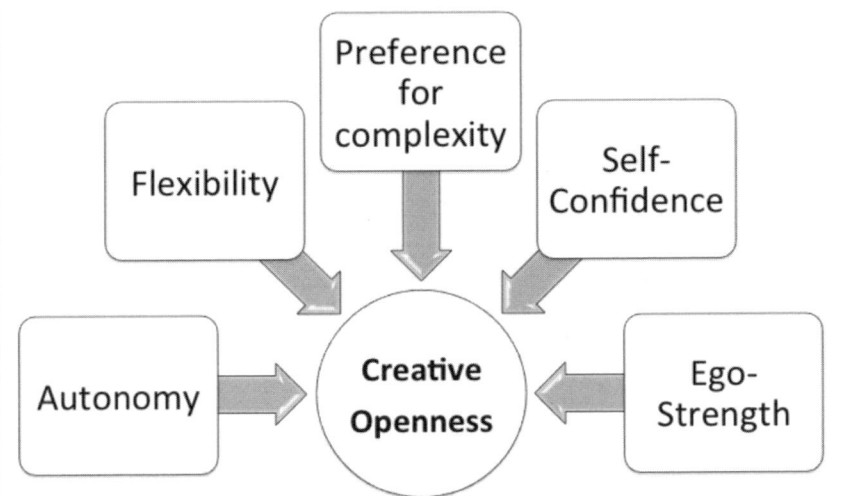

**Graduate Students Learning Objectives:**

- Build alliances among people and groups with diverse interests
- Claim legitimacy for the work/partnership/project and public agency for children and youth
- Negotiate agreements between the possible, the probable and the desired
- Practice nonviolent communication and active listening
- Negotiate multilingual groups
- Craft narrative structures in multiple registers
- Foster participants' creative risk taking and symbolic literacies including knowledge of the creative process
- Grasp educational system
- Parse community's diverse aesthetic languages and use them appropriately and ethically
- Assess and leverage ensemble participation and creative capacity
- Foster collaborative risk taking and structure participatory making
- Honestly and collaboratively reflect on and hone aesthetic structures
- Form purposeful relationships and networks; sustain them through inclusive and democratic planning; negotiate difficulties with transparency; reflect together on the import of the project; and collaboratively assess its successes and failures
- Give equal weight to process and product
- Structure creative flow from abstract concept to concrete product

(*continued*)

- Understand the principles and methods of collaborative evaluation and assessment

**Project description**
Make the world a better place by:
   Partnering in small groups, adult artists and youth artists will:

   a. Decide on an issue or problem they wish to address and the scale by which they wish to be judged
      - Define impact.
      - Craft evaluation protocol.
   b. Conduct background research
   c. Devise a creative solution and art action
   d. Present an "informance" to an appropriate and public audience toward change
   e. Present an overview of the community cultural development project and publically evaluate success

**Project theory of change**

- Change will be understood as emergent.
- Projects decided upon by the groups must be small enough to present the possibility of change.
- We will use the Animating Democracy Impact Continuum (included below) to understand how projects can make a "difference." Change will be understood primarily at the individual level as learning/knowledge and asset development in collaborative efficacy.
- Each small group will create their own change theory with adult input and help.

**Project requirements and budget**
Minimal. Time in partnership. A classroom for the use of the residency graduate classwork, appropriate support from teachers and administration for audience building.

**Project time line**
   Jan 29 Meet at elementary school: introduction by teacher
   Feb 5 Meet at ASU: Adult resident artists plan first day small group residency programs. Include space to set project, decide upon impact and evaluation methods. For both the project as a whole and for the adult

*(continued)*

learners. The kids will grade the adults cumulative work/partnership with them.
Feb 12 Residency 2–3
Feb 19 Adult resident artists plan unit residency with tentative audience, et cetera. Residency 2–3
Feb 26 Residency 2–3
March 5 Residency 2–3
March 12 SPRING BREAK
March 19 Residency 2–3
March 26 Residency 2–3
Week of April 2 Residency 2–3
Week of April 9 AIMS testing, no meetings
April 16 Independent meetings with teams
April 23 School presentations/informances
April 30 Residency 2–3: Last class day, pizza celebration/final evaluation

**Project risks**

- Youth may feel unhappy with what they create.
- Interpersonal difficulties may arise.
- Adults may have difficulty communicating with their young partners.
- Adults may feel unsure or unhappy about what they create.
- School and district administration may dismiss youth's collaborative efficacy and deny access to public-making.

**Exit criteria & evaluation protocols**
The final day will be a pizza party plus final public evaluation presented to the whole class by each of the small groups. Each small group will develop evaluation protocols and data gathering with partnering teacher and Etheridge Woodson input. Fifth graders will evaluate/grade their facilitating artists through the use of a rubric developed collaboratively. Graduate students will also complete a written self-evaluation and meet individually with Etheridge Woodson. The project will not seek photo release permission from the class as a whole so all photographs and video will be kept private. Individual groups however may seek photo/video permission from parents/guardians if youth participants decide on a project requiring such. The partnering teacher will document the project for action research as an ELD case study in authentic, contextual English language use.

*(continued)*

| Objective | Data source | Responsibility | When completed |
|---|---|---|---|
| Common Core Standards | Decided on by small groups | Individual groups | Ongoing/presented 30 April |
| Vocabulary Targets | Decided on by small groups | Individual groups | Ongoing/presented 30 April |
| Creative Openness | Self-assessment questionnaire/census | Etheridge Woodson | 30 April |
| Graduate Student Performance | Rubric created by partnering teacher and 5th grade students | 5th grade students | 30 April |
| Graduate Student Objectives | 1. Narrative self evaluation 2. Etheridge Woodson evaluation | Individual graduate students and professor | Completed by 7 May |
| Individual Project Objectives and Theory of Change | Decided on by small groups | Individual groups | On going/presented 30 April |
| Overall Partnership Success | Final partner meeting | Partnering teacher and Etheridge Woodson | 1 June |

**Organization/Artist information**

This graduate-level project is grounded in the praxis—theories and practice—of community-based arts with various communities of location, spirit, experience, or tradition. Community-based art projects bring artists together with communities to create art rooted in the needs, values, desires, triumphs, and challenges of that community. The students in this course are masters and doctoral level students drawn from the Herberger Institute for Design and the Arts and all activities take place under the supervision of Professor Stephani Etheridge Woodson. All students have AZ state fingerprint clearance cards and commit to the following values:

- mutual respect among persons
- deliberative democracy
- the human right of all individuals to take part in cultural life.

This project proposal outlines a process of engagement while leaving space for the individual groups to construct their own small-scale projects. Five groups tackled five different issues decided on collaboratively, set their own metrics of success, and developed their own theories of change. As both groups of learners (the 5th graders and the graduate students) were imbedded in classes, the partnering teaching and I included our own necessary learning objectives. Evaluation and assessment was ongoing but primarily shared at the end of the process as dictated by the needs of the projects and the course work/learning environment. I cover principles of project assessment more completely in Section 3.8.

### 3.7.4 Project Management

Project management is a large field with several professional organizations and best practices standards. CCD processes share many of these same management requirements. Chrislip (2002) notes,

> The [...] project director needs a high level of credibility with the stakeholder group. The director must work constructively with stakeholders as well as funders, media, and the broader community. Supporting staff members need skills in writing memorandums, scheduling meetings, taking care of logistics needs, transcribing meeting notes, contacting stakeholders by telephone, and so on. [Responsibilities include]:
> - Communicating with stakeholders
> - Meeting logistics
> - Financial management
> - Resource development
> - Coordinating steering committee, stakeholder, and other working group meeting schedules
> - Organizing outreach to media, the public, and formal organizations
> - Working with process and content experts
> - Documenting the process
>
> (90)

In my experience, outlining job responsibilities ensures that crucial tasks do not get overlooked. Who is the primary communication contact? Who handles meeting logistics? Financial management and resource development? Assigning different individuals to each of these tasks highlights the need for coordination meetings, and will be necessary for large and complex projects.

For small-scale projects like the example above, one person can serve as the overall project director easily. Again, the importance of the project proposal here cannot be overstated. A clear and careful proposal provides well-defined guidelines for project management.

Although we cannot plan for all contingencies, I have had certain topics or issues come up again and again, either in my work or in the work of colleagues. The first has to do with collective authorship and ownership—particularly relevant when project outcomes include a written and potentially publishable script. When a group of artists labor together to create a piece of art, who owns that art? I believe a more expansive way to consider this issue asks what do you want to do with the art? For example, do you understand the script as a commercial property? I have never seen a community-based performance-work successfully recreated in another community. The work of community-based theatre by its nature is not commercial and does not travel. Like a library, I believe the art created thusly belongs to everyone—TFY CCD practices craft *publics*. That being said, TFY CCD artists will want to have unlimited use of the work for their own professional growth and development. You will want to be able to include exerts in your portfolio, to write about your experiences, or share the work at conferences or with other potential partners. Additionally, there may be instances where CCD artists partner with commercial institutions or craft training or experiential engagements with commercial potential. In these cases, TFY CCD artists should reserve those rights from the outset while making the reasons explicitly clear to project partners. As a salaried academic, I do not depend on independent contractor income, as do many individual artists or small nonprofit theatres—I have the ability to be generous with my time and craft. Artists deserve to make a living from their work, but they are morally obligated not to "steal" the creativity of their community partners. Nor should artists even create the appearance of impropriety—the onus to initiate this discussion falls onto the artist or artistic company. I use Creative Commons copyright licenses—and apply these to all material generated by a project when I am able. Created for sharing and disseminating material online, Creative Commons has six licenses with diverse restrictions or freedoms on each. In my experience, project partners generally wish that the material created is shared widely and freely—in fact, often the placemaking strategy depends on this freedom. Of course, this does not apply across the board. Also note, if collaborating youth are under eighteen, you will need explicit permission from both the youth and the youth's legal guardian to use images, video, or audio featuring the child. In certain scenarios, for example hospitals, mental health, or detention facilities, privacy laws preclude any video or pictorial representation. Who maintains the archive of waivers, and what rights the waivers guarantee should also be worked out during the project planning stage.

Open or closed studio should also be something you, your partnering organization, and collaborating youth discuss. Can anyone join rehearsals? Will younger siblings be invited to participate? Parents? How fluid an environment will you promote? Many of the youth with whom I work, serve as primary caregivers for younger siblings before and after school. I am a more-the-merrier kind of woman, but never knowing who will come to studio can make for tense planning. You will need to think about these aspects. Additionally, will you require transportation? Will you need to transport youth? How will you handle permissions, insurance, and safety—for both you and your collaborating youth? Again, these aspects need to be clearly outlined during planning stages. Often, partnering organizations have policies in place already covering photo releases, transportation, et cetera. They will likely require crossover training to address their safety concerns. Over the years, I have been trained to drive multiple kinds of vehicles, attended safety courses, anti-bullying courses, safe zone courses, warning signals for suicide, and been fingerprinted, background-checked, and drug-tested tens of times. No training is wasted; knowledge is power. Please do not feel insulted or as if your partners do not trust you. Rather, their due diligence brands your project partners as thoughtful, honorable people with their youths' best interests at heart. Lack of such protocols should be a warning sign of a muddled organization.

> **KEY IDEAS**
>
> - TFY CCD builds projects and partnership focused on capacity and capabilities development not needs.
> - TFY CCD projects function within a context of abundance, cooperation, and joyfulness.
> - TFY CCD projects create spaces for human meaning making.
> - TFY CCD artists cannot plan projects on their own.
> - Project planning and development depends on nested cooperation working through action items and "if then" choices.
> - Clear intentions produce better outcomes.
> - Project proposals include project title, key personnel contact information, executive summary, a placemaking approach/goal, CCD objectives, project description, project theory of change, project requirements and budget, project time line, project risks, exit criteria and evaluation protocols, and organization/artist information.
> - Logistics matter
> - All projects have similar life cycles

## 3.8 DOCUMENTATION, EVALUATION, AND ASSESSMENT

Vicki Flerx (2007) helpfully articulates several key introductory ideas around program evaluation and assessment:

*What is program evaluation?*
- A process by which staff/stakeholders are able to determine progress toward goals
- An assessment of the extent to which an intervention or service achieves its objectives
- A determination of congruence between the performance of a program and its objectives

*Why perform program evaluation?*
- To make decisions about whether to continue or modify an intervention or service
- To determine strengths/barriers related to success
- To determine additional resource needs
- To determine if the program works
- To determine cost/effectiveness

*What are five things about evaluation that make people nervous?*
- Do not know how
- Do not have the time
- Not good at statistics
- Not enough money
- Too much paperwork
- Fear that evaluation may show that the program is not working

*Why do evaluation?*
- More likely to achieve its goals if they are defined and measured
- Evaluation provides a tool for obtaining and maintaining funding and support
- Evaluation helps the organization know if its activities are reaching the intended groups
- Evaluation identifies the effective elements of the project and the areas that need improvement
- Evaluation documents organizational efforts and allows the organization to inform itself and others about what did and did not work
- Evaluation will help the organization figure out if its program is working as intended.

(Flerx 2007: 157–158)

I am a strong believer in evaluation and assessment. If we care about what we are doing then we evaluate ourselves in a manner making the most sense to us. While we live in a data-driven world and most funders now require program assessment and evaluation, we cannot allow other's frames to drive our assessments. I can always grow more competent in my chosen art practice, and frankly, I feel no interest in maintaining creative stasis or the cultural status quo. Toward that end, my assessment practices generate avenues of exploration and challenge while letting me know what I am doing well. As Smith (2010) points out,

> [...] belief, enthusiasm, and commitment are not enough. Regardless of whether a professional is working in health settings, child welfare programs, schools, or counseling agencies, it is not sufficient to simply believe in what one is doing [...] professionals who do not take program evaluation seriously appear to not care about the program, the results of the program, or the results of their practice.
>
> (Smith 2010: 17, 8)

Evaluation may sound intimidating, but solid planning makes the process relatively simple. My key point here is that evaluation and assessment planning occurs at the beginning of projects in collaboration with community partners and youth participants as part of the full planning processes. Muriel Harris (2010) notes, "a participatory model for evaluation views evaluation as a team effort that involves people internal and external to the organization with varying levels of evaluation expertise in a power-sharing and co-learning relationship" (7). Again, TFY CCD assessments should be collaborative, reciprocal, generative, rigorous, and practical, reflecting the core values of CCD itself. So, what do you need to know both to document TFY CCD and to structure solid project evaluations?

### 3.8.1 Documentation

Documentation captures the essence of a project to communicate scope and sequence to project partners, participants, funders, and stakeholders. As an exit strategy, the usefulness of a culminating documentary slide show, video, or hard copy photo/project memory book cannot be underestimated. In addition, documentation of past projects becomes work samples for future projects and/or funding requests. So what counts as documentation?

- Project proposals
- Permission slips and publicity waivers

- Asset maps
- Photographs
- Videos
- Worksheets, devising prompts, and session designs
- Creative writing, sketches, and devising/devised material
- Scripts
- Publicity material or other ephemera
- Closing ceremonial items (memory books, et cetera)
- And final project reports

Basically, any material generated can be archived. I use a cloud service (such as Dropbox or Sugarsync) to organize my files and I back up on both a personal and a work server. The high-quality cameras now standard with almost all cell phones have revolutionized my documentation practices. I can pull out my phone and take quick photographs or snippets of video and I use my camera to document both people and objects. My phone serves handily as a camera, a photocopier, a voice recorder, and a video recorder. Given the prevalence of cell phones, project partners and participants become documentation partners. Having multiple "eyes on the prize," too, allows me to see the work through multiple viewpoints during the devising process. Here, the usefulness of a cloud service means that we can share folders quickly and easily upload material. Google docs and Google spreadsheets can also be usefully employed for collaborative documentation (and assessment). Closed Facebook pages and groups can also work as documentation hubs and have the added benefit of archiving discussion around works-in-progress. As I use digital media frequently in my work, I have found iPads useful for multiple purposes. I often designate one iPad solely for documentation. iPads can be set up to automatically sync to the Apple cloud server or manually sync to other cloud services. The drawback of using digital media to document projects and partnerships can be data inundation. Now, instead of having no images of our work and work-in-progress, I end up with hundreds, sometimes thousands. Remember though, quality counts. Documentation serves a different purpose than project evaluation. Documentation answers the question *what happened* while project assessment address both *how well* did the project happen and did the project *succeed*? Each have their role to play in any project or partnership.

### 3.8.2 Specialized Research Terminology

Project evaluation uses special terms that can be intimidating to the uninitiated. First, however, I want to distinguish between *program evaluation* and *research*.

While program evaluation uses research protocols, the questions asked are too specific to be generalized to larger populations as a whole, and thus cannot be considered research. Harris (2010) has a helpful chart distinguishing between research and program evaluation.

|  | **Research** |
|---|---|
| Assessment of specific programs or projects | Results are generalizable |
| Designed to improve the program/project | Designed to prove a relationship |
| Focus on why and how an intervention worked | Focuses on an endpoint |
| Questions crafted by stakeholders and project artists | Questions dictated by researcher's agenda |
| Assesses the value of the community cultural development project | Assesses whether the intervention worked |

(Harris 2010: 3)

Program/project/partnership evaluation uses research protocols but does not count as research. They share processes and terminology however. When institutions like the US Department of Health and Human Services or the US Department of Education call something *evidence-based practice*, they mean activities validated through experimental protocols; research designed to prove causal relationships. In order to prove cause and effect, research designs have to build overwhelming and statistical proof between independent variables (program inputs) and dependent variables (program outcome). In other words, the causal relationship focus in research design protocols expresses whether a program activity (independent variable) caused a program outcome (dependent variable). To craft overwhelming and statistical evidence of a causal relationship, research designs need to include a *control group*. Control groups are statistically similar populations who do not participate in program activities (access to the independent variable). Researchers then measure for the dependent variable in both groups looking for causation. If researchers randomly assign individuals to either the group participating in program activities or the control group, we call that *randomization* and the research counts as *experimental*. If participants are not randomized into *treatment* and *control* populations, the study is *quasi-experimental*. Randomization increases research *internal validity* or the degree to which one can claim causality between variables. When we talk about *validity* in research or program evaluation, we discuss whether we measure what we intend to measure. Randomly assigning individuals to either control or treatment group helps eliminate certain forms of bias.

Causality can be difficult to prove and involves controlling as many independent variables as possible in order to isolate the contributing variable. The statistical relationship between any two variables is called *dependence*, and variables can relate in multiple ways. The relational connection between variables is called *correlation*. Correlation does not equal causation. The surprisingly funny blog, "Spurious Correlations," maintained by Harvard student Tyler Vigen (http://www.tylervigen.com/) highlights this truism by charting causally bogus but statistically dependent variables. For example, did you know that US spending on science, space, and technology correlates 0.992082 with US suicides by hanging, strangulation, and suffocation? Clearly, budgetary allocations in space exploration do not cause suicides, but the variables exhibit statistical dependence to a high degree. Methodologically, researchers generally divide research protocols into *quantitative, qualitative,* and *mixed methods*. Quantitative data can be counted, statistically analyzed and mathematically manipulated:

> Quantitative data analysis includes a set of rules and procedures and statistical concepts based on the science of [statistics]. This is how structured data such as yes/no answers, number of years or amount of time in the program, checklists, rating scales, and scales measuring substantive concepts and goals are analyzed.
>
> (Smith 2010: 305)

Researchers looking for patterns and qualities of phenomenon use qualitative methodologies. Interviews, open-ended surveys, project descriptions, participant observation, field notes, participant journals, focus groups, case studies, meeting minutes, et cetera provide qualitative data. Flerx notes, "Process data collected through qualitative methods [...] are usually analyzed by identifying categories, themes, patterns" (Flerx 2007: 174). Mixed methods protocols combine quantitative and qualitative data.

Bradley Cousins and Jill Chouinard (2012) define "evaluation" as "systematic inquiry leading to judgments about program merit, worth and significance, and program decision making [...]" (10). Thus, while program and project evaluation cannot be considered research per se, the systematic inquiry process relies on research protocols and processes to establish *value*. Donald Yarbrough, Lyn Shulha, Rodney Hopson, and Flora Caruthers note,

> Valueing is at the heart of each decision and judgment made throughout an evaluation. The utility of the evaluation is dependent, in part, on the extent

to which program and evaluation stakeholders can identify and respect the value perspectives embedded in each facet of the evaluation.
(Yarbrough, Shulha, Hopson, and Caruthers 2011: 37)

Value then happens contextually, collaboratively, and culturally. Economist David Throsby (2001) has some interesting things to say about *value* in cultural systems. Throsby points out that in both culture and economics, value is an "expression of worth, not just in a static or passive sense but also in a dynamic and active way as a negotiated or transactional phenomenon" (Throsby 2001: 19–20). *Program evaluation then passes judgment on the value of the program's interventions into social and cultural lives.* In his 1938 book, *Logic: The Theory of Inquiry,* John Dewey acknowledges the importance of humans' psychosocial space by pointing out that the end result of the inquiry processes is not truth per se but warranted assertability. Program evaluation does not determine truth but rather makes defensible claims. Throsby writes, "[…] it should not be difficult to accept that cultural value is a multiple and shifting thing which cannot be comprehended within a single domain. Value is, in other words, both various and variable" (Throsby 2001: 28). Negotiating variability in such a way as to make warranted claims as to a program's value highlights the importance of methodological rigor in assessment protocols.

### 3.8.3 Rigor

In the context of program or partnership evaluation, rigor alludes to exactness and precision in the inquiry and analysis process. While not generalizable, rigorous program evaluation nevertheless adheres to standard social science protocols established to increase evaluators' ability to certify their claims—the evaluation's warranted assertability. Basically, crafting rigorous evaluation designs allows us to measure what we say we are measuring, calculate agreed-upon upon outcomes, and negotiate the psychosocial space of appearance between participants, stakeholders, and community partners. Rigorous evaluation design involves several key components:

- Asking the right questions
- Carrying out the evaluation
- How we measure
- Who we measure or sampling
- Collecting the data
- Data analysis

The involved conceptualization and planning process I advocate earlier in this section helps streamline assessment questions. Knowing what questions to ask depends on the interrelation of the project design and project theory of change. If both the project design and the theory of change are clearly conceived, defining success in desired outcomes/impacts will be apparent. SMART objectives are specific, measurable, attainable, realistic, and time limited. Additionally, using the project planning logic model helps TFY CCD artists to articulate well-defined associations among inputs, activities, outputs, and outcomes. At a pragmatic level, project evaluation explores whether or not a project had access to necessary resources, engaged in the planned activities, in the promised manner, and produced the promised project outputs. Did we accomplish what we said we would do? If not, why not? Evaluation experts speak to "formative" and "summative" designs. Formative evaluation examines the processes of a project while summative assessments evaluate goals and outcomes. In TFY CCD, project processes and outcomes twine tightly; project outcomes relate back to project goals and objectives through relationships articulated in the project's theory of change and the deliberative democratic environment. The planning questions discussed in Section 3.7 link directly to evaluation questions:

1. Who is your community?
2. What is your placemaking goal?
3. What is the condition your program/project/partnership wants to address?
4. What resources are needed to make the program possible? What capital systems, behaviors, structures, assets, or capacities will you leverage? How will you negotiate building capabilities? What are the project/project's objectives?
5. What change are you hoping to achieve?
6. What is the change environment?
7. What does your program/project plan do to create the desired change?
8. What products will result from program activities?
9. What defines success? What level or amount of change needs to occur for you and your allies to feel successful? Short-term outcomes? Long-term outcomes?
10. If you achieve these outcomes, will the conditions in #2 and #3 be addressed?
11. Is it logical to believe that the products of your program activities (#8) have the potential to produce your desired outcomes and results (#5)?
12. What indicators will you use to evaluate your project's effectiveness, efficiency, impact, sustainability, and relevance?

If we have done a good job in planning projects, then assessment questions will be obvious.

The design of the evaluation should be as rigorous as is practical. Practically, I do not run experimental or quasi-experimental protocols without hiring an external evaluator. In general, the TFY CCD artist functions as project director, primary artist-in-residence, and project evaluator: a heavy load. The benefit of working in CCD, however, can be found in the number of people invested in achieving success. Once we design our evaluation plan, carrying it out together does not feel so intimidating. Include the evaluation protocol on the project proposal with a clear worksheet of what indicators will be used and who will be responsible for gathering the data. With younger youth, I use what a friend calls "shoe box organizing." Using small boxes, we decorate them and paste one evaluation question per box. Anytime anyone has an idea or hears a story or piece of evidence answering the question, they document it and drop in the box. Online folders can accomplish the same process here too. Smith (2010) outlines nine steps in program evaluation:

1. Describe the program (or the need to be assessed in conducting a needs assessment study).
2. Define the program activities and/or the goals of the program (or the needs if a needs assessment study).
3. Design or plan the study by selecting a type of study (e.g., an experimental study comparing different forms of the program, a survey of consumers, or a qualitative-formulative study involving personal interviews with a small number of consumers).
4. Choose a method of data collection (e.g., handed-out or mailed questionnaire, personal interview, direct observation, focus group, data from case records).
5. Decide on the type of sample you will have (e.g., a convenience sample of consumers who are available to you, a random sample from the population of consumers).
6. Construct the data collection instrument (e.g., the questionnaire or personal interview guide).
7. Implement the study by collecting the data.
8. Analyze the data using the techniques of quantitative or qualitative date analysis.
9. Report the results of your study: the findings, conclusions, implications, and limitations of your study.

(Smith 2010: 40–41)

I use mixed methods evaluation protocols both because I feel that mixed methods allow for more rigor and because what we want to know often does not fall cleanly into either quantitative or qualitative methodological camps. For example, gathering data on how many neighbors participate in a performance/salon discussion involves counting. Gathering data on what was discussed during the salons and how participants feel about the discussions involves qualitative data. Information can be gathered in multiple kinds of ways: surveys, census, questionnaires, interviews, focus groups, participant observation, field notes, journaling, photovoice, story circles, memory boxes, et cetera. I understand data gathering to be a core part of the creative process and I build the evaluation structure into the devising and art action protocols. For example, an installation project crafted by homeless youth in downtown Phoenix focused on raising awareness of and building effective connections between art-walk audiences and the homeless youth resource center. The project particularly focused on aesthetically exploring how homeless youth experience time. The youth created a walk-through experience in which each room explored time differently. As audiences were leaving, youth engaged them in evocative questions designed to poetically punctuate the installation project. Audiences could respond to the questions using sticky notes that were then incorporated into the installation. A roving youth with a voice recorder captured descriptive observational data along with brief audience interviews. In this way, data gathering for later evaluative use functioned creatively. How you gather data and your sample method relate of course. In the above example, we offered the evaluative/ punctuation experience to all of our audience (and by comparing total audience numbers to the number of sticky notes we got a rough response rate). The roving interviewer, however, used convenience sampling (those people approached who were interested in responding). We also counted the number of people taking the center's informational brochure away with them and added a check box to the organization's volunteer worksheet (How did you hear about the organization? A First Friday Performance) to track higher levels of interest.

The data collection instrument/measurement matters here. Knowing what questions to ask and what to measure depends on setting clear indicators and knowing success levels. For a project addressing homeless pets, the project team used the number of pounds of pet food collected as their indicator of success. For a project raising awareness around the emotional costs of gossip, the team performed convenience sampling once a week over a six-week period to track changes in awareness. In both cases, the evaluation methodology was integrated into the project processes themselves and fed the creative approach of the CCD team.

When designing interview questions, surveys, or pre- and post-tests, we need to keep several things in mind in order to build rigorous instruments:

- First, the measurement's validity. Is the question you are asking actually measuring what you think it is?
- Second, the measurement's reliability. Does the instrument consistently measure the same thing? If I administer the instrument multiple days, will it return the same information?

One way to address internal validity is to ask the same question in multiple ways and compare and contrast the answers statistically. Another is to use already validated instruments and questionnaires. While unfortunately many instruments are copyrighted and must be purchased, many can be found freely available or under Creative Commons license. The Harvard Family Research Project publishes a useful table of resources on their website (and maintains a database of relevant research) at http://www.hfrp.org/out-of-school-time/publications-resources/measurement-tools-for-evaluating-out-of-school-time-programs-an-evaluation-resource2#table1-2. Resources, such as Lester (2000), also been collected into volumes and can be found in many public libraries or ordered through interlibrary loan. The National Endowment of the Arts offers research advice particularly circulating around their system map of how art works (2012). Arts Ed Search (http://www.artsedsearch.org/) maintains a user-friendly database of research along with suggested research topics and policy implications. Rigor in the data collection also means paying attention to informed consent and ethical participation structures. Harris notes:

> During the data-collection process, the rights of individuals must be respected and their welfare must be protected. It is also important to protect privacy and confidentiality in data collection and in reporting the results. Protecting the rights of individuals requires that researchers do not coerce anyone to participate in a study. In addition, participants have the right to know and understand all the research procedures. If they consent to participate they must be treated in a caring, considerate, and respectful way. All their interactions must be kept confidential, and their data remain anonymous unless they have been notified otherwise.
>
> (Harris 2010: 122)

The National Institute of Health has an online, free education module outlining research with human subjects that project directors should download. You can find this resource at http://phrp.nihtraining.com.

Once you collect the data, rigor comes into play in the methodological approach to analyzing the information. I have zero statistical skills and tend to default to percent change, sum, average, and mean, which are all easily calculated automatically on spreadsheets. There are several webinars, YouTube videos, and online resources helpful when parsing quantitative data. Qualitative data analysis, also called *coding* and *content analysis*, is a process of moving through the data and looking for themes. I understand coding and content analysis as dramaturging the data. Again, multiple resources exist articulating qualitative methodologies. I highly recommend my colleague Johnny Saldaña's *The Coding Manual for Qualitative Researchers*, published by Sage. I tend to code qualitative date first for key repeated elements using the direct words of the participants (in vivo). Then I code for themes. Like planning and conducting the research, analyzing data functions cooperatively too. While the TFY CCD artist generally serves as lead, working collaboratively and generatively means moving through the processes of evaluation together. The young man who collected audio clips of interviews and descriptive observations used the clips to craft a spoken word piece recording his reflections. Another youth edited the audience interviews into a 122 second overview/remix using GarageBand.

In order to craft rigorous formative and summative valuation, art actions themselves must also be included in the evaluation and assessment plan. Here, we acknowledge that art actions have both extrinsic value and intrinsic value. Remember, if the art action does not first function *as art*, we lose our ability to transfer and build capital effectively. Throsby notes,

> Thus, without being exhaustive it may be possible to describe an artwork, for example, as providing a range of cultural value characteristics including:
> 
> - Aesthetic value (… beauty, harmony, form, et cetera, aesthetic characteristics)
> - Spiritual value (religious or secular based, understanding, enlightenment and insight)
> - Social value: "The work may convey a sense of connection with others, and it may contribute to a comprehension of the nature of the society in which we live and to a sense of identity and place"
> - Historical value (how it reflects the conditions of life at the time it was created, and how it illuminates the present by providing a sense of continuity with the past)
> - Symbolic value: "Artworks and other cultural objects exist as repositories and conveyors of meaning. If an individual's reading of an artwork involves the extraction of meaning, then the work's symbolic value embraces the nature of the meaning conveyed by the work and its value to the consumer"

- Authenticity value: This value refers to the fact that the work is the real, original and unique artwork which it is represented to be. There is little doubt that the authenticity and integrity of a work have identifiable value per se, additional to other sources of value listed above

(Throsby 2001: 28–29)

I wrote elsewhere in this text about system understandings of creativity highlighting the need to build expert appraisal processes into the process and product. Paying attention to our craft means setting standards for artistic excellence and achievement and then measuring our attempts. How can we measure these attempts? Again, economist David Throsby writes,

Several different assessment methods might be brought into play in evaluating cultural value, drawing on a number of specific valuation methods used in the social sciences and the humanities, including the following:
- Mapping (contextual framework).
- Thick description (interpretive description … which rationalizes otherwise inexplicable phenomena by exposing the underlying cultural systems et cetera at work, and deepens the understanding of the context and meaning of observed behavior).
- Attitudinal analysis: Various techniques may be referred to under this heading including social survey methods, psychometric measurement, et cetera and a variety of elicitation techniques might be employed. Such approaches are likely to be useful especially in assessing social and spiritual aspects of cultural value. They may be applied at the individual level to gauge individual response, or at an aggregate level to study group attitudes or to seek out patterns of consensus.
- Content analysis: This group of techniques includes methods aimed at identifying and codifying meaning, appropriate for measuring various interpretations of the symbolic value of the work or other processes under consideration.
- Expert appraisal: The input of expertise in a variety of disciplines is likely to be an essential component of any cultural value assessment, especially in providing judgments on aesthetic, historical and authenticity value, where particular skills, training and experience can lead to a better informed evaluation. Some testing of such judgments against accepted professional standards via a peer-review process is likely to be desirable in some cases in order to reduce the incidence of hasty, ill informed, prejudiced or quixotic opinions.

(Throsby 2001: 29–30)

Each of Throsby's suggestions can be useful. I tend to default, however, to semiotic analysis rooted in both performative components, such as:

1. Duration—time, rhythm, dynamics, tempo, kinesthetic response, repetition.
2. Embodiment—real bodies and characters, spatial relationships, kinesthetic response, timbre.
3. Ensemble—collaborative group, spatial relationships.
4. Gesture—expressive and behavioral.
5. Reenactment of an original, (story/memory), melody.
6. Imaginative location—architecture (solid mass, texture, light, color), topography, setting.
7. Sound/music—rhythm, dynamic, melody, harmony.
8. Spectacle—shape, gesture, architecture, topography.
9. Text—texture, timbre, melody, rhythm.
10. Form—genre and shape, bracketed experience.

and the creative process relationships of self-to-self, self-to-ensemble, and ensemble-to-community. Patrice Pavis (2003) has a useful and elaborate semiotic questionnaire in his book, *Analyzing Performance: Theatre, Dance, and Film*. I have adapted this instrument multiple times productively and recommend the book.

I understand assessment and evaluation as a key component of TFY CCD. Articulating what we want to change means being responsible for addressing whether or not we productively accomplished what we set out to achieve. The process of plan-play-evaluate highlights both mindfulness, in general, and aesthetic reflective practice specifically. I counsel approaching evaluation not as an aggravating add-on to the end of the art but as part of the creative process and public-making strategy. In the next and final segment of Section 3, I discuss final project reports.

**KEY IDEAS**

- The very act of evaluation increases project success rates.
- Belief and enthusiasm in our work is not enough, we must also measure and assess to warrant our claims.
- Solid project planning makes the project assessment simple.
- We follow a participatory evaluation model, understanding the process as a team effort.

- TFY CCD assessments should be collaborative, reciprocal, generative, rigorous, and practical, reflecting the core values of CCD itself.
- Documentation captures the essence of a project to communicate scope and sequence to project partners, participants, and stakeholders.
- Documentation answers the question *what happened* while project assessment address both *how well* did the project happen and did the project *succeed*?
- Plan documentation and data management. Cloud services can be useful.
- Program/project/partnership evaluation uses research protocols but does not count as research as it cannot be generalized.
- Evaluation uses specialized terminology drawn from both the scientific method and social science domains.
- Program evaluation passes judgment on the value of the program's interventions into social and cultural lives.
- Value is a transactional term.
- Methodological rigor in assessment protocols allows us to make warranted claims and key assertions.
- The design of the evaluation should be as rigorous as practical.
- Rigorous research design involves asking the right questions, carrying out the evaluation, how we measure, who we measure or sampling, collecting the data, and data analysis.
- Rigor in the data collection also means paying attention to informed consent and ethical participation structures.
- In order to craft rigorous formative and summative valuation, art actions themselves must be included in the evaluation and assessment plan.
- Art actions have both extrinsic value and intrinsic value, measured separately.

## 3.9 FINAL PROJECT/PARTNERSHIP/PROGRAM REPORTS

If the proposal frames TFY third space activities, the final project report closes that loop. Final reports (or yearly reports in longer partnerships) have a few more components than project proposals, as reports gather the documentation and assessment material as well as a synopsis of activities and events. I tend to use lots of visual material in final project reports as photographs add to narrative in uncountable ways. My aim, however, remains no more than ten pages not including appendixes. These reports have a bit more fluidity than do project proposals: for example some include session designs while others do not—depending on relevance. Be aware, some funders and partnering organizations have their own specific formats or online databases that they would rather you use for final reports. My generic outline for the final report is:

1. Project name and relevant dates and personnel
2. Project synopsis (include projected cost and actual cost)
3. Project placemaking approach
4. Project CCD objectives
5. Project theory of change and outcomes
6. Project activities
7. Project outcomes
8. Project successes and challenges
9. Conclusions and future plans (if relevant)
10. For more information contact X.

The *project name, relevant dates and personnel* are self-explanatory. The *program synopsis* functions like an executive summary and should include the planned and actual cost of the program. The *project placemaking approach, CCD objectives*, and *theory of change/desired outcomes* can be pulled directly from the proposal document, unless they have morphed and/or been adapted over the life of the project. Be direct. What specific change were you trying to accomplish? If your goal, objectives, and/or outcomes changed discuss that here, speaking to why and how new goals, objectives, and/or outcomes were chosen. In my experience, these categories do morph especially when youth have not been a part of the planning process from the beginning. In other cases, artists and youth discover the reality on the ground so different from their expectations they radically redesign their projects.

As a category, *program activities* tend to be a bit more complex. Like the planning model, program activities divide into inputs and outputs. Starting with a sentence that locates the program activities in time and space, summarize the program's actions. List the number and kind of activities/outputs: workshops; performances; videos; trainings; salon sessions; interviews; workbooks; policy recommendations; blogs; brochures; conversations et cetera. What resources/inputs made this program possible? What capital systems did you leverage? Think globally here: space; volunteer hours; CCD artist hours; community partner staff hours; funds; in-kind donations, et cetera. What did the program participants bring to the table, for example, bridging capital, political capital, familial capital, cultural capital, resistant capital, et cetera? How did they become connected with the project? Describe the general demographics of your participant population if relevant. How many participants who started the project finished it? What was the percent completion rate? If individuals dropped out can you tell us why? The average hours spent in the program will be helpful here too. This information often works best in a data table rather than in prose. Use both raw numbers and percentages if possible.

*Project outcomes* loop back to the theory of change. Did the program achieve the change sought? How do you know this? What is the participant satisfaction rate? What is the satisfaction rate for project partners? Volunteers? The intended audience? Again, tell us how you gathered this data. What other changes occurred because of the program? Unintended or unanticipated results? If possible, discuss how the program affected the community partner and/or partnering organizations. Use narrative and story to summarize while also telling us how you gathered and analyzed your data. Data tables work well here too but only when nested in narrative. Address primary outcomes before you speak to any surprise or additional results.

*Project success and challenges* addresses program quality beyond the outcome numbers. How did the project compare with the standard of artistic excellence that you set for yourself? Vignettes work really well here, as do quotes from outside eye reviewers or media coverage. What do the project participants, partners, and audiences say about the strengths and weaknesses of the art action and the project? Reflective practice lives at the core of TFY CCD and is manifest here. Speak frankly about mistakes or creative dead ends and how the program learned and adapted. In particular, discuss how planned activities morphed to meet the needs and desires of the youth involved. What changed and why? What lessons were learned? How were project risks or vulnerabilities managed? Here you would also discuss positive or negative unintended effects.

*Conclusions and future plans*: Overall, what would you say is the value of this project, program, or partnership? What benefits were derived from the investments? In addition, only rarely will a group of youth leave a TFY CCD program not fired up for their next project. Even if the TFY CCD partnership will not continue, this is the place to let the funder and partners know what the youth would like to do next. You might make specific recommendations as to partnering artists or organizations to pursue for future projects. As an outsider, too, the TFY CCD artist might have recommendations for small changes that could have big impact. Again, this would be the location for that data. TFY CCD moves from a space of abundance and the final report should reflect those values. We are the change we want to see in the world. The project report explicitly claims that space.

**KEY IDEAS**

- Final project reports close projects down while looking forward to the future.
- Use narrative and story to summarize while also telling us how you gathered and analyzed your data.
- Data tables and pictures are both useful.
- Be honest: be reflective.

# Works Cited

Ackroyd, J. (2007), "Applied theatre: an exclusionary discourse?" *Applied Theatre Researcher,* #8.

Adams, D. and Goldbard, A. (2001), *Creative Community: The Art of Cultural Development,* New York: Rockefeller Foundation.

Adams, D. and Goldbard, A. (eds), (2002), *Community, Culture and Globalization,* New York: Rockefeller Foundation.

Alkire, S. (2002), "Dimensions of Human Development," *World Development,* 30/2, pp. 181–205.

Alkire, S. (2005), *Valuing Freedoms: Sen's Capability Approach and Poverty Reduction,* Oxford, United Kingdom: Oxford University Press.

Alrutz, M., Listengarten, J., and Wood, M.V.D. (eds), (2012), *Playing with Theory and Theatre Practice,* New York: Palgrave Macmillan.

Althusser, L. (1969), *For Marx,* New York: Pantheon Books.

Amabile, T.M. (1999), "Consensual assessment," In Runco, M.A. and Pritzker, S. (eds), *Encyclopedia of Creativity,* San Diego, CA: Academic Press, pp. 346–349.

Anderson, L., Krathwohl, R., Airasian, P., Cruikshank, K., Mayer, R., Pintrich, P., et al. (eds), (2001), *Taxonomy for Learning, Teaching, and Assessing: A Revision of Bloom's Taxonomy,* New York: Longman.

Animating Democracy (2013), Typical Social and Civic Outcomes [online], http://animatingdemocracy.org/social-impact-indicators/typical-social-and-civic-outcomes. Accessed 30 August 2012.

Arendt, H. (1958), *The Human Condition,* Chicago, IL: University of Chicago Press.

Arendt, H. (1969), "Communicative Power," In Lukes, S. (ed), (1986), *Power,* New York: New York University Press, pp. 59–74.

Avolio, B.J., Gardner, W.L., Walumbwa, F.O. (eds), (2005), "Preface," *Authentic Leadership Theory and Practice: Origins, Effects and Development,* San Diego, CA: Elsevier, pp. xxi–xxix.

Baber, P.S. (2010), *Cassie Draws the Universe,* iUniverse.com.

Barone, T. and Eisner, E.W. (2012), *Arts Based Research,* Los Angeles, CA: Sage.

Baumeister, R.F. (1991), *Meanings of Life*, New York: Guilford Press.

Beaulieu, L.J. (2002), "Mapping the assets of your community: a key component for building local capacity," Southern Rural Development Center. Report SRDC-227. PDF, http://srdc.msstate.edu/trainings/educurricula/asset_mapping/asset_mapping.pdf. Accessed September 2013.

Bebbington, A. (1999), "Capitals and capabilities: a framework for analyzing peasant viability, rural livelihoods and poverty," *World Development*, 27, pp. 2021–2044.

Bedard, R.L. and Tolch, C.J. (eds), (1989), *Spotlight on the Child: Studies in the History of American Children's Theatre*, New York: Greenwood Press.

Begg, A. (2000), *Empowering the Earth: Strategies for Social Change*, Cambridge, United Kingdom: Green Books, Ltd.

Bem, D.J. (1970), *Beliefs, Attitudes, and Human Affairs,* Belmont, CA: Brooks/Cole Publishing Company.

Bennett, T., Grossberg, L. and Morris, M. (eds), (2005), *New Key Words: A Revised Vocabulary of Culture and Society,* Malden, MA : Blackwell Publishing.

Benson, P.L. (2007), "Developmental assets: an overview of theory, research, and practice," In Silbereisen, R.K. and Lerner, R.M. (eds), *Approaches to Positive Youth Development*, Thousand Oaks, CA: Sage, pp. 33–58.

Berry, K. (2001), *The Dramatic Arts and Cultural Studies*, New York: Falmer Press.

Bhabha, H.K. (1990), "The third space: interview with Homi Bhabha," In Rutherford, J. (ed), *Identity: Community, Culture, Difference*, London: Lawrence and Wishart, pp. 207–221.

Bhabha, H.K. (2004), "The commitment to theory," In *The Location of Culture* (2nd edn), London: Routledge, pp. 28–56.

Biggeri, M., Ballet, J., and Comim, F. (2011), *Children and the Capability Approach* [online], New York: Palgrave Macmillan, http://www.myilibrary.com?ID=336011. Accessed 17 September 2013.

Boal, A. (1985), *Theatre of the Oppressed,* Leal McBride**,** C.A. and Leal McBride M. O. (trans), New York: Theatre Communications Group.

Bogart, A. (1995), *Viewpoints*, Lyme, NH: Smith and Kraus, Inc.

Bohman, J. (1996), *Public Deliberation: Pluralism, Complexity and Democracy*, Cambridge, MA: MIT Press.

Borrup, T. (2006), *The Creative Community Builder's Handbook: How to Transform Communities Using Local Assets, Art, and Culture*, Saint Paul, MN: Fieldstone Alliance.

Bourdieu, P. (1977), *Reproduction in Education, Society and Culture*, Nice, R. (trans), London: Sage Publications.

Bourdieu, P. (1984), *Distinction: A Social Critique of the Judgment of Taste*, Nice, R. (trans), Cambridge, MA: Harvard University Press.

Bourdieu, P. (1993), *The Field of Cultural Production: Essays on Art and Literature*, In Johnson R. (editor and introducer), New York: Columbia University Press.

Boyte, H.C. (2004), *Everyday Politics: Reconnecting Citizens and Public Life*, Philadelphia, PA: University of Pennsylvania Press.

Boyte, H.C. and Kari, N.N. (1996), *Building America: The Democratic Promise of Public Work*, Philadelphia, PA: Temple University Press.

Boyte, H.C. and Shelby, D. (2009), *The Citizen Solution*, St. Paul, MN: Minnesota Historical Society Press.

Bringle, R.G., Clayton, P.H., and Price, M.F. (2009), "Partnerships in service learning and civic engagement," *Partnerships: a Journal of Service Learning and Civic Engagement*, 1, pp. 1–20.

Brown, D.M. (2013), "Young people, anti-social behaviour and public space: the role of community wardens in policing the 'ABSO Generation,'" *Urban Studies*, 50, pp. 538–555.

Burnham, L.F. (2005), "Listen up: sojourn theatre's lessons in community dialogue," *Community Arts Network*, http://wayback.archive-it.org/2077/20100906202945/http://www.communityarts.net/readingroom/archivefiles/2005/09/listen_up_sojou.php: N.P.

Butler, J. (1990), *Gender Trouble*, New York: Routledge.

Caillois, R. (1961), *Man, Play, and Games*, Barash, M. (trans), New York: Free Press of Glencoe.

Certeau, M.de (1984), *The Practice of Everyday Life*, Rendall, S.F (trans), Berkeley, CA: University of California Press.

Chan, A., Hannah, S.T., and Gardner, W.L. (2005), "Veritable authentic leadership: emergence, functioning, and impacts," In Garder, W.L., Avolio, B.J., and Walumbwa, F.O. (eds), *Authentic Leadership Theory and Practice: Origins, Effects and Development*, San Diego, CA: Elsevier, pp. 3–41.

Chatterton, P., and Hollands, R. (2003), *Urban Nightscapes: Youth Cultures, Pleasure Spaces and Corporate Power*, London: Routledge.

Chrislip, D.D. (2002), *The Collaborative Leadership Fieldbook: A Guide for Citizens and Civic Leaders*, San Francisco, CA: Jossey-Bass.

Cleveland, W. (2012), "Arts-based community development: mapping the terrain," In Borwick, D. (ed), *Building Communities, Not Audiences*, Winston-Salem, NC: ArtsEngaged, pp. 296–308.

Cohen-Cruz, J. (2010), *Engaging Performance: Theatre as Call and Response*, New York: Routledge.

Cohen, A.P. (1985), *The Symbolic Construction of Community*, New York: Tavistock Publications.

Cohen, D. (2006), *The Development of Play* (3rd edn), New York: Routledge.

Cohen-Cruz, J. (2005), *Local Acts: Community-Based Performance in the United States*, New Brunswick, NJ: Rutgers University Press.

Cousins, J.B. and Chouinard, J.A. (2012), *Participatory Evaluation Up Close: An Integration of Research-Based Knowledge*, Charlotte, NC: Information Age Publishing.

Crocker, D.A. (1992), "Functioning and capability: the foundations of Sen's and Nussbaum's development ethic," *Political Theory*, 20, pp. 584–612.

Crocker, D.A. (2007), "Deliberative participation in local development," *Journal of Human Development*, 8, pp. 431–455.

Cropley, A. and Cropley, D. (2009), *Fostering Creativity: A Diagnostic Approach for Higher Education and Organizations*, Cresskill, NJ: Hampton Press.

Csikszentmihalyi, M. (1990), *Flow: The Psychology of Optimal Experience*, New York: HarperCollins.

Csikszentmihalyi, M. (1996), *Creativity: Flow and The Psychology of Discovery and Invention*, New York: HarperCollins.

Dasgupta, P. and Serageldin, I. (eds), (1999), *Social Capital: A Multifaceted Perspective* [online], Washington, DC: World Bank, http://documents.worldbank.org/curated/en/1999/09/439794/social-capital-multifaceted-perspective. Accessed 3 October 2013.

De Bono, E. (1992), *Serious Creativity: Using the Power of Lateral Thinking to Create New Ideas*, New York: HarperCollins.

DeFilippis, J., Fisher, R., and Shragge, E. (2010), *Contesting Community: The Limits and Potential of Local Organizing*, New Brunswick, NJ: Rutgers University Press.

Dewey, J. (1938), *Logic: The Theory of Inquiry*, New York: Holt, Rinehart and Winston.

Diamond, E. (1997), *Unmaking Mimesis*, New York: Routledge.

Dolan, J. (2005), *Utopia in Performance: Finding Hope at the Theater*, Ann Arbor, MI: University of Michigan Press.

Drèze, J. and Sen, A. (2002), *India: Development and Participation* (2nd edn), Oxford: Oxford University Press.

Eccles, J. and Gootman, J.A. (eds), (2002), *Community Programs to Promote Youth Development*, Washington, DC: National Academy Press.

Eiselt, S.B. (2012), *Becoming White Clay: A History and Archaeology of Jicarilla Apache Enclavement*, Ann Arbor, MI: University of Utah Press.

Ellison, J. (2005), "From the director: the naming of cats," *Imagining America Newsletter*, 6, pp. 1–2.

Ellsworth, E. (2005), *Places of Learning: Media, Architecture, Pedagogy*, New York: Routledge-Falmer.

Emory, M. and Flora, C. (2006), "Spiraling up: mapping community transformation with community capitals framework," *Community Development*, 37, pp. 19–35.

Etheridge Woodson, S. (2003), "A meditation on ideology, truth, and personal ethics," *Youth Theatre Journal*, 17, pp. 119–129.

Finnis, J. (1980), *Natural Law and Natural Rights*, Oxford, United Kingdom: Clarendon Press.

Finnis, J. (1983), *The Fundamentals of Ethics*, Oxford, United Kingdom: Oxford University Press.

Finnis, J. (1996), "Is natural law theory compatible with limited government?" In George, R.P. (ed), *Natural Law, Liberalism, and Morality*, Oxford, United Kingdom: Oxford University Press, pp. 1–26.

Finnis, J. (1997), "Commensuration and public reason," In Chang, R. (ed), *Incommensurability, Incomparability, and Practical Reason*, Boston: Harvard University Press, pp. 215–233.

Finnis, J. (1999), "Natural law and the ethics of discourse," *Ratio Juris*, 12, pp. 354–373.

Flerx, V.C. (2007), "Building capacity for self-evaluation among community agencies and organizations," In Motes, P.S. and Hess, P.M. (eds), *Collaborating with Community-Based Organizations through Consultation and Technical Assistance*, New York: Columbia University Press, pp. 137–187.

Flora, C.B. (1995), "Social capital and sustainability: agriculture and communities in the Great Plains and the Corn Belt," *Research in Rural Sociology and Development*, 6, pp. 227–246.

Flora, C.B. (2004), "Community dynamics and social capital," In Rickert, D. and Francis, C. (eds), *Agroecosystems Analysis*, Madison, WI: American Society of Agronomy, Inc., Crop Science Society of America, Inc., Soil Science Society of America, Inc., pp. 93–107.

Fraser, N. (2000), "Rethinking recognition," *New Left Review*, 3, pp. 107–120.

Fraser, N. (2001), "Recognition without ethics?" *Theory, Culture, Society*, 18, pp. 21–42.

Gaiman, N. (2013), *Make Good Art*, New York: William Morrow.

Gamble, D.N. and Weil, M. (2010), *Community Practice Skills: Local to Global Perspectives*, New York: Columbia University Press.

Gardenswartz, L., Cherbosque, J., and Rowe, A. (2010), "Emotional intelligences and diversity: a model for differences in the work place," *Journal of Psychological Issues in Organizational Culture*, 1, pp. 74–84.

Gardner, H. (1998), "The ethical responsibilities of professionals," The Good Work Project Report Series, Number 2, Harvard University. Revised February 2001.

Gardner, H. (2006), *Multiple Intelligences: New Horizons in Theory in Practice*, New York: Basic Books.

Gardner, H., Csikszentmihalyi, M., and William D. (2001), "The good work project a description," The Good Work Project Report Series, Number 1, Harvard University.

Gardner, W.L., Avolio, B.J., and Walumbwa, F.O. (eds), (2005), *Authentic Leadership Theory and Practice: Origins, Effects and Development*, San Diego, CA: Elsevier.

Geertz, C. (1973), *The Interpretation of Cultures: Selected Essays*, New York: Basic Books.

Giroux, H. (2000), *Stealing Innocence: Youth, Corporate Power, and the Politics of Culture*, New York: St. Martin's Press.

Gladwell, M. (2000), *The Tipping Point: How Little Things Can Make a Big Difference*, Boston: Little Brown.

Glasl, F. and Kopp, P. (1999), *Confronting Conflict: A First-Aid Kit for Handling Conflict*, Stroud, United Kingdom: Hawthorne Press.

Goldbard, A. (2006), *New Creative Community: The Art of Cultural Development*, Oakland, CA: New Village Press.

Gomez-Peña, G. (1996), *The New World Border: Prophesies, Poems & Loquera for the End of the Century*, San Francisco, CA: City Lights Books.

Govan, E., Nicholson, H., and Normington, K. (2007), *Making a Performance: Devising Histories and Contemporary Practices*, New York: Routledge.

Grady, S. (2000), *Drama and Diversity*, Portsmouth, NH: Heinemann.

Gramsci, A. (1973), *Letters from Prison*, New York: Harper & Row.

Green, G.P. and Haines, A. (2002), *Asset Building and Community Development*, Thousand Oaks, CA: Sage Publications.

Greer, R.O. (1994), "Of the people, by the people, for the people: the field of community performance," *High Performance*, 16, pp. 23–27.

Griffin, P. (1997), "Introductory module for the single issue courses," In Adams, M., Bell, L.A., and Griffin, P. (eds), *Teaching for Diversity and Social Justice: A Sourcebook*, New York: Routledge, pp. 61–81.

Grisez, G., Boyle, J., and Finnis, J. (1987), "Practical principles, moral truth and ultimate ends," *American Journal of Jurisprudence*, 32, pp. 99–151.

Gropnik, A. (2010), "How babies think," *Scientific American*, 303, pp. 76–81.

Grudin R. (1982), *Time and the Art of Living*, New York: Houghton Mifflin Company.

Gutmann, A. (1999), *Democratic Education*, Princeton, NJ: Princeton University Press.

Gutmann, A. and Thompson, D. (2004), *Why deliberative democracy?* Princeton: Princeton University Press.

Habermas, J. (1989), *The Structural Transformation of the Public Sphere: An Inquiry into a Category of Bourgeois Society*, Burger T. and Lawrence, F. (trans), Cambridge, United Kingdom: Polity Press.

Hall, E.T. (1977), *Beyond Culture*, Garden City, NY: Anchor Books.

Harris, M.J. (2010), *Evaluating Public and Community Health Programs*, San Francisco, CA: Jossey-Bass.

Heap, B. and Simpson, A. (2005), "A lesson for the living: promoting HIV/AIDS competence among young Zambians," *Youth Theatre Journal*, 19, pp. 89–101.

Heath, S.B. and Roach, A. (1999), "Imaginative actuality: learning in the arts during the nonschool hours," In Fiske, E.B. (ed), *Champions of Change: The Impact of the Arts on Learning*, pp. 19–34. The Arts Education Partnership and the President's Committee on the Arts and the Humanities, www.aep-arts.org. Accessed 6 January 2004.

Himmelman, A.T. (1994), "Communities working collaboratively for change," In Herrman, M. (ed), *Resolving Conflict: Strategies for Local Government*,

Washington DC: International City/County Management Association, pp. 27–47.

Hughes, L.W. (2005), "Developing transparent relationships through humor in the authentic leader-follower relationship," In Garder, W.L., Avolio, B.J., and Walumbwa, F.O. (eds), *Authentic Leadership Theory and Practice: Origins, Effects and Development,* San Diego, CA: Elsevier, pp. 83–106.

Huizinga, J. (1950), *Homo Ludens: A Study of the Play Element in Culture*, Boston: Beacon Press.

Human Development and Capabilities Association (2005), "Briefing note: capability & functionings: definition & justification" [online], http://hd-ca.org/publication-and-resources/introductory-recommended-readings. Accessed 5 October 2013.

Jackson, M.-R. and Herranz, J. (2002), *Culture Counts in Communities: A Framework for Measurement*, Washington, DC: The Urban Institute.

Jackson, S. (2000), *Lines of Activity: performance, historiography, Hull-House domesticity,* Ann Arbor, MI: University of Michigan Press.

Kershaw, B. (1992), *Politics of Performance: Radical Theatre as Cultural Intervention*, London: Routledge.

Knight, K., Schwarzman, M., et al. (2005), *The Beginner's Guide to Community-Based Arts*, Oakland, CA: New Village Press.

Knowles, R. (2004), *Reading the Material Theatre*, Cambridge, United Kingdom: Cambridge University Press.

Kosnik, C. (2014), *The Adolescent's Voice: How Theatre Participation Impacts High Schoolers and College Students*, Dissertation, Arizona State University.

Kuftinec, S. (2003), *Staging America: Cornerstone and Community-Based Theatre*, Carbondale, IL: Southern Illinois University Press.

Kumar, K. (2013), *Evaluating Democracy Assistance*, Boulder, CO: Lynne Rienner Publishers.

Laden, A.S. (2001), *Reasonably Radical*, Ithaca NY: Cornell University Press.

Lawlor, K. (2008), "Knowing beliefs, seeking causes," *American Imago*, 65, pp. 335–356.

Lefebvre, H. (1991), *The Production of Space*, Nicholson-Smith D. (trans), Cambridge, MA: Blackwell.

Lesko, N. (2001), *Act Your Age! A Cultural Construction of Adolescence*, New York: Routledge/Falmer.

Lester, P.E. (2000), *Handbook of Tests and Measurement in Education and the Social Sciences* (2nd edn), Lanham, MD: Scarecrow Press.

Lewis, J.P. (2007), *Fundamentals of Project Management* (3rd edn), New York: AMACOM.

Linden, R.M. (2002), *Working Across Boundaries: Making Collaboration Work in Government and Nonprofit Organizations,* Hoboken, NJ: Jossey-Bass.

Loden, M. and Rosener, J.B. (1991), *Workforce America: Managing Employee Diversity as a Vital Resource*, Homewood, IL: Business One Irwin.

Lord, C. (2012), "Sowing new beans: the making of memory and the measuring of impact," *Counting New Beans: Intrinsic Impact and the Value of Art*, San Francisco, CA: Theatre Bay Area, pp. 23–53.

Lord, C. (ed), (2012), *Counting New Beans: Intrinsic Impact and the Value of Art*, San Francisco, CA: Theatre Bay Area.

MacDonald, G.B. and Valdivieso, R. (2001), "Measuring deficits and assets: how we track youth development now, and how we should track it," In Benson, P.L. and Pittman, K.J. (eds), *Trends in Youth Development: Visions, Realities, Challenges*, Boston: Kluwer Academic Publishers, pp. 156–186.

Markusen, A. and Gadwa, A. (2010), "Creative placemaking" [online], National Endowment of the Arts, http://arts.gov/sites/default/files/CreativePlacemaking-Paper.pdf. Accessed 15 September 2012.

Martin, R. (2006), "Artistic citizenship: an introduction," In Campbell, M.S. and Martin, R. (eds), *Artistic Citizenship: A Public Voice for the Arts*, New York: Taylor & Francis, pp. 1–22.

Masayesva, V. and Younger, E. (eds), (1983), *Hopi Photographers/Hopi Images*, Tucson, AZ: Sun Tracks and University of Arizona Press.

Maslow, A.H. (1943), "A theory of human motivation," *Psychological Review*, 50, pp. 370–96.

McBride, C. (2005), "Deliberative democracy and the politics of recognition," *Political Studies*, 53, pp. 497–515.

McConachie, B. (1998), "Approaching the 'Structure of Feeling' in grassroots theatre," *Theatre Topics*, 8.1, pp. 33–53.

McKay, R.B. and de la Puente, M. (1995), "Cognitive research on designing the CPS supplement on race and ethnicity," In *Proceedings of the Bureau of the Census' 1995 Annual Research Conference*, Rosslyn, VA, pp. 435–445.

McKean, B. (2006), *A Teaching Artist at Work: Theatre with Young People in Educational Settings*, Portsmouth, NH: Heinemann.

McKnight, J. and Block, P. (2010), *Abundant Community: Awakening the Power of Families and Neighborhoods* [online], Oakland, CA: Berrett-Koehler Publishers, http://www.mylibrary.com?ID=314939. Accessed 10 September 2013.

Milner, M. (1994), *Status and Sacredness: A General Theory of Status Relations and an Analysis of Indian Culture*, London: Oxford University Press.

Morse, S.W. (2004), *Smart Communities: How Citizens and Local Leaders Can Use Strategic Thinking to Build a Brighter Future*, San Francisco, CA: Jossey-Bass.

Motes, P.S. and Hess, P.M. (eds), (2007), *Collaborating with Community-Based Organizations through Consultation and Technical Assistance*, New York: Columbia University Press.

Naidus, B. (2009), *Arts for Change: Teaching Outside the Frame*, Oakland, CA: New Village Press.

National Cancer Institute (2005), *Theory at a Glance: A Guide for Health Promotion Practice* [online], Washington, DC: U.S. Department of Health and Human Services, http://www.cancer.gov/cancertopics/cancerlibrary/theory.pdf

National Clearing House on Families and Youth (2007), *Putting Positive Youth Development into Practice* [online], Health and Human Services, Family and Youth Services Bureau, http://ncfy.acf.hhs.gov/sites/default/files/PosYthDevel.pdf. Accessed 8 July 2012.

National Research Council: Committee on Scientific Principles for Education Research (2003), *Scientific Research in Education*, In Shavelson, R.J. and Towne, L. (eds), Center for Education, Division of Behavioral and Social Sciences and Education, Washington, DC: National Academy Press.

Newton, R. (2006), *Project Management Step by Step: The Proven, Practical Guide to Running a Successful Project, Every Time*, Harlow, United Kingdom: Pearson Education.

Nicholson, H. (2005), *Applied Drama: The Gift of Theatre*, New York: Palgrave-McMillian.

Nussbaum, M. (2000), *Women and Human Development*, Cambridge, United Kingdom: Cambridge University Press.

Nussbaum, M.C. (2011), *Creating Capabilities: The Human Development Approach*, Cambridge, MA: Belknap-Harvard University Press.

Osterloh, M. (2007), "Human resources management and knowledge creation," In Ichijo, K. and Nonaka, I. (eds), *Knowledge Creation and Management: New Challenges for Managers*, Oxford, United Kingdom: Oxford University Press, pp. 158–175.

Pavis, P. (2003), *Analyzing Performance: Theatre, Dance, and Film*, Williams, D. (trans), Ann Arbor, MI: University of Michigan Press.

Pellegrini, A.T. (2009), *The Role of Play in Human Development*, Oxford, United Kingdom: Oxford University Press.

"People, Land, Arts, Culture, and Engagement: Taking Stock of the PLACE Initiative" (2013), Tucson Pima Arts Council Report, http://www.tucsonpimaartscouncil.org/wp-content/uploads/2011/08/PLACEreport-FINAL-web.pdf

Phakama (2012), "Our approach" [online], http://www.projectphakama.org/our-approach. Accessed 24 June 2013.

Phillips, R. and Shockley, G. (2010), "Linking cultural capital conceptions to asset-based community development," In Green, G.P. and Goetting, A. (eds), *Mobilizing Communities: Asset Building as a Community Development Strategy*, Philadelphia, PA: Temple University Press, pp. 92–111.

Pine, J. and Gilmore, J. (1999), *The Experience Economy*, Boston: Harvard Business School Press.

Pinholster, J. (2013), Shared Link Post [Facebook], 17 February, www.facebook.com/jakepin?fref=ts. Accessed 18 June 2013.

Pittinsky, T.L. and Tyson, C.J. (2006), "Leader authenticity markers: finding from a study of perceptions of African American political leaders," In Garder, W.L., Avolio, B.J., and Walumbwa, F.O. (eds), *Authentic Leadership Theory and Practice: Origins, Effects and Development*, San Diego, CA: Elsevier, pp. 253–279.

Poulsson, S. H.G. and Kale, S.H. (2004), "The experience economy and commercial experiences," *The Marketing Review*, 4, pp. 267–277.

Prentki, T. (2003), "Save the children? Change the world," *Research in Drama Education*, 8, pp. 39–54.

Project for Public Spaces, "What is placemaking?" [online], http://www.pps.org/reference/what_is_placemaking/. Accessed 4 April 2013.

Prout, A. (2005), *The Future of Childhood*, New York: Routledge.

Putnam, R.D. (2000), *Bowling Alone: The Collapse and Revival of American Community*, New York: Simon & Schuster.

Qvortrup, J. (1994), "Childhood matters: an introduction," In Qvortrup, J., Bardy, M., Sgritta, G., and Winersberger, H. (eds), *Childhood Matters: Social Theory, Practice and Politics*, Aldershot, United Kingdom: Avebury.

Rebstock, M. and Roesner, D. (eds), (2012), *Composed Theatre: Aesthetics, Practices, Processes*, Bristol, United Kingdom: Intellect Press.

Reeler, D. (2007), "A three-fold theory of social change and implications for practice, planning, monitoring and evaluation," Centre for Developmental Practice, http://www.cdra.org.za/threefold-theory-of-social-change.html. Accessed 12 November 2013.

Reisman, J., and Gienapp, A., with contributions from Langley, K. and Stachowiak.S. (2004), *Theory of Change: A Practical Tool for Action, Results and Learning*, Report prepared for Annie E. Casey Foundation by Organizational Research Services [online], http://www.aecf.org/upload/publicationfiles/cc2977k440.pdf. Accessed 1 October 2013.

Richards, G. (2011), "Creativity and tourism: the state of the art," *Annuals of Tourism Research*, 38, pp. 1225–1253.

Robison, L.J., Schmid, A.A., and Siles, M.E. (2002), "Is social capital really capital?" *Review of Social Economy*, 60, pp. 1–21.

Rohd, M. (2012), "The new work of building civic practice", *HowlRound* [online], http://www.howlround.com/the-new-work-of-building-civic-practice. Accessed 1 June 2014.

Rokeach, M. (1969), *Beliefs, Attitudes and Values: A Theory of Organization and Change*, San Francisco, CA: Jossey-Bass.

Rosenberg, M.A. (2003), *Nonviolent Communication: A Language of Life* (2nd edn), Encinitas, CA: PuddleDancer Press.

Runco, M.A. (2007), *Creativity Theories and Themes: Research, Development, and Practice*, Burlington, MA: Elsevier Academic Press.

Runco, M.A. and Chand, I. (1995), "Cognition and creativity," *Educational Psychology Review*, 7, pp. 243–267.

Russell, B. (1938), *Power: A New Social Analysis*, London: Allen and Unwin.

Saldaña, J. (2009), *The Coding Manual for Qualitative Researchers*, Los Angeles: Sage.

Sampson, R. (2012), *Great American City: Chicago and the Enduring Neighborhood Effect*, Chicago, IL: University of Chicago Press.

Sawyer, K.R. (2003), *Group Creativity: Music, Theater, Collaboration*, Mahwah, NJ: Lawrence Erlbaum Associates.

Sawyer, K.R. (2006), *Explaining Creativity: The Science of Human Innovation*, Oxford, United Kingdom: Oxford University Press.

Search Institute (2006), "40 Developmental Assets [online], http://www.search-institute.org/developmental-assets. Accessed 5 October 2013.

Sen, A. (1999), *Development as Freedom*, New York: Anchor Books.

Sen, A. (2006), "What do we want from a theory of justice?" *The Journal of Philosophy*, CIII(5), pp. 215–238.

Sepe, M. (2009), "Creative urban regeneration between innovation, identity and sustainability," *International Journal of Sustainable Development*, 12, pp. 144–159.

Skelton, T. and Gough, K.V. (2013), "Introduction: young people's Im/mobile urban geographies," *Urban Studies*, 50, pp. 455–466.

Smedley, A. (1996), "American anthropological association statement on 'Race,'" AAA Executive Board, http://www.aaanet.org/stmts/racepp.htm. Accessed 5 June 2013.

Smith, M.J. (2010), *Handbook of Program Evaluation for Social Work and Health Professionals*, Oxford, United Kingdom: Oxford University Press.

Smithson, C.W. (1982), "Capital, a factor of production," In Greenwald, D. (ed), *Encyclopedia of Economics*, New York: McGraw-Hill, pp. 111–112.

Snyder-Young, D. (2013), *Theatre of Good Intentions: Challenges and Hopes for Theatre and Social Change*, New York: Palgrave Macmillan.

Studdert, D. (2005), *Conceptualizing Community: Beyond the State and Individual*, New York: Palgrave Macmillan.

Svich, C. (2013), "Unruly drama," *HowlRound* [online], http://www.howlround.com/unruly-drama. Accessed 26 August 2013.

Szkupinski Quiroga, S., Underiner, T., Etheridge Woodson, S., Winham, D., and Todd, M.A. (2012), "Cultural Engagements in Nutrition, Arts and Sciences (CENAS)" Grant. Proposal to the National Institute of Health.

Tannen, D. (1998), *The Argument Culture*, New York: Random House.

Taylor, C. with commentary by Gutmann, A., Rockefeller, S. C., Walzer, M., and Wolf, S. (1992), *Multiculturalism and "the Politics of Recognition,"* Princeton, NJ: Princeton University Press.

Taylor, P. (2003), *Applied Theatre: Creating Transformative Encounters in the Community*, Portsmouth, NH: Heinemann.

Thompson, J. (2005), *Digging Up Stories: Applied Theatre, Performance and War*, Manchester, United Kingdom: Manchester University Press.

Thompson, J. (2006), *Applied Theatre: Bewilderment and Beyond*, Bern, Switzerland: Peter Lang.

Thompson, J. (2009), *Performance Affects: Applied Theatre and the End of Effect*, New York: Palgrave Macmillan.

Throsby, D. (2001), *Economics and Culture*, Cambridge, United Kingdom: Cambridge University Press.

U.S. Bureau of the Census, (2010), *Income, Poverty, and Health Insurance Coverage in the United States: 2010*, Report P60, n. 238, Table B-2, pp. 68–73.

U.S. Department of Health and Human Services, Bureau of Health Professions, (2005), *Transforming the Face of Health Professions through Cultural and Linguistic Competence Education: The Role of the HRSA Centers of Excellence*, www.hrsa.gov/culturalcompetence/cultcompedu.pdf. Accessed 18 February 2012.

Valdez, J. (2001), *Deliberative Democracy, Political Legitimacy, and Self-Determination in Multicultural Societies*, Boulder, CO: Westview Press.

van de Water, M. (2012), *Theatre, Youth, and Culture: A Critical and Historical Exploration*, New York: Palgrave Macmillan.

Von Oech (2008), *A Whack on the Side of the Head: How You Can Be More Creative* (25th Anniversary edn), New York: Business Plus Publishing.

Wangh, S. (2013), *The Heart of Teaching: Empowering Students in the Performing Arts*, New York: Routledge.

Weber, M. (1968), *Economy and Society: An Outline of Interpretive Sociology*, New York, Bedminster Press.

Weigler, W. (2001), *Strategies for Playbuilding: Helping Groups Translate Issues into Theatre*, Portsmouth, NH: Heinemann.

Wheatley, M. (2002), *Turning to One Another: Simple Conversations to Restore Hope to the Future*, San Francisco, CA: Berrett-Koehler Publishers.

Williams, R. (1961), *The Long Revolution*, London: Chatto & Windus.

Williams, R. (1977), *Marxism and Literature*, Oxford, United Kingdom: Oxford University Press.

Yarbrough, D.B., Shulha, L.M., Hopson, R.K., and Caruthers, F.A. (2011), *The Program Evaluation Standards: A Guide for Evaluators and Evaluation Users*, Thousand Oaks, CA: Sage.

Yosso, T.J. and Garcia, D.G. (2007), "'This is No Slum!' A critical race theory analysis of community cultural wealth in Culture Clash's *Chavez Ravine*," *Aztlán: A Journal of Chicano Studies*, 32, pp. 145–179.